ELVIS, MARILYN, AND THE SPACE ALIENS

ELVIS, MARILYN, and the SPACE ALIENS

Icons on Screen in Nevada

ROBIN HOLABIRD

UNIVERSITY OF NEVADA PRESS | *Reno & Las Vegas*

University of Nevada Press | Reno, Nevada 89557 USA
www.unpress.nevada.edu

Photographs by Robin Holabird
Cover illustration by Jeff Rogers

LIBRARY OF CONGRESS CATALOGING-IN-PUBLICATION DATA
Names: Holabird, Robin, 1954– author.
Title: Elvis, Marilyn, and the space aliens : icons on screen in Nevada / Robin Holabird.
Description: Reno : University of Nevada Press, 2017. | Includes bibliographical references and index. | Description based on print version record and CIP data provided by publisher; resource not viewed.
Identifiers: LCCN 2016041580 (print) | LCCN 2016058633 (e-book) | ISBN 978-0-87417-465-6 (e-book) | ISBN 978-1-943859-24-5 (paperback)
Subjects: LCSH: Motion picture industry—Nevada. | Motion pictures—Production and direction—Nevada. | Television—Production and direction—Nevada. | Nevada—In motion pictures. | BISAC: PERFORMING ARTS / Film & Video / History & Criticism. | SOCIAL SCIENCE / Popular Culture.
Classification: LCC PN1993.5.U758 (print) | LCC PN1993.5.U758 H65 2017 (e-book) | DDC 384/.809793—dc23
LC record available at https://lccn.loc.gov/2016058633

The paper used in this book meets the requirements of American National Standard for Information Sciences—Permanence of Paper for Printed Library Materials, ANSI/NISO Z39.48-1992 (R2002).

FIRST PRINTING

Manufactured in the United States of America

Contents

Acknowledgments

Like movies, books take the collaborative input of people. *Elvis, Marilyn, and the Space Aliens* benefitted with help from numerous quarters:

The Nevada Film Office—directors Charlie Geocaris, Bob Hirsch, and Eric Preiss, along with an assortment of staff members, including Kristin Anderson, Tina Baldassare, David Cadwalleder, Jeanne Corcoran, Ed Harran, Eric Joseph, Carrie Keiser, Veronica Quarles, Mikki Reissman, Larry Rossi, and Julie Wilcox. Thanks for your help during the process of working with, interviewing, and photographing the people and places in this book.

The government officials who used their influence to help during my tenure at the Nevada Film Office—Gov. Richard Bryan (who created the office), Gov. Kenny Guinn, Gov. Bob Miller, Lt. Gov. Lonnie Hammargren, Lt. Gov. Lorraine Hunt, Lt. Gov. Brian Krolicki, Reno Mayors Bob Cashell and Jeff Griffin, plus Reno city council member Sharon Zadra among them.

The Association of Film Commissioners, International—Bill Lindstrom, Joe O'Kane, Leigh Von Der Esch, Barbara Shore, and my Lake Tahoe compatriots Kathleen Dodge and Beverly Lewis. Thanks for sharing ideas about bringing location filming to the community and for the opportunity to learn even more by writing for and editing *Locations* magazine.

The Nevada writing community—Steve Blust, Terri Farley, Forrest Hartman, Christine Kelly, Eric Moody, David Sundstrand, and, oh yes, my husband, Nevada Bottle Book author Fred Holabird. Thanks for advice, support, faith, and cheerleading.

The television program producers and filmmakers who bring their projects to Nevada—thanks for your wisdom in recognizing Nevada's fabulous locations. And keep on working here!

ELVIS, MARILYN, AND THE SPACE ALIENS

Introduction

What do Elvis, Marilyn, and space aliens have in common? They're all pop culture icons with great scenes in Nevada movies. They make an odd combination, a fun connection I experienced during my twenty-one years as a government film commissioner. Despite the authoritarian-sounding commissioner title, my job involved creativity when I helped movie and television producers find Nevada locations for their projects. These projects brought jobs to the state and gave it lasting attention if icons joined the picture—familiar names like James Bond, Rocky, Indiana Jones, and the Showgirls. Famous places work, too—Area 51, Bonanza's Ponderosa Ranch, the Mustang Ranch, Las Vegas, and Reno. They share Nevada links and fit the definition of icons as enduring symbols and objects of great attention and devotion. People love them.

The Nevada connection occurs in surprising ways, as I found just after the 9/11 attacks while sitting in a speeding subway train whooshing through Manhattan tunnels. Two teenagers squinted as they questioned the passenger to my right, a woman with short, cropped reddish hair.

"Were you one of my teachers?" a girl asked, focusing carefully on the woman's friendly face. "You look familiar."

Dressed elegantly in a dark pantsuit with an oriental motif, actress Rue McClanahan resembled the southern belle Blanche Devereaux she portrayed on *The Golden Girls* for seven years. Since Rue and Blanche spent time in my living room—at least on television—I felt comfortable enough to join the conversation.

"You weren't my teacher, but thanks for your great work," I said, and Rue smiled. I continued, "I really didn't expect to see someone like you on a subway."

Government workers from Nevada like me, sure, we travel cheaply on mass transit. But a classy actress carried the clout to demand limo service and special treatment.

Rue laughed and explained the subway got her out of the theater district faster than other options.

"I'm just so glad to be here," she continued, referring to the recent attacks that took down the Twin Towers.

Aboveground, smoke smoldered and puffed light gray against the night sky where the air took on a slightly sweet, rotting scent. But here in the subway tunnels, things felt close to normal. As always, dim lighting gave a surreal sense as tunnel walls rushed by in kaleidoscope forms. The air touched extra coolness on skin, possibly because fewer tourists traveled as passengers. People stayed away from Manhattan those first few weeks after the attacks, and Rue wondered if I was a local.

"No, I'm from Reno," I answered.

I figured Rue knew the small Sierra Nevada community's name, and she might even remember its iconic arch proclaiming "Reno the Biggest Little City in the World."

"Reno," she cried excitedly. "That's in my play!"

My eyes widened with hope. Reno, in a new play? This might impact me, because plays often turn into movies.

"What's the play?" I asked.

"It's *The Women,*" she said proudly.

"Of course!" I said enthusiastically, but with a disappointed twinge. Experts already turned *The Women* into a 1939 movie, with a musical remake in 1956 (a non-Reno version followed later in 2008). The play and original movie made my hometown a divorce-linked icon with lines like "Let's get Reno-vated."

"So tell me," Rue asked conspiratorially. "Do people still go to Reno to get divorced?"

I stifled surprise—divorce happens everywhere these days.

Yet Reno and its iconic role as Divorce Capital of the World still lived on in this Manhattan subway train, influenced by both a play and a movie that audiences first saw more than fifty years ago.

This way that movies and television affect attitudes about Nevada hits me repeatedly. Projects shooting in the state provide immediate impact when producers spend millions of dollars by hiring crewmembers and paying for accommodations, locations, and other services. But these projects' lingering effect comes from the images they portray, the way famous people and places connect in a wild, wonderful, and wacky world vastly different from Middle America.

Nevada blends beautifully with extreme and intense pop culture icons. Try Elvis Presley. Does he wear a white jumpsuit with sequins? That came in Las Vegas when he revitalized his career for concerts shown in *Elvis:*

That's the Way It Is. Or maybe you conjured the hot, skinny Elvis singing "Viva Las Vegas," his deep voice throbbing harmoniously with neon lights in the movie's title city. The iconic Marilyn Monroe hugs a tree in a classic poster made from a scene shot in the Nevada movie *The Misfits*. Meanwhile, the archetypical-looking alien of *Paul* spent time as a research subject at Area 51, one of the state's iconic locations.

Nearly everyone knows about Area 51, the rumored government research center for space aliens and remnants of unidentified flying objects. The state also houses such iconic places as the Nevada Test Site, which gained world renown for exploding atomic bombs—and if you believe the movies—causing giant mutants. Another iconic location, Las Vegas, serves as the worldwide catchphrase for Party Central.

Nevada remains on peoples' minds and in their homes with box office blockbusters, top-rated television shows, and classics readily available to rent, buy, stream, and watch every day. Some works linger for decades as icons in their own right. Though it ended decades ago after fourteen seasons, *Bonanza* still draws millions of viewers. *CSI* ran more than fifteen years and made Crime Scene Investigations a household concept that sent its staff searching for clues at a museum dedicated to Liberace, an icon beneath the many candelabra once stored there. Nevada's swinging nightlife epitomizes the hip, glamorous stars of *Ocean's Eleven*, either Frank Sinatra or George Clooney, in a franchise attracting millions of new viewers.

Nevada means the Old West for the Cartwrights in *Bonanza*; it supplies the New West with the Corleones, present in two *Godfather* movies, where fostering the forbidden lets iconic gangsters further their crimes. And Nevada serves as the Future West for mechanical aliens in *The Transformers*, a box office hit based on iconic toys adored by millions.

Nevada's unusual venues let *The Hangover* partiers wake up to find strippers, tigers, and Mike Tyson filling their days and all seem natural in a city whose slogan promises "What happens in Vegas stays in Vegas." Despite the slogan, movies and television make what happens in Nevada cross well beyond state borders into millions of homes and theaters.

But the Vegas slogan accurately reflects a tradition of accepting the traditionally unacceptable. Nevada once offered the nation's only refuge for gambling, boxing, divorce, and quick marriages. It remains the only state with legal brothels. Nevada stays vital with open spaces and open minds that put a unique spin on stories featuring intense and iconic characters.

While iconic people pass temporarily through the state, Nevada's places remain. Elvis has left the building and Marilyn no longer walks through downtown Reno, but you can follow their footsteps at some of the locations listed in this book's final sections. Better yet, you can watch movies and television shows to get a sense of places to experience throughout Nevada, whether you live here or arrive as a tourist. Movies and television influence sights to see, as Caesars Palace demonstrated by offering several *Hangover* specials.

My favorite travel inquiry came when a man called asking for help finding a location from a movie called *The Doctor*. The scene involves a striking moment of freedom as two cancer patients break away from treatment. They hit the road to Winnemucca but spontaneously stop at a beautiful lake and dance, their figures silhouetted against a setting sun.

The caller explained why he wanted to find the exact spot. After his girlfriend's cancer diagnosis, she watched *The Doctor* repeatedly for inspiration. As she approached her first cancer-free anniversary, he wanted to surprise her with a visit to the place where her favorite scene in her favorite movie filmed.

"Do you know the movie I mean?" he asked doubtfully.

Various state agencies already passed him around to others before someone finally suggested the Nevada Film Office.

"You're in luck," I said. "You're talking to the person who found that site for *The Doctor*'s production team."

"Did it film near Winnemucca?" he asked. "Do I just take Interstate 80 there?"

Actually, no one driving I-80 accidentally stumbles across the dirt road off a little-used highway featuring the lonely, eerie beauty that the producers wanted.

"I'll mark it on a map and send directions," I said, feeling pleased to contribute to a meaningful moment in someone's life.

Finding locations repeatedly showed me how much I love the diverse state I call home. My job also let me pursue my adoration of film. I drove producers, directors, and writers to different areas as we talked about their works. I chatted with many talents who figure in *Elvis, Marilyn, and the Space Aliens,* among them the creators of the iconic television shows *Bonanza* and *CSI*. I worked with a couple of former Directors Guild of America presidents, George Sidney and Taylor Hackford, along with Oscar winner Clint Eastwood.

I spent time around Eastwood in 1988 when *Pink Cadillac* filmed in Northern Nevada. Wearing casual slacks and a blazer, I dropped by the Fuji Park rodeo grounds in Carson City. I checked out filming at an abandoned drive-in outside Fallon in Nevada's rural farmland. I looked in on Hazen and other locations to make sure the production process rolled smoothly.

Leaving John Ascuaga's Nugget in Sparks one afternoon, I realized Eastwood strolled just ahead of me on the casino floor where some scenes filmed. In front of him, two women carried their luggage toward the valet pickup area. Amidst the pinging of slot machine tunes and bells, the lanky actor picked up his pace and came up behind the women.

"Ladies, may I take your bags?" he asked.

They slowed and turned around, with stiff body language implying what they planned to say.

They started telegraphing "No thanks, we're fine" to the tall guy in jeans.

But they looked up into the craggy face, seeing features famous for saying "Go ahead, make my day." Recognition and shock registered as Eastwood made their day by taking their bags and walking them to valet parking.

Many months later, Eastwood returned to Reno for a special screening of *Pink Cadillac,* followed by a party at a local nightclub. I put aside my casual work outfit and replaced it with an ivory dress. A premiere and party with stars deserved the dress, bought just for this occasion.

Dance music pulsed in the nightclub as I wandered toward a wall where I flowered and surveyed the dimly lit room. It didn't take long to spot Eastwood. Besides having one of the most recognizable set of features in the universe, he stands six-foot-four with surprisingly long legs. He relaxed on the other side of the room, leaning against a wall. He gestured like he wanted someone to come over. I looked around to see who—a couple of nearby people faced away from Eastwood. Was he motioning at me? I must be mistaken. Why would "the man with no name—Dirty Harry—Clint Eastwood" motion at me? Hoping not to make a fool of myself, I raised my hand and pointed at my face. He nodded. Well, then. I pushed my way through some of the partiers and walked over to Eastwood.

I may even have sputtered a puzzled-sounding greeting, no more original than "Hi?" Eastwood took my hand, cradling it in both of his. This felt good.

"Robin," he said as my brain quickly registered a startling concept.

He knows my name?

"Robin," he said, still holding my hand. "I just wanted to tell you how nice you look tonight."

I immediately became an instant proponent of Eastwood winning every award he's ever nominated for.

Eastwood's manner also gives insights about his moviemaking technique. He pays attention to the smallest of details and catches everything going on around him, even if he doesn't show it. He knows how to make people feel special, a useful skill in directing actors Gene Hackman, Morgan Freeman, Tim Robbins, Sean Penn, and Hilary Swank in Oscar-winning performances.

Eastwood often enhances his movies by filming in real locations rather than sets.

"I've done it," he told me in Reno. "I've made movies where you have sets and fake walls, but it doesn't pull you into the movie as well."

Other filmmakers took the time to tell me their views about Nevada locations, among them Taylor Hackford. After his huge success and Oscar nomination for the movie *Ray*, he joined his wife Helen Mirren on a project called *Love Ranch*, loosely based on a real-life legal brothel. Taylor, I discovered in frequent e-mails, loves researching old files and articles. After we passed information back and forth, he wanted to explore brothels in person.

He asked me to set up appointments and take him to northern Nevada's legal brothels to talk with management. Though hesitant to let gawkers in, brothel owners opened their doors wide for a big name director married to the cinematic queen.

Luckily, Taylor wanted more than chauffeur duties from me.

"Don't hesitate," he urged. "Join in and ask questions."

No problem; like many local women, I never visited brothels but maintained a high level of curiosity about them.

A big guy with a closely trimmed white beard, Taylor strides comfortably into any location, always curious to experience something new.

He got a surprise when we wandered down the narrow hallway of the famous Moonlite Bunny Ranch brothel with owner Dennis Hof, recognizable from the HBO series *Cathouse*. As we edged down the hallway, a door opened and a woman walked out, standing tall in heels that added even more definition to her shapely legs. The skimpy shoes matched her red-thong bikini, whose minimal top accentuated huge breasts popping out like large, round soccer balls.

Dennis introduced the woman to Taylor, but I missed her name while staring in astonishment at her body proportions.

"So," I heard Dennis say, "Give Taylor a Bunny Ranch handshake."

Before anyone blinked or moved, the bikini top vanished. With a swift shift to the left, the woman grabbed Taylor's head from behind and mashed his face into her breasts, rubbing back and forth. Taylor came up for air as she headed toward the film's producer, Marty Katz, and followed the same procedure.

She aimed for me as I turned my face to the walls, throwing my arms up like a suspect avoiding police brutality.

"No, that's okay, really!" I cried.

Unruffled and thoroughly professional, Taylor continued the tour as if nothing happened. And as he hoped, he found useful information to include in his film—though not a Bunny Ranch handshake.

Taylor's experience reflects the evolving nature of Nevada's reputation as the number one place to go for fun, glamour, and craziness. With firsthand insight on shows I dealt with from 1987 to 2008, I easily answer questions about projects, from *Reno 911* to *The Hangover* to *Independence Day*.

"Do the cops in Reno really wear such tight shorts?" (Not on the job.)

"Is Las Vegas really that fun?" (It can be.)

"Are there really aliens at Area 51?" (I hope so.)

Both timely and timeless, such projects strengthen Nevada's unique role as an ideal location for icons adored by millions.

1

Elvis and the Impersonators

We call him "The King," and Las Vegas serves as his glittery Camelot. Elvis Presley only made one feature film in Las Vegas but, ever since, the man and the place blend as a unified force. Dynamic, bright, and sparkly, Elvis and Las Vegas come from the same flashy fabric. A sleek, trim dynamo when cameras rolled for *Viva Las Vegas* in 1964, Elvis thrived in a city where nightlife included showgirls, the Rat Pack, and mobsters.

"Elvis took me to Vegas in the early sixties," recalled his Army buddy and road manager, Joe Esposito, at a Las Vegas convention where he peddled documentary footage of The King.

Dressed in a dark mock turtleneck sweater covered by a black sport coat, Esposito looked more like a casual businessman than a key member of Elvis's famous Memphis Mafia, the tightly knit group of friends that surrounded the singer, protected his privacy, and shared the spoils of fame. A young soldier with dark locks when he first met Elvis during the singer's Army stint in Germany, Esposito lost some hair, gained a trim, white beard, but never wavered in his loyalty to The King and their shared memories.

Las Vegas provided many of those memories.

"We drove down with a bunch of guys and went to the Sahara. We came for a week—we stayed five weeks. That's when Vegas was Vegas. Every showroom had a major act, and all of the big acts were in the lounges. We went to every act, every showroom. We had a great time. He enjoyed it tremendously because it was a twenty-four-hour town. The sun would rise, and we went to bed like Count Dracula."

By the time Elvis returned for *Viva Las Vegas*, he had made fifteen movies, most of them ranging from bland to bad.

"All his movies are travelogues, thirty-one films of him singing to a dog, a cat, a kid," recalled Esposito.

Viva Las Vegas continues that trend, though with extra panache to push it into iconic pop culture status.

"*Viva* was a better story, better crew, and good director," said Esposito.

That director, George Sidney, never buckled under the Elvis mystique. Sinatra, not Elvis, played on the sound system in his Las Vegas Country Club home. Photos of him working with Judy Garland, Gene Kelly, and other MGM stars filled his office walls. At eighty-six, Sidney's memory remained sharp and detailed. Wearing a dapper gray suit and ascot, he clearly enjoyed discussing work.

Sidney's office included photos of Elvis, but the director noted the two never hung out like buddies.

"At the end of the workday, he went off with his troupe," recalled Sidney. "He was polite, but it was hard to get to know him."

Sidney preferred his *Viva* co-star, Ann-Margret, who held a place of honor in his home. A framed picture of her as the *Flintstones* caricature Ann-Margrock, graced the kitchen wall near an original still life by Georgia O'Keefe.

A couple of years later, Ann-Margret sat on a Nevada set in Genoa when Sidney's name came up. Still sporting her famous red hair, Ann-Margret's face softened and her blue eyes misted.

"Oh, Mr. Sidney," she sighed. "He was so wonderful."

This came decades after she first worked with him. With five Golden Globe Awards, two Oscar nominations, and a handful of Emmy nominations, plus the star stature to headline a television movie, *'Til the River Runs Dry*, she still danced, still sang, and still sold out stage shows. And she still called her *Viva Las Vegas* director Mr. Sidney.

Sidney's stature as president of the Directors Guild of America for sixteen years meant current directors called to talk with him. He knew all his era's Hollywood legends and made decisions that helped launch careers for Judy Garland and Frank Sinatra. He understood musicals, directing film versions of *Annie Get Your Gun* and *Bye Bye Birdie*. Since *Birdie* spoofed an Elvis-style singer, Sidney seemed a natural to work with the real thing.

He had never watched an Elvis movie before getting the *Viva* gig, so he studied a couple of the singer's projects. Sidney immediately spotted a consistent flaw: directors always focused on Elvis, ignoring the leading lady.

"You need to go 'boy-girl, boy-girl,'" he explained.

As an A-list director, Sidney's clout allowed him to make many changes in the tentatively titled *Las Vegas Days*, which he promptly renamed *Viva Las Vegas*. One involved switching Ann-Margret's character from showgirl to swimming instructor and letting a bathing suit enhance her performance.

Sidney made other changes. He turned Elvis into an underfinanced race-car driver who earns money gambling and waiting tables in an exciting casino environment. Originally, the singer supported his race-car hobby by working on a drill rig in the desert.

"Who wants to see Elvis do that?" Sidney wondered.

Sidney tinkered with projects throughout his career, and he loved exploring new directions. He shot in 3-D long before it became a mainstay in new, millennium-era movies. His picture *Anchors Away* features a memorable scene where Gene Kelly dances with the famous cartoon mouse of *Tom and Jerry*, an early example of live action melding with animation.

Viva Las Vegas took a more traditional path, reflecting Sidney's tastes, including a love for speed. Sidney got Elvis all shook up by riding a Harley Davidson to work the first day on set, destroying the singer's image of a staid, old-school director. Sidney followed the motorcycle stunt the next day by arriving in a Bentley race car.

Sidney's passion for flashy, colorful cars shows up throughout *Viva Las Vegas*, with fast, flamboyant vehicles on picturesque routes throughout the region. Elvis zips along Blue Diamond Road by Red Rock Canyon and flashes through the flame-colored red sandstones of the Valley of Fire, an hour's drive north from Las Vegas.

In another scene using popular visitor sites, Hoover Dam provides a backdrop, with Lake Mead presenting a chance for water ski action. The giant, neon cowboy, Vegas Vic, waves and welcomes visitors to the old city's heart on Fremont Street during the film's climatic Grand Prix car race.

Las Vegas casts its spell as a party town with sunshine, nightlife, and beautiful people like Elvis with his jet-black pompadour hair or Ann-Margret with her high cheekbones and Swedish bombshell allure.

Both gorgeous stars seem in their natural habitat amid sun-dappled pools and nighttime neon as they spar and sing through eleven numbers. That much music in a movie running only eighty-five minutes leaves little room for detailed storytelling or complicated character development. Performers and songs take the spotlight.

Decades later, the "Viva Las Vegas" tune thrives. Simply staged in the movie, it begins with hands thumping on bongo drums to a lively beat. The camera pans as Elvis opens a set of saloon door props, bobbing briskly through as he sings the opening lyrics about bright lights setting his soul on fire.

Meanwhile, Elvis sets millions of fans on fire, looking hot in skintight black slacks and an open red shirt, a "V" revealing his chest, with a matador-style black jacket broadening his shoulders and narrowing his waist. Rather than dance, he bounces to the song's beat, moving left to glide with a showgirl in lacy black and pink, then switching to the right and a different girl in a glittering gold bodice and towering white feathered hat. Two other showgirls join the mix, adding mauve to the limited color palate of vivid hues.

Written by Doc Pomus and Mort Shuman, the song went to number twenty-nine on the *Billboard* record charts, the flip side of the more heavily promoted "What'd I Say." Frequently covered by other musicians, "Viva Las Vegas" paints an iconic image of the city, with its references to neon, one-arm bandits, and a place that turns day into night and vice versa.

As for Ann-Margret, she sings strongly, but her most memorable number comes with her moves. Wearing a simple ensemble of black tights and orange top, she shimmies to an instrumental, jazzy dance set in the University of Nevada, Las Vegas gym. Another highlight joins her with Elvis in a bantering duet called "The Lady Loves Me," easing smoothly through the Flamingo Hotel pool area.

The setting lets Ann-Margret start by wearing a red one-piece bathing suit, with white buttons down the chest to draw the eyes of those who initially fail to notice her fine form. As the sport-coated Elvis strums the guitar he just happens to be carrying, Ann-Margret moves behind a screen to change into a yellow undergarment, carrying out a matching wraparound skirt to finish the scene. Both sexy and warm, Ann-Margret matches Elvis's intense screen magnetism.

"She was on fire," recalled Sidney.

That chemistry makes *Viva Las Vegas* stand apart from other Elvis pictures, according to Esposito.

"It was a hot movie. It's definitely one of his best," said The King's friend, quickly adding, "Of course, a lot were terrible."

Decades after its release, *Viva Las Vegas* remains fun and entertaining to watch, with the title evolving into an iconic catchphrase for the city.

Elvis reached a movie zenith with *Viva* as his top-grossing film. Meanwhile, his singing career headed downward, as the Beatles, Rolling Stones, and other Brits invaded America with number-one releases. Rather than surrender, Elvis reinvented himself by returning to the risk-taking city that embraces change, Las Vegas.

Elvis: That's the Way It Is explores how Presley developed his landmark show, first seen at the International Hotel, now the Westgate. Released in 1970, the documentary comes in several forms, including the original theatrical release on videocassette. A severely edited version aired on television in 2007 as *Kingdom: Elvis in Vegas*. A 2000 remastering bests the others by changing 40 percent of the material from the theatrical version.

The revised documentary improves the project by eliminating talking-head shots of enraptured fans crying "Elvis! Elvis! Elvis!" Instead, rehearsal footage shows the singer and his skeleton band as top-rate musicians who love their work. Their clever melding of "Little Sister" and "Get Back" stands out with raw, forthright musical honesty. The medley grabs an Elvis hit and one from the competing Beatles, forming a perfect union with a lean band that lets Elvis's rich vocals shine.

Before getting to music, the movie opens with a shot of the International Hotel and a stunningly empty Las Vegas Strip. Action backtracks to rehearsals, next focusing on shows taking place over a span of six different performances in Las Vegas. Fans and newcomers can't help falling in love with the Elvis presented here, a beautiful man in top form and voice. His new white jumpsuit highlights his martial arts skills and love for superhero costumes. Trimmed to a thirty-two-inch waist, Elvis mixes a fashion model body with movie-star hotness. Best of all, he exudes excitement about breaking new ground with energetic covers of sixties pop songs.

That energy goes missing in a one-hour 2007 British documentary called *Elvis: Destination Vegas*. With no material from the Elvis Presley Estate or authorized sources, the program features remarkably poor, grainy footage.

Narration befuddles. At one point, a voiceover says that Elvis's Vegas performances of mainstream songs represent career low points. The narrator then acknowledges that millions adore lush covers of "My Way" and a repertoire of material developed at Elvis's casino shows.

The program also features questionable math. The documentary says our world includes 80,000 people registered as Elvis impersonators.

"If that trend continues," intones the worried narrator, "then one out of every three people will be an Elvis impersonator by the year 2030."

Scary but. . . really? After all, most households have two parents and maybe one or two children, so the movie predicts an Elvis impersonator in every household. Compared to *Elvis: Destination Vegas*, the documentary *Elvis: That's the Way It Is* remains the most insightful look at the pairing between man and place. Esposito helped promote *That's the Way It Is*, but lists his favorite documentary as 1981's *This Is Elvis*, for which he served as technical consultant. The project features Esposito throughout, including having fun as he and Elvis goof off by riding tiny cycles on the film set.

The documentary contains sequences with performers reenacting events, narrated in first person by an impersonator and interspersed with real footage, like Elvis wearing a tux and singing to a hound dog on Steve Allen's show. A friendly overview, scenes half-heartedly acknowledge the singer's womanizing, drug problems, and weight issues.

"We tried to make sure it was as real as possible. It showed good and bad and talked about Elvis's problems," said Esposito.

Besides the International Hotel concerts, Las Vegas plays a role when

Elvis marries his longtime fiancée, Priscilla, at the Aladdin with Esposito as co-best man. The union proved short-lived.

"Being married to a big star is not easy," said Esposito, continuing, "I understand why they broke up. We were all out there being a bunch of wild guys. That's why his marriage ended."

The marriage serves as fodder for a two-part, 1988 television movie, *Elvis and Me,* based on Priscilla Presley's memoir and listing Las Vegas as one of its filming locations.

By the time *Elvis and Me* aired, the biographical picture ("biopic") genre regarded The King as fodder deserving regular chewing. The singer's first major biopic came just two years after his 1977 death with the broadcast of the ABC Movie of the Week, *Elvis.*

The program starts with highway shots over title credits, quickly flashing on the famous "Welcome to Fabulous Las Vegas" sign. Actor Kurt Russell, hair dyed black and combed big, twitches nervously while waiting to go on stage at the International Hotel. With no big venue performances in nine years and record sales melting, Elvis realizes he faces the choice between comeback or failure as he flashes back on his life.

Director John Carpenter uses that International show as framework for the Elvis legend and the capricious nature of stardom. Vegas represents the make-it or break-it gamble, the chance for Elvis to reclaim his crown as The King or fade off as just another name on old fifties hits.

Kurt Russell fully embodies Elvis, whom he worked with during *It Happened at the World's Fair.* Russell jokes that he got a kick out of the job, literally, because one scene has him nailing Elvis in the shin.

Though just a boy in that movie, Russell absorbed a lot about Elvis's day-to-day style, transforming the experience into in a dynamic, Emmy-nominated performance. Russell speaks the famous Elvis drawl, repeating words the real man said in published interviews. But when it comes to music, the voice belongs to country hit-maker Ronnie McDowell, who reached the charts with Elvis intonations in a tribute song called "The King Is Gone." Russell lip-syncs naturally, and his work impresses those in the know.

"Russell was the best Elvis," said Esposito, with a fond smile.

Esposito liked the *Elvis* biopic and saw himself played by an up-and-coming actor named Joe Mantegna, later known to millions for the television show *Criminal Minds.*

Esposito barely shows up in the 2005 two-part CBS Movie of the Week called *Elvis: The Miniseries.* Vegas takes a backseat, too. Instead of the Las Vegas International Hotel show, *Elvis: The Miniseries* frames its story around a 1968 televised "Comeback Special." The story includes Elvis's affair with Ann-Margret during *Viva Las Vegas* and shows his wedding party, without mentioning that it took place at Aladdin Hotel Casino. Aside from a stock shot of the old Vegas skyline, *Elvis* uses the city in name only, with most location work done in Louisiana. As the program ends, Elvis plans to tour Las Vegas.

The newer television movie differs from the original biopic by getting rights to use Elvis's original master recordings.

"Elvis did all the singing, or else I wouldn't be standing here," Irish actor Jonathan Rhys Meyers said after winning a Golden Globe for the title role in the miniseries.

Singing like Elvis features strongly in *Almost Elvis,* John Paget's 1991 documentary showcasing a group of real-life impersonators trying to win the official "Images of Elvis" contest in Memphis. To succeed, they obsess over The King.

"I have nothing against Elvis impersonators," said Elvis expert Esposito during his pitch selling footage of the real thing. But then his eyes flashed anger. "It's the ones who walk off the stage and still think they are Elvis," Esposito's voice rose. "You are not Elvis—there's only one Elvis," he said, jabbing his finger at an imaginary impersonator.

The competitors in *Almost Elvis* understand this, acknowledging that no one but Elvis combined the perfect package of voice, moves, looks, and magic for iconic status. Still, his impersonators mix in as many Elvis qualities as they can.

Judges give voice top priority. Looks factor in, too, a problem for several contenders, including a woman, a fifteen-year-old, and a black guy named Robert Washington. Meanwhile, competitor Irv Cass worries about weight as he downs bacon and eggs in the morning plus hamburgers and fries at night. Still, Cass made a living playing The King in Las Vegas during the Legends in Concert show at the Imperial Palace and Harrah's.

Almost Elvis spends a portion of its hour-long running time at a quarter finals competition in Las Vegas. There, job opportunities included positions at Graceland Wedding Chapel, where an Elvis impersonator marries visitors with the vows, "I'll always be you're A-Number-1 hunka-hunka burning love." Freelancers performed at various Las Vegas Strip corners, but the easiest way to guarantee an Elvis sighting came at such shows as "Legends in Concert."

Interviewed in *Almost Elvis,* "Legends" producer John Stuart describes Las Vegas as the Elvis Town and "the place that embodies the spirit of Elvis." Stuart envisions "Legends" as a show that "pierces heavenly veils" and allows classic performers like Judy Garland to sing again. The program moves up the heavenly circle and finishes at the pinnacle. Who would close such a show? Says Stuart, "Undoubtedly, it would be Elvis."

As a result, someone who looks, dresses, and sings like Elvis has closed more shows than anyone else in Las Vegas, and The King himself performed more shows there than anywhere else. The "Legends" show spread worldwide to cruise ships and various cities and remained a Las Vegas staple for more than twenty-five years, linking the city and singer together in the minds of visitors and moviemakers. Set a movie or television show in Las Vegas, and it makes sense to use the singer, his songs, or his impersonators.

This explains why robbers wear Elvis-style jumpsuits in *3000 Miles to Graceland*, a Las Vegas casino heist picture. The robbers pass through unnoticed during a Riviera convention for Elvis impersonators.

Star Kurt Russell reprises that special feeling a jumpsuit provides by playing one of the lead robbers, and viewers see other familiar faces in tight, sparkling suits, including Kevin Costner, David Arquette, and Christian Slater.

These men in white quickly shed their fun clothes to change the mood with a gruesome, vicious shootout that kills casino workers and customers. Presley's influence remains with the fleeing criminals when his songs "Trouble," "Such a Night," and "My Way" layer the soundtrack. Russell led his costars in a frequently televised music video promoting the movie.

Sometimes backing a movie with Elvis songs provides nothing more than a pulsing soundtrack. *Elvis Has Left the Building* makes that point in a straight-to-DVD project from Joel Zwick, the director of the highly successful comedy *My Big Fat Greek Wedding*. The gimmick of killing off Elvis impersonators failed to catch fire in this film—except when one of them turns into a hunka-hunka burning love after a cigarette hits his cheap, flammable jumpsuit.

Others die in mysterious ways, including one played in freeze frame by Tom Hanks. The dead impersonators share the coincidental presence of Kim Basinger, on her way to Las Vegas and an Elvis impersonators' contest. A plethora of cheap suits and bad hair implies world salvation lies in eliminating Elvis impersonators.

The *3000 Miles to Graceland* and *Elvis Has Left the Building* scripts borrow from reality since Elvis impersonator conferences meet regularly in Las Vegas. Mainstream movie viewers first learned about this trend from *Honeymoon in Vegas*. Planning to marry in Las Vegas, Sarah Jessica Parker and Nicolas Cage arrive to find Bally's swarming with impersonators, tagged with the nickname "Elvi" during the 1996 production. Several Nevada casting companies auditioned hundreds of Elvi.

"It's amazing," Sally Lear reported during preproduction. Her Reno-based Nevada Casting Group joined the Elvis hunt, where prey included a Sikh Elvis in wraparound headgear.

"He was singing something like 'I don't smoke dope, I don't drink bourbon, all I wanna do is shake my turban!'"

She seemed all shook up.

"There are no limits," she said, and the movie's final titles make that point by listing more than a dozen Elvi, including credits for "Oriental Elvis" and "Black Elvis."

But *Honeymoon in Vegas* expanded the field when director/screenwriter Andy Bergman invented the notion of impersonators leaping from airplanes as "Flying Elvi." Bergman's *Honeymoon* production team contacted local Las Vegas skydivers.

"He had no idea these guys would become instant celebrities," reads the official "Flying Elvi" webpage.

The troupe since switched from movie fantasy to Las Vegas reality, performing for parties, commercials, and other events by diving from 5,000 to 12,000 feet at speeds up to 160 miles per hour. Their movie gig drew thousands to the Bally's parking lot to watch the landing during filming. Cage joins the skydivers, hitching a ride and unwillingly leaping out the plane—though perhaps wearing that white jumpsuit gave Cage an edge in wooing one of his future wives, Elvis's daughter Lisa Marie.

Elvis lives on through his music and movies, and his popularity spans several locations. Graceland and Memphis remain the Mecca for Elvis, but Nevada serves as an important stop in the pilgrimage, a tie cemented by the blending of both film and song in *Viva Las Vegas*. The man and his symbiotic relationship with the city thrive. All over town, the King's rich tones emanate on stage or through outdoor speakers with lyrics crying "Viva Las Vegas." Meanwhile, with intense energy, bright color, and unremitting excitement, Las Vegas responds with a call of "Viva Elvis."

2

Marilyn and the Divorcees

Marilyn Monroe's magic joined a powerhouse lineup to cast a spell on Reno when *The Misfits* production team arrived in 1960. With *Gone with the Wind* star Clark Gable heading the cast, producers planned to topple that film's box office and Academy Awards records. They blended *African Queen* action skills from director John Huston, a physical and cinematic giant. They added intellect from Pulitzer Prize–winning playwright Arthur Miller as screenwriter. And, there was Marilyn.

She scattered magic with every step, and locals displayed fairy-dust memories decades later. Almost anyone who lived in Reno that summer *The Misfits* filmed tells a story. Uwe Nikoley fondly recalls walking out of the downtown Majestic Theater and stumbling across the production team. He stopped, enthralled. Envisioning a future watching this same movie up on the big screen, he used his twelve-year-old confidence to walk straight up to the biggest man he saw.

"What's this movie on?" Uwe asked.

"On film, son," bellowed the man Uwe now recognizes as director John Huston. "We're shooting this movie on film!"

The stories still get told because everyone remembers anything to do with Marilyn. And Nevada stands out in those memories because Reno gave Marilyn what every actress wants—the role of a lifetime. Playwright Arthur Miller wrote the script after he established a six-week residency in Nevada so he could divorce his wife and marry Marilyn.

During his Nevada stay, Miller saw elements of a great film as characters around him rowed their courses off the mainstream of American life. Cowboys rode nearby, seeing their lifestyle fade into the sunset. Rodeo riders broke into pieces but kept on moving. Women fell apart as their dreams of marriage and stability shattered. These lost misfits came together in a landscape that both suited and challenged them.

The movie's still shots show land and people distinguished by sharply contrasting tones. Marilyn's light hair and dark clothes stand apart with classic photographic images that continue to haunt fans. One shot grabbed worldwide attention, frozen into a popular poster plastering countless walls of smitten fans in the years after Marilyn's death. It came from a sequence when Marilyn's new "misfit" friends show her the real Nevada in "God's country," at an isolated, partially built house on the west side of Pyramid Lake. Moving freely, Marilyn's Roslyn takes a turn with a new friend, then continues dancing on her own, gliding out the door and into a yard where a cottonwood grows.

The dance ends as she hugs the grizzled tree whose bark resembles folds and wrinkles of a wizened wise man. Frozen in time, this eye-catching simplicity stood apart from other posters.

Wearing an almost backless black dress, Marilyn's face rests just left of center at the top of the shot. She looks at the camera, her bleached blonde hair framing a half-formed smile and eyes slightly hooded. Her elbow bends at the bottom right, clasping the tree as if pulling it closer. Can Marilyn, this soft and vulnerable force of nature, actually make a hard, stoic tree lean into her?

Why not? Marilyn had that impact on people. Her blond-bombshell allure and heartrending ache cast her as the quintessential girl ready to be wooed and rescued by the American male.

For all the intensity the production inspired, *The Misfits* struggled in theaters. Decades later, *The Misfits* earned a place in the National Film Registry, officially designating it as a project worth preserving at the Library of Congress. Back in the sixties, it earned a Directors Guild nomination for John Huston and a Golden Globe for Marilyn as World Film Favorite rather than the plethora of Oscars originally envisioned for everyone involved. Gable's final performance failed to generate award sympathy or lure a big enough audience to help the movie instantly take back its $4 million cost. And no one knew that Marilyn would never finish another film.

Her involvement inspires 2002's *Just a Dream*, whose backdrop features a big production company filming in a tiny desert town. That title word "dream" repeats *The Misfits* theme about fantasy, including the ones Marilyn and Roslyn face. Their dream marriages turned nightmare; they seek refuge in divorce. Nevada stood apart from the rest of the nation with the equivalent of no-contest divorce decrees for people establishing state residencies at ranches and boarding houses. Like millions who briefly became Nevadans, Roslyn fears the coming changes her divorce implies, a universal emotion that Marilyn's performance captures beautifully.

Screenwriter Miller patterned Roslyn on Marilyn; they bear similar names and traits. Is it Marilyn, or Roslyn, who feels trapped by her heart-breaking beauty? Her looks and voluptuous body mesmerize men who want more than sex. They hope to catch her happy façade, not perceiving the deep loneliness preventing her from finding a home and happiness anywhere.

Reno better suits Roslyn's friend Iz, played by Thelma Ritter. Iz loves what she calls "the leave-it state" in one of her many wisecracks.

"Anything goes," explains Iz, "but don't complain if it went."

Reno's divorce industry upends marriage and family, and Roslyn looks more comfortable outside the city, where director Huston shoots Marilyn in soft focus so her ethereal beauty contrasts the sharp, harsh land around her. That physical difference between person and place intensifies imagery for a look and performance that crystallize Marilyn's vulnerability and instinctive understanding about what makes men tick. By the end of *The Misfits*, Marilyn's Roslyn seems on a better path, though her final line asks a key question: "How do you find your way back in the dark?"

The Divorcees

Marilyn Monroe's *Misfits* character epitomizes a woman gambling on new beginnings by using Nevada to end her marriage. The cinematic tradition arose from Reno's real-life reputation as the world's most famous place to split, highlighted in the 1927 movie title *Reno Divorce*. Writer Walter Winchell created the term "Reno-vated" in his newspaper column, co-opted by playwright Clare Boothe Luce after she qualified for her own divorce by establishing Nevada residency at the Washoe Pines dude ranch.

The experience morphed into her 1936 hit play, *The Women*, later turning into a popular 1939 movie. F. Scott Fitzgerald contributed to the screenplay, keeping Reno in the mix as the iconic place where wealthy people fled to avoid scandal. Socialites made the process a vacation.

In this first film version of *The Women*, several socialites arrive at a dude ranch and shuck their gowns for rustic attire more suited to Liberace than Annie Oakley. Waiting for her divorce, a countess decorates her plaid shirt with a massive string of pearls.

Another newcomer dresses lightly despite chill mountain air. Cinching a flimsy blouse at her narrow waste, a wide, white belt accessorizes with no realistic need as it wraps around shorts too tight to budge a millimeter.

While the dude ranch fashions of *The Women* raise questions about practicality, the terrain passes by in a Reno mountain setting, reportedly filmed about thirty miles west of the city near the small logging community of Truckee, California.

Besides its view of a divorce ranch for pampered dudettes, *The Women* affected the nation's view of Reno as "Divorce Capital" when Paulette Goddard,

Mary Boland, and Norma Shearer take a train to their western destination. They toast "Reno: The biggest little city in the world" and "Reno: American cradle of liberty." The city, says one, represents "a beautiful emblem of the Great Divide."

These Reno references seared the region into the minds of millions for generations to come, and *The Women* plays an essential role in any basic discussion of divorce-trade movies. The black-and-white comedy spiced itself with a ten-minute color fashion show interlude. Another trick limited the cast to women, without a single male appearing on screen. A clever story and major stars make the most of bright dialogue.

Booth's biting wit crackles as Joan Crawford, Rosalind Russell, and top actresses take aim with verbal darts. Fun as *The Women* remains today, it reflects its times. Mannered acting borders on posturing, and Shearer sheds any trace of regional dialect in stiffly delivered speech patterns. Today's viewers find it even more difficult accept how *The Women* readily celebrates a double standard between the sexes, with attitudes that rub like a ragged razor on feminist sensibilities.

Just as 1939 audiences knew why *The Women* went west, those who saw *Charlie Chan in Reno* expected divorce. Before leaving his Hawaii base to help a friend accused of murder, the famed Chinese detective calls his spouse "just so honorable wife will not misunderstand contemplated visit to Reno." At eighty minutes, *Charlie Chan in Reno* ignores anything resembling detecting skills or techniques.

Its biggest success lies in painting a portrait of Reno at its height as Divorce Capital, emphasized by two special features on the 2007 digitally remastered DVD. The specials note that, even though this Charlie Chan movie pales compared to other top 1939 releases like *The Women* and *Gone with the Wind*, it maintains historical interest with a surprisingly accurate view of the divorce process.

Typical for its time, the black-and-white movie filmed on Southern California stages, using stock footage of the original Reno Arch to open the story. Establishing shots continue when neon casino signs whiz by for Club Eldorado, Owl, and Royal as a cabbie drives his fare to the fictitious Hotel Sierra, modeled on the Riverside. He hits his passenger with observations she prefers avoiding.

"It's the biggest little city in the world, and by gosh, it's the wildest," he tells the distraught woman.

"I guess these divorcees figure as long as they're changing partners, they might just as well dance," he adds, continuing her misery with "I guess divorce ain't much more than a matter of travelin'. You check out of the state of matrimony and land in the state of Nevada."

Reno's fame as America's Divorce Capital never assured location filming, but it often gave the city passing reference in projects.

"I'll see you in hell before I see you in Reno," quotes a district attorney prosecuting Tim Robbins for killing his philandering wife in *The Shawshank Redemption.*

The resulting life sentence in prison suggests that a quickie divorce in Reno represents a better choice than homicide—but without that murder conviction, fans would never experience what turned out to be one of the most popular movies of all time.

Divorce meant a trip to Reno when Walter Winchell's column about celebrity breakups provided the title *Phffft!* in 1954. Sure enough, blonde comedian Judy Holliday plays a well-known soap opera writer whose marriage ends at Reno's courthouse on Virginia Street by the Truckee River. Rather than head north a few blocks for an establishing shot of the arch, director Mark Robson filmed a small version of the city's famous icon on a corner across from the courthouse. Looking at the domed building with trepidation, Holliday walks through majestic marble hallways into a stately courtroom and leaves shocked at the event's brevity.

Such projects linked Nevada and divorce in the mind of Victoria Tennant when she wrote *Edie & Pen* in the mid-nineties. The comedy features a staid wife ending her marriage in the place where it started. While in Reno, she bumps into the reason she needs a divorce: her husband's sexy, ditzy girlfriend.

"Reno was fundamental to the story," said Tennant with her dignified British accent.

"I knew in advance I had to set it where two women could meet getting divorces. I came to Reno to research that aspect of the movie," she explained.

"When I was first here, I looked at the visual impact of the casinos and landscape and imagined what it would be like to see the movie in this setting, and I thought this would be a very good choice," the actress continued.

Tennant, who played Steve Martin's love interest in *L.A. Story* before marrying him, also chose Reno as a place where "the weird and wonderful" seem natural.

"I like that a wide variety of people came here: a worldly lady from New York, a girl from the wrong side of the tracks in San Diego, a Greek cab driver, eccentric hotel people, cowboys."

Stockard Channing and Scott Glenn make a well-suited romantic couple, while Louise Fletcher lends prestige by playing a judge. Jennifer Tilly stands out, demonstrating the comic timing that earned the leggy brunette an Oscar nomination in Woody Allen's *Bullets Over Broadway*. Tilly plays a bimbo frequently, using her high-pitched voice and questioning tones to seal the deal. No dummy, she often wins big at televised Las Vegas Poker Championships.

Gregarious and friendly, she demonstrated good community relations by happily posing for photos with Reno police officers. Dressed skimpily in a black-and-white bodice, she lifted one long leg and bent it at the knee in a mock showgirl position. On a fluke, the officers surrounding her spontaneously imitated her pose and raised their legs too.

While some stars hide in trailers between scenes, the almond-eyed Tilly mingled comfortably with people like me. Outside what is now the Grand Sierra Resort, we stood in a food line assembled for the crew.

"You know what I like best about this role?" she asked me as we piled our plates with spicy Caesar salad.

"Wmm?" I wondered, mouth slightly full, as I taste tested appetizing offerings.

Smiling brightly, Tilly continued, "I don't have to kiss anyone in this movie, so I can eat all the garlic I want!" She added another spoonful of garlicky dressing and smiled even more broadly. She proved warm and funny—much like the character she plays in *Edie & Pen*.

By the time *Edie & Pen* filmed, quick divorces came easily almost anywhere. But that was not the case for women in 1959, when *Desert Hearts* takes place. Director Donna Deitch based her screenplay on Jane Rule's book, *Desert of the Heart*, following its lesbian love story with respect that earned the film cult status long before 2015's *Carol* made mainstream rounds. The 1985 project inspires fans to find real locations—though the one most sought for its extended and sensitively filmed love scene lies in private lodging at the Riverside Hotel apartments. The movie also includes the last motion picture footage of the defunct Mapes Hotel, its elegant, glass-encircled Sky Room hosting a celebratory wedding party. The privately owned Capurro family ranch near Pyramid Lake provides another key location for the main character to establish Nevada residency.

The movie opens at Reno's railroad station, an older structure now barely noticeable between bigger, looming buildings like a national bowling stadium. As *Desert Hearts* begins, Patsy Cline's mournful song "Leavin' on Your Mind" plays in the background, its throbbing vocals and sad lyrics mirroring emotions for Helen Shaver, an actress better known in her native Canada than the United States.

Shaver stands stiffly as steam disperses and reveals her full form, dressed conservatively in a gray suit, dark blonde hair knotted tightly and mostly hidden under a tidy, small hat. She means for her rigid, upright stature to hide how lost she feels, but her unease shows. She travels to the

Divorce Capital from New York, explaining, "I just want to be free of who I've been."

She finds freedom in vacant desert and Reno's neon casinos representing the potential for change, a point director Deitch appreciated.

"I was really drawn to the central metaphor of the novel, comparing the risk and gambling in Reno to what the characters need to do," Dietch told me. "There's something we're all afraid to risk, to bet on, to take a chance with."

Reno represents that risk, and *Desert Hearts* joins other films following the metaphor. With its divorce ranches, Western hospitality, memorable people, casino games, and beautiful surroundings, Reno offered the opportunity to end one dream and start another. Thousands of women—including Marilyn Monroe's Roslyn—came to Reno and began living that dream.

Following *Misfits* Trails Today

Producers still ask for *Misfits* locations. One inquiry led to a *The Making of the Misfits* documentary for a 2001 episode of *Great Performances* on the public television network PBS. By then, several decades had passed since *The Misfits* filmed, and many of its locations vanished, imitating the movie's theme of a lost lifestyle.

In Reno, only a couple of sites remain. Though locals walk the same steps Marilyn and Kevin McCarthy take into the Washoe County Courthouse on South Virginia Street, the empty corner of 1960 now features big buildings. A few steps away from the courthouse, the Truckee River meanders through town, while a nearby, refurbished bridge provides a tempting spot to throw away bad memories represented by wedding rings.

Down the street, a *Misfits* hangout remains at Harrah's, but the tiny operation with manual slot machines transformed into a skyscraper featuring updated gaming technology. Casino space fills the Harrah's bar where Marilyn Monroe, Clark Gable, Eli Wallach, and Thelma Ritter hook up, while a *Misfits* plaque on a wall outside honors the memory.

Finding specific *Misfits* locations north of Reno provides challenges. The tree Marilyn hugged at an isolated home grows bigger every year, but the site at Quail Canyon Ranch rarely opens to the public. Driving its location off Pyramid Highway's Mile Marker 29 reveals highway as lonely as the time when the movie's misfits head out that way. Breathe deep, and you catch the sage scent that Roslyn describes as "green perfume." The Pyramid area remains refreshingly preserved by the local Paiute tribe, and impressive vistas surround the lake's many beaches, with one providing a plausible excuse for Marilyn to wear a bathing suit.

Tracking *Misfit* trails means stopping in Dayton, about forty-five minutes east of Reno. People jam Dayton as they arrive for the movie's rodeo, but today the historic main street usually stands empty, its few Western-style buildings looking more like a ghost town than a popular hangout. Dayton's other *Misfits* claims disappeared, including the rodeo grounds where Montgomery Clift's character competes. The Odeon Bar interior closed long ago, no longer letting *Misfits* fans salivate over memories of Marilyn playing paddleball. The building itself still stands, the name battered into deeper states of decay with the passing of every season.

Just a few miles up the road from Dayton in Stagecoach, off-road drivers race on a dry lakebed where people and horses met for the film's finale. Producer Gail Levin brought the film's surviving creators back to the place now known as Misfits Flat to tell their stories about *The Making of the Misfits*.

"You can still feel the spirit of Marilyn and *The Misfits* out here," she said, closing her eyes and taking in air as she prepared for another segment of her project.

Relatively small with smatterings of new housing to the west, Misfits Flat plays time machine. Look out in the distance and the old days come back. It's easy to imagine a herd of mustangs thundering down from the surrounding hills onto bleached, bare ground. Listen carefully and the muffled shouts of troubled souls whisper in the wind.

The spot worked perfectly for *The Misfits*, highlighting director John Huston's trademark skill with strenuous location work. Long credited with leading to a heart attack that killed Gable shortly after the movie's completion, the thirty-minute finale shows horses running wild on an expanse of flat desert, emphasizing all the characters' fear of being reigned in.

Seeing herself in these beautiful animals, Roslyn cries over plans to butcher the horses. She begs an aging cowboy for freedom—the horses and hers. The cowboy puts up a fight but ultimately recognizes the tragic twist that transforms those iconic symbols of the free West—wild mustangs—into dog food. Catching horses, he realizes, "is like ropin' a dream now." His dream faded, but more than fifty years after that lament, *The Misfits* movie survives.

A Misfit Remembers

Even famous people inclined to act blasé about big names brighten with their memories of *The Misfits*. The project stood out for Hollywood actor Kevin McCarthy, who played the husband Marilyn's character Roslyn divorces. McCarthy returned to Northern Nevada for a 1991 television movie called *Dead on the Money*, where kids flocked to him for autographs because they recently saw him in a popular *Goulies* movie.

Later, in a quieter mountain setting, I approached him with questions about his work on the original *Invasion of the Body Snatchers* and *The Misfits*.

"What was it like working on such great films?" I asked.

We stood on location in the Sierra Nevada, looking over granitic rock formations into a distant vista of peaks rising more than 10,000 feet. Behind us, blue Steller's Jays squawked in a smattering of gnarly trees that knew how to deal with all weather extremes.

"Well," drawled the lean-jawed actor, still looking trim. "There's a lot to tell." He patted the chair next to him. "Sit down."

I hesitated. The canvas chair by McCarthy clearly bore the label "Eleanor Parker," who earned three best actress Oscar nominations in the fifties. More dauntingly, Parker played the baroness who almost stole Christopher Plummer from Julie Andrews in *The Sound of Music*. I did not want to annoy this woman.

"Sit down," McCarthy repeated. I didn't want to annoy him, either, so I sat. McCarthy, wearing a pale yellow golf cap tilting over a full head of graying hair, leaned back comfortably and told his stories.

His *Misfits* connection came from friendship with Montgomery Clift, set to play a rodeo rider in the film. Clift put in a good word for his buddy.

"I was excited when I heard I had a role in the movie," McCarthy recalled. "This was a big picture."

When the screenplay arrived, McCarthy saw that spare dialogue gave him about thirty words.

"I was crushed. So I quoted them an outrageous price, something that worked out like $100 a word. I knew they wouldn't go for it."

Around this time, I sensed a presence behind me. I looked, and Eleanor Parker stood regally with her hand on the chair where I sat—her chair.

My apology never finished as she interrupted.

"Don't move," she said. "I'm enjoying every word."

"So," continued McCarthy, the production company went for his outrageous fee. His next step involved investing that money toward looking great. He might only be on screen a couple of minutes, but the handsome actor would make the most of it.

"I bought a new suit, a beautiful suit," McCarthy said, adding, "Then I got on set and Huston just glared at me."

"What's that?" Huston asked, glowering at the actor's fashion magazine attire.

"My suit," McCarthy answered.

"It's all wrong," Huston growled. "You should look like a used car salesman," he grumped.

"Like him," the director continued, pointing to a crew member in a shiny suit.

And, in the way that moviemakers punt, McCarthy traded suits. McCarthy spent his big screen minutes wearing someone else's cheap clothes while Marilyn looked gorgeous.

3

Space Aliens and Area 51

When screen legend Indiana Jones rolls into Nevada, he hits one of the state's definitive icons, Area 51. He hunts a crate left in a warehouse following a mysterious incident involving Unidentified Flying Objects at Roswell, New Mexico. Establishing titles over the screen's barren desert images in 2009's *Indiana Jones and the Kingdom of the Crystal Skull* put the hero in Nevada, while the hangar wall behind him bears a large "51." No matter that the scene filmed in New Mexico. Everyone knows you find Area 51 in Nevada, despite military denials such a facility exists.

But where else to put aliens? Boasting the seventh-largest surface area among states in the nation, much of Nevada looks like a dictionary definition for "middle of nowhere." Its isolation easily hides aliens, according to popular mythology about Area 51, two hours north of Las Vegas in Lincoln County. The story catapulted worldwide in the late eighties when Bob Lazar told Las Vegas television viewers he once worked inside Area 51 at Papoose Lake, where the military keeps aliens and their aircraft remnants in nine underground hangars.

Since then, the story has crept into many projects, including *Independence Day*, marketed as *ID4* for its July 4, 1996 release. Before finishing the script, writers ran a survey to see how much Area 51 background information viewers needed to understand the story. Not much, it turned out.

The real problems arose from several quarters. One issue came when the US military refused cooperation with the project if it maintained the Area 51 reference. Of course, the producers always expected complications, knowing the difficulties associated with filming in a location where the property's managers deny its mere existence. The producers responded by finding a different site to pass as a military facility, choosing the location where soldiers put together the first atomic bomb.

Years after making the bomb, the military abandoned Wendover Air Force Base in Utah and turned it over to city management. Located right next to the Nevada border, off Interstate 80, the base retains several hangars, an airstrip, some old barracks, plus a terrific view of the Nevada desert extending into Elko County. Nevada always benefits from film projects in Wendover, Utah, because crews prefer staying in West Wendover, Nevada, where casino resorts supply upscale lodging suitable for big stars like Will Smith.

Other *Independence Day* stars saw more of the state when the Nevada Commission on Tourism designated an official Extraterrestrial Highway in 1996. *Independence Day* director Roland Emmerich joined actors Jeff Goldblum and Bill Pullman for a trip to Rachel, Nevada, where they spearheaded an official ribbon cutting to showcase the new E.T. Highway signs for the ninety-eight miles of State Route 375. The ceremony also honored *Independence Day* and its use of Area 51 by placing an "ID4" plaque outside Rachel's biggest business, the Little A'Le'Inn. The movie and new signs continue to lure tourists intrigued by the region's alien connections.

Independence Day shows Area 51 as a gathering place for the United States president and other leaders as they determine how to fight a worldwide alien invasion. Simple and action-packed, the movie's award-winning special effects rolled past any logistical flaws and turned *Independence Day* into the 1996 box office champ. *Independence Day* cemented knowledge about Area 51 for millions of people all over.

When *Independence Day* finally generated a sequel called *Resurgence* in 2016, original star Will Smith dropped out. Director Emmerich, plus stars Pullman and Goldblum, remained, along with the Area 51 setting and Wendover area locations. This round, West Wendover, Nevada made it into the final cut, though it was hardly acknowledged by most viewers. The city's Wendover Will shows up in a brief establishing shot, as one group of characters heads toward Area 51, about sixty miles away, according to their dialogue. MapQuest disagrees, logging it at nearly 300 miles (but forget using Area 51 as your destination from West Wendover, as MapQuest offers its version of "huh?" or "WTF" when queried; the Little A'Le'Inn, instead, makes for an acceptable destination).

Despite Central Intelligence Agency officials acknowledging Area 51 in 2013, filming there provides daunting challenges beyond getting permission. The two-and-a-half-hour drive from Las Vegas to the region runs longer than producers like, though their reward includes the striking desolation that true isolation delivers. Flat desert scrub stretches out in two directions, bisected by an incredibly straight road heading miles into a horizon that seems to end the world. A tiny fraction of the view reveals trailers in Rachel, another reason why the real location rarely shows up in big projects. Film crews—and especially stars accustomed to penthouse suites—

require the usual comforts found in one of those big-city rooms with private baths, phone service, and television transmission.

On top of that, finding supplies proves difficult when only two businesses dominate a town with no gas station. A non-singing Glenn Campbell runs one operation, the Area 51 Research Center. Down the road lies the Little A'Le'Inn, filled with alien dolls, statues, and other souvenirs.

The Inn represents a must-see place for alien addicts, such as those in 2011's *Paul*, which moviemakers filmed on set rather than on location. As stars Simon Pegg and Nick Frost sit at a bar, drinking coffee from a green mug decorated like an alien's head, the owner pushes souvenirs, such as a bumper sticker reading, "Watch the Skies." They call her Pat Stevens in the movie, and she looks like *Glee*'s Emmy winner Jane Lynch.

Like her movie counterpart, the real Pat Travis enjoys chatting with customers.

Pretty much everyone gets around to the obvious question.

"Have you ever . . ."

Before you can finish the sentence, Pat jumps right in with a response.

"The answer is yes.

"Yes, three times aliens looking like regular people visited the restaurant. One stayed a couple of days and never ate or used a restroom. A different alien knew surprising things and foretold the future."

With a round face quick to turn up in a smile, Pat enjoys these interactions with her long-distance visitors, whether they come from Earth or some other world.

"It's fun," she said of the business she bought in 1988, adding "I've been blessed." The blessings have included animators scouting her place and using "Ale E Inn" for the 2002 Oscar-winning animated short *The ChubbChubbs!*.

Rachel lies near Tikaboo Peak, where a crew from the *UFO Hunters* television series hiked for the closest possible view of the facility for civilians. In a 2009 episode, thirteen "Hunters" hauled three cameras and the equivalent of a 1,100- millimeter telephoto lens up a rocky, dusty path to capture images of the secret base. Even without carrying heavy equipment, hikers find the route challenging.

Getting to the trailhead requires a four-wheel drive vehicle on twenty-two miles of dirt road off U.S. Highway 93's mile marker LN 32.2. Once the four-wheel reaches its limits, passengers transform into hikers and trek up a steep, poorly detailed path to reach the vista. At 8,000 feet, the summit offers views of the surrounding terrain and buildings by Groom Lake. The site lies twenty-six miles away, requiring binoculars for a decent view.

Besides regularly starring in UFO documentaries for specialty networks like the History Channel, Area 51 gets passing references in fictional pieces. No one bothers to explain Area 51's alien connection when drivers take a *Fast Lane to Vegas* and accidentally end up on the military facility where women-in-black grab them for research. As characters in a sexploitation film, the girls wear black only briefly. By 2003, *Looney Tunes: Back in Action* featured Area 52, where research includes tickling aliens to see how they react. Writers assumed most kids got the joke.

Since Area 51 activities involve poking, prodding, and other physical insults, any self-respecting alien should stay away. For instance, the alien called Starman hopes to get home by picking up a craft in Arizona. He accidentally goes beyond state lines into Las Vegas, but the mistake proves useful. As it turns out, alien powers work wonders on a slot machine at the Union Plaza on Main Street, providing enough cash to handle expenses for the rest of the Earthly trip. Many of *Starman*'s road scenes filmed on Nevada highways, where state transportation authorities proved more flexible than those in Arizona when it came to closing sections of the interstate.

Starman follows the school of peaceable aliens, with Jeff Bridges earning an Oscar nomination as a wise and gentle force. The script showcases Bridges' great 1984 body when he arrives on earth completely nude for the kind of humanoid mutation found in stories told at the Little A'Le'Inn.

That humanoid-alien routine works for two teenage creatures when they crash-land in *Race to Witch Mountain*. Aliens organize in Las Vegas and fit right in at the Planet Hollywood casino, where people with antennas and green faces wander the floor, part of a sci-fi geek conference. From Vegas, the aliens flee with Dwayne "The Rock" Johnson to Witch Mountain, just over the Nevada border in California. The 2009 family-friendly variation of a successful set of Disney pictures opened strongly, relying heavily on Johnson's appeal.

Of course, as *Independence Day* points out, some aliens threaten humanity. Playing a lone invader from a dying world in *What Planet Are You From?*, Garry Shandling needs to impregnate a woman so that alien spawn can take over Earth. He hits a roadblock by targeting a woman who insists on marriage before sex. Nevada steps right in, offering a vast array of Las Vegas wedding chapels and honeymoon accommodations. The couple selects the Bellagio, whose famous spurting fountains provide appropriate symbolism for what turns out to be an Energizer Bunny wedding night adventure.

Rather than send a lone alien to take over the world, armies come down in 1996 when *Mars Attacks!*. Director Tim Burton purposely imitates a trashy fifties feel, using a huge budget to create comedy suited to his skewed tastes. Besides revealing a fondness for the bad movies he adored as a kid, Burton indulged in nostalgia from childhood Vegas stays at the

Landmark with its distinct tower. He wanted the building in his movie but faced problems when city officials announced its impending destruction. A "lemonade from lemons" practical director at times, Burton sent location manager Kokayi Ampah and a second-unit production team to capture the Landmark implosion before regular filming began. Images of the crumbling building melded into scenes with Jack Nicholson as a casino owner trying to weather the Martian attack on Las Vegas.

By 2007, aliens once again threatened the world when *The Transformers* attacked Nevada, aiming for a state icon, Hoover Dam. Based on a popular set of toys manufactured by Hasbro, *The Transformers* create history-changing legend. The bit about Hoover Dam being built to provide water for everyone? Forget it. According to *The Transformers*, the government used that story to cover up its need to store the massive metallic alien called Megatron. The dam also holds a special cube powered to tip the balance of power between good and bad alien Transformers.

Spectacular special effects enhance a story inspired by a series of toys featuring moving parts that transform from typical-looking cars to super-powered robots. Kids who loved their Transformer toys grew into passionate, sentimental fanboys and flocked to theaters. Director Michael Bay fulfilled their dreams by continuing his flair for extreme special effects on a large and noisy scale. Besides spending vast resources on special effects, Bay used his clout and money to get into Hoover Dam, where filming had been scaled back after 9/11 and further terrorist threats.

Before that, the dam boasted a long and extensive history in movies and television, with a surprising appeal to aliens. Decades before *The Transformers* movie, the dam drew attention from the good alien Superman, when his nemesis Lex Luthor plots to flood California to create a new Nevada-Utah shoreline. Despite its dated 1978 effects, with miniatures on stage, the entire project holds up, enhanced by Christopher Reeve in his iconic screen role.

The dam's lure to space folk showed up even before *Superman* in a television pilot called *The Aliens Are Coming*. Terrible dialogue propels the plot when researchers spot aliens near the dam.

"We don't know if they're hostile, friendly, or fiendishly mutant," says one actor in a performance of some merit since he never cracks up laughing during the line.

Juvenile special effects contribute to the mess, including an alien resembling a deformed Keno game, with ping-pong balls in twisted tubing that circles its body. The alien's head blends football and motorcycle helmets for an odd combination.

The 1980 show proudly boasts stars Tom Mason and Melinda Fee. Meanwhile, Ed Harris shows up in smaller print. Yes, the guy who has since earned four acting Oscar nominations, a future not predicted with his first reaction to alien invasion.

"Holy Toledo!"

While *The Aliens Are Coming* offers hope to aspiring performers beginning their careers in absolute garbage, the project's ongoing significance comes from allowing history buffs the chance to see Hoover Dam in detail. Management granted film permits despite the script's description of the dam as a "primitive but functional" source of hydroelectric power.

"They were wonderful," recalls location manager Bill Bowling. "They let us go everywhere."

Extensive aerials show the dam's enormity, while interior shots highlight its complexity. The general public still visits Hoover Dam, but sees less of it than before the 9/11 attacks that took down the World Trade Center towers in New York City. Terrorists, it turns out, agree with aliens and consider Hoover Dam a prime target.

The Aliens Are Coming hits masterpiece status, though, compared to *The Creeping Terror*. Argyle Nelson's infamous project forever links the state and aliens in the minds of bad movie fans because it lists Lake Tahoe, Nevada as a location. Painful to watch, it took top prize as the Most Laughable Concept of an Outer Space Monster in the 1980 book *The Golden Turkey Awards*. The competitive field for WBAM (Worst Bad Alien Movie) includes 1965's *The Wizard of Mars*, with such familiar elements as a yellowish road leading to a city ruled by a leader whose face is magnified through projection, just like that other sorcerer from Oz.

Director David Hewitt, who later helped with special effects for major Hollywood releases like 1989's *Honey, I Shrunk the Kids*, envisioned substance for *The Wizard of Mars*. That must be why his wizard never shuts up.

"Death gives life meaning," proclaims the wizard during an interminable monologue.

As the wizard, John Carradine gets huge billing for a partial day's filming. Slides of the universe superimpose over Carradine's disembodied face, nearly hiding it. The film's trailer highlights the actor's brief presence by blaring "John Carradine is . . . (dramatic music) . . . *The Wizard of Mars*.' Reissued later under a different title, the movie promo suffered when somebody forgot to change things for "John Carradine is . . . (dramatic music) . . . *The Horrors of the Red Planet*.

As bad films go, *The Wizard of Mars* claims decent use of Nevada locations. The Stillwater area, near Fallon, vaguely resembles Mars. The marsh leads to the Lehman Caves in Great Basin National Park, an hour east of

Ely. The caves feature impressive dark formations that look like giant sand castle drippings frozen in rock.

The caves bring Ridley Scott's *Alien* to mind because the spooky, closed-in feeling fit his movie. Make no mistake; Scott shot *Alien* elsewhere. Instead of hosting Scott's fabulous classic, the Lehman Caves claim *The Wizard of Mars,* where locations outclass anything else about the movie. Sadly, no other feature film seems destined to bring cameras inside the spectacular caves since the National Park Service limits crew size to protect a rare and delicate interior.

Rather than continue *The Wizard of Mars* trend of using Lehman Caves, filmmakers seek the red planet in Nevada's Valley of Fire State Park. This worked for a couple of minutes toward the end of the Arnold Schwarzenegger hit *Total Recall.* Natural reddish hues at the Valley of Fire combine with warbled sandstone, joining in a geologic pattern continuing through Utah and Arizona's Zion, Bryce, and Grand Canyon National Parks. State park status keeps the valley remarkably undeveloped with few signs of human exposure.

Located about an hour from Las Vegas, the Valley of Fire features an expanse of land that suited an icon of science fiction, *Star Trek.*

As always, the Starship Enterprise and its crew have many missions: ". . . to explore strange new worlds; to seek out new life and new civilizations; to boldly go where no man has gone before."

By 1994, the original series cast had ventured boldly through four movies.

Meanwhile, a follow-up series called *Star Trek: The Next Generation* developed the courage to boldly explore otherworldly dimensions in feature films. Producers decided to combine characters from the two series into a movie called *Star Trek: Generations.* This justified William Shatner's Captain Kirk meeting up with Patrick Stewart's Captain Picard, teaming up both leaders of the Enterprise. Their voyage leads them boldly to another strange new world, a planet called Veridian 3.

Using the Valley of Fire for Veridian 3, the filmmakers achieved the plant-free, rock-dominated look needed to evoke a barren planet. Vacant land suited their need to build a retro set of wobbly stairs and platforms for a rocket launch, ending the Enterprise and several worlds as we know them. Once filming finished, the crew tore down the *Star Trek* set, but Valley of Fire remains a short drive from Las Vegas for Trekkers on pilgrimages.

Space nuts easily find other potential planets in Nevada at the Lehman Caves, Cathedral Gorge, Pyramid Lake, and the Black Rock Desert, two hours north of Reno. And with any luck, they might spot an alien light show near Area 51. Startling in their isolation and distinctiveness, these locations show Nevada personifying the phrase "out of this world."

Visiting Area 51

Imitating *Paul*'s sci-fi geeks, my coworkers demonstrated dorkiness during our Rachel scout as we entered the Little A'Le'Inn wearing bobbing antennae attached to headbands purchased just for this visit.

"Cute," said the proprietor, Pat, eyes rolling and adding with a hint of sarcasm, "Never seen that before."

She welcomed us for a weekend stay at the Inn where trailers served as motel rooms. This allowed a night hunt for strange sights in the sky. Our first goal required locating the misleadingly named black mailbox and a sky promising bizarre star shows.

Painted white to confuse UFO aficionados who kept stealing it, the black mailbox boasts protective, bulletproof metal on a tall post sunk several feet into concrete, thus deterring souvenir hunters. My group got there near midnight and lay spread-eagled on the highway, staring upwards. Sky looms blacker in areas lacking a softening city glow, so the Milky Way shines thicker and brighter. Beautiful lights danced in the sky, but no laser rays struck us.

So far, our biggest danger came from the fenceless open range around E.T. Highway as we drove the twenty miles from Rachel to the mailbox. Cattle wander onto asphalt and blend right in. While the possibility of alien abduction seemed scary, the potential of crashing into a cow appeared more likely.

Giving up on seeing strange lights in the sky, we took a nine-mile dirt road from the mailbox to an entrance posted with military signs.

"RESTRICTED AREA" blares one.

It concludes with "Use of deadly force authorized."

Another sign bears total tourist bait: "Photography is prohibited."

Journalist and UFO expert George Knapp calls this "the money shot" for visitors, either on their own or with organized explorations like Adventure Photo Tours.

The signs reminded me of one scene in the "Dreamland" episode of *The X-Files* television show about verifying spooky tales. Like the show's protagonist Fox Mulder, we headed to the Area 51 border in the dark. The nearly full moon illuminated a hill but, even so, we needed a night spotting scope to see anything. The scope revealed a Ford truck parked on one side behind the entrance. Inside, two men watched us through their own night spotting scopes. A sensor system resembling a Tinkertoy man loomed on the other side of the entrance. Whatever this region holds, it gets more attention than typical empty space at midnight that lies nine miles up a dirt road just off a highway that's already in the middle of nowhere.

Watching the Worst Bad Alien Movie Ever

Boasting Lake Tahoe locations and a unique award, 1964's *The Creeping Terror* spent many years on my "gotta see this" list. Authors Michael and Harry Medved nominated it as "worst film ever" and gave the movie extra cache by presenting it with a Golden Turkey Award for Most Laughable Concept of an Outer Space Monster.

But Jurassic viewing opportunities made *The Creeping Terror* hard to find in those unimaginable days before video and recording devices. That's right, not available on videotape, DVD, or Blu-ray. Certainly not streaming.

The movie finally showed up on *Mystery Science Theater 3000* (*MST3K*), a program that ridicules trashy movies. The show was broadcast past my bedtime, but I bought a copy of the video and rushed to insert the seventy-five-minute opus into a video machine, eagerly watching for Lake Tahoe.

Of course, this also meant watching the story of a spaceship crash that traps one alien and sends the other out to creep its terrorism. Viewing *The Creeping Terror* proves to be a surprisingly painful process. Yes, *MST3K*-related website Daddy-O's Drive-In Dirt noted bad traits like "lots of narration and little dialogue because the soundtrack reportedly was lost in Lake Tahoe, Nevada, where the locations shots were made." A review titled "The Carpet Wore Tennis Shoes" gives some idea of quality, along with the video box description of the aliens as "erect penises." Actually, the monsters resemble a bedspread turned into a kid's entry for a Chinese New Year parade.

The aliens took me back to age seven when local kids took Dad's eight-millimeter camera and filmed a caveman story with neighbors on our Southern California street. A couple of us got under a fake, furry, black-and-white panda bear rug and used a cornucopia as a trunk, our interpretation of a wooly mammoth. We terrorized the hero, professional actor Ralph Hart, who played Vivian Vance's son Sherman from 1962 to 1965 on *The Lucy Show*. He planned to beat us to death with a club that looked a lot like a baseball bat.

Our zero budget and compressed time frame showed. Without a chance to practice, we failed to coordinate leg movements when Ralph swung at us. Our last, pitiful shot shows us kids spilling out from the mammoth blanket and with quick, embarrassed moves, trying to hide back under it. This devastating blow ended my movie career in the neighborhood. Ralph danced with Marian the Librarian in 1962's *The Music Man*, but he eventually quit pictures, too.

The Creeping Terror's creator, Argyle Nelson, obviously wore the tough skin it takes to force one's way into the film industry—despite making embarrassing mistakes. He also proved more successful than us because he got his movie distributed. Still, ours was better because it only lasted thirty seconds.

Our budget prevented sound or music, but *The Creeping Terror* features a soundtrack—six notes played over and over and over again. This, plus a song at a hootenanny scene, inspires the fast-forward icon, but that would be cheating. To fully experience *The Creeping Terror*, you have to sit through it all, sound and music included. No zipping through numerous, pointless cloud shots, though that might cut off ten minutes of running time. Fast-forwarding during alien attacks promises a welcome reprieve, too, since the creeping terror waddles so slowly that victims practically hurl themselves into the terror's mouth.

This makes *The Creeping Terror* far more deserving of the top Golden Turkey Award than the Medved Brothers' eventual winner, *Plan 9 from Outer Space*. *Plan 9* at least offers a perverse last chance to see the iconic screen Dracula, Bela Lugosi. *Plan 9* also inspired the fine movie *Ed Wood* and resulted in a best supporting actor Oscar for Martin Landau, so some good came of it. No such positive future lay in store for *The Creeping Terror*.

Like *Plan 9*, the *Terror* ups its Awful Quotient by hiring its director to act. Argyle Nelson audaciously plays the lead, taking the hopeful moniker Vic Savage. Argyle's. . .uh, Vic's. . .overpowering pompadour proves a distraction, taking away from visions of Tahoe and a sense of why the filmmaker chose to work in the region. Does the area possess unique qualities to lure the story of these unforgettable alien creatures?

No. The name Tahoe lacks importance for an Angel County, California setting. Trees and scrub look suspiciously like Angels Camp in Calaveras County rather than the higher-altitude evergreens of Lake Tahoe. This leads to a truly fearsome possibility, at least for this book.

What if cameras never opened lenses on Nevada? Nothing on screen or in the story offers proof. Rumor filtered to the Nevada Film Office that a local or two claimed to have heard of someone who knew someone else who worked on the movie at Lake Tahoe, but no one ever confirmed the stories.

With or without a claim to write off the viewing as Nevada research, watching *The Creeping Terror* proves a truly terrifying experience. But one thing stands out, frightening and haunting me to this day: I actually paid real money for this video. Too bad I lacked visionary powers to predict the development of YouTube, which now plays the movie for free.

4

The Godfather and Mobsters

Prologue

When the Godfather decided to conduct business in Nevada on screen, he forever associated the Mafia with the state and its reputation for fostering the forbidden. Though everyone today accepts the instrumental role organized crime played in transforming Las Vegas from dusty desert to glamorous resort, decades passed before Nevada and the word *Mafia* came together in a single movie. Granted, hints about the connection abounded. *Las Vegas Shakedown* from 1956 implied organized crime. Same with *Guns, Girls and Gangsters* in 1959.

Still, it took the iconic 1974 *Godfather* sequel to formally connect the word *Mafia* with crime and imbed Nevada's Mob ties in the public mind. Until *The Godfather*, gangsters lived back east and bore features of the growling Edward G. Robinson, a scowling Humphrey Bogart, or a sneering James Cagney. They joined Paul Muni as the first Scarface and television's *The Untouchables* in Chicago, among other metropolitan areas where real-life criminals like Al Capone ruled.

Part I: The Godfather

Author Mario Puzo put a different spin on the mobster genre when his book *The Godfather* took testimony that various government commissions made public. The writer blended fact and fiction into a cohesive and dramatically compelling tale, reaching mega–best-seller status. That success guaranteed a movie version, and Puzo joined forces with director Francis Ford Coppola to write a screenplay emphasizing themes of family loyalty called *Omertà*. Coppola proved a visionary director who took *The Godfather* beyond page imaginings.

Winning the Academy Award for Best Picture, the film immediately slotted in the record books for sheer brilliance. As time passes, its position shifts on different lists, but it generally makes an appearance on those looking at the best films ever made. In 2010, it topped Everyone's a Critic online, stepping down to number two in the Internet Movie Database. A more formal 1998 voting, organized by the American Film Institute, listed the hundred best movies, and rated *The Godfather* the third-greatest film ever made. *Sight and Sound* puts it at number twenty-one.

This gives *The Godfather* huge credibility in setting the groundwork for assumptions about Nevada's Mob connections, ideas other moviemakers used as blueprints for their own projects. Following *The Godfather* pattern makes sense according to retired mayor Oscar Goodman, a longtime Las Vegas resident and former criminal attorney whose clients included gangster Meyer Lansky.

"From the characters I used to represent, the people I used to deal with, it's 100 percent accurate—the best," he said, looking across at old Las Vegas from his mayor's office on the tenth floor of city hall.

"It's very, very realistic, said the mayor, a snappy dresser with a friendly face that belies courtroom toughness.

"It's very good. I mean, *Omertà* meant something, it was a Real McCoy. It wasn't the present-day Mob. The reason you don't hear about them is they're a bunch of wannabes, they're Mickey Mouses," insisted Goodman. (In the years since Goodman made his comments, Russian and Armenian "wannabes" do prove threatening in such projects as 2016's second season of *Bosch* on Amazon.)

While *The Godfather* novel represents a community well known by the mayor of Las Vegas, the movie planted its roots back in the East, with power struggles between competing factions of The Family, who value their own blood but turn on a spigot for outsiders and enemies.

In this scenario, mandatory loyalty tops all virtues; vices vary in acceptability, with gambling serving as an effective tool for dealing with unreported cash. The first *Godfather* movie acknowledges this as it leads toward its finale.

By then, Marlon Brando's Don Corleone turns operations over to his son Michael. Michael sees ripe pickings in 1952's Vegas, with location and time established in skyline shots and the marquees of headliners Patti Page, Joe E. Lewis, Dean Martin, and Jerry Lewis.

Michael urges a casino owner to gracefully back out of his business, filmed on location at the Riviera. Refusing to let go, the owner becomes part of *The Godfather*'s final choreography of retribution and gunplay that remains screen legend.

The scene's intensity helped *The Godfather* win the Oscar for Best Picture and become a box office blockbuster. That kind of success inspired others to explore and copy similar themes.

Part II: Founding Vegas

Spiraling off *Godfather* concepts, novelist/screenwriter Jackie Collins provides her own variation on how the Mob started Las Vegas in *Lucky/Chances*, a 1990 television miniseries based on two of her books.

Collins' hero, Gino Santangelo, dreams of a fabulous Las Vegas and convinces reputable socialites to invest in his vision. Construction problems lead him to his daughter's godfather, who neglects to mention a penchant for laundering money and running drugs.

This new godfather maintains his nefarious doings decades later when "The Goddaughter," Lucky, needs an investor for her own Las Vegas casino.

Played by Nicolette Sheridan, Lucky gets the money and shows her design acumen, arriving at her desert construction site in a slinky white dress and spike heels. She demonstrates admirable strength and coordination, staying upright and clean the whole time despite her dirty business. The miniseries earned an Emmy nomination for costuming.

In between wardrobe changes, Lucky builds the grandest hotel in town, effectively played by the old MGM (now Bally's). The hotel features extensive floor space with a ceiling adorned by massive rows of glittery, elegant chandeliers.

Lucky eventually determines that working with the Mob entails complications. For one thing, she learns her godfather ordered the murders of both her brother and mother. The tiny mom role features Sandra Bullock, who was lucky to be killed off quickly and avoid any lingering association with trashy soap operas and questionable history lessons.

Some *Lucky/Chances* ideas about Las Vegas repeated views covered earlier in *The Neon Empire*, a 1989 television movie-of-the-week based on a story by journalist Pete Hamill. Producers thought *The Neon Empire* and its Junior Moloff character eliminated the need for any other story about Las Vegas Mob roots.

"This project will probably kill those Bugsy projects in development," producers said, while scouting small gambling towns dotting Northern Nevada.

"Our movie is about the birth of an area out on a desert highway. It's where real-life mobster Bugsy Siegel built the Flamingo Hotel," explained producer Richard Maynard in a publicity packet.

"Like our Junior Moloff character, Siegel was a dreamer. What Moloff sees in Las Vegas are opportunities to become legitimate, to be recognized as an entrepreneur."

Though producers scouted both Las Vegas and Reno, they used the small Arizona town of Florence for filming.

"Florence is about the same age as Las Vegas," said production designer Peter Wooley after scouting Northern Nevada towns like Yerington.

"What Florence never did was get into that frenzy of the 1950s, putting new fronts on old buildings."

Rather than refurbish anything with years on it, Las Vegas visionaries blew up outdated buildings to erect glass and concrete towers decorated with miles of neon. This lack of a forties-period look also proved a problem for *The Marrying Man*, another project set in early Las Vegas with a character based on Bugsy.

Part III: Bugsy

Pretty much any producer planning a project about early Las Vegas seeks something resembling Bugsy Siegel's original Flamingo Hotel. Low slung like a Spanish hacienda, the hotel featured a tubular tower rising many feet above the building, a beacon for a stand-alone destination on the town's outskirts.

Huge pink neon letters spelled out "Flamingo" across the roof, where trap shooters and golfers played. Inside, visitors stayed in one of seventy-seven rooms and saw the decade's top entertainers. The unique design never caught on in the rest of Nevada, so finding a filmable substitute proved difficult.

Meanwhile, Bugsy's original Flamingo remnants disappeared in 1993, enveloped by a standard hotel tower. Development spread like a virus around it, destroying any hint of isolation. Bought out several times, the Hilton name graced it before Caesars Entertainment took over and revised the name to Flamingo Las Vegas.

A couple of nods toward the Flamingo's notorious past hide amidst property sites. Guests watch shows at Bugsy's Cabaret, which eventually hosted Mormon superstars Donnie and Marie Osmond belting out such hits as "Sweet and Innocent."

The nod to Bugsy's preoccupation with entertainment continues across the property where visitors emulate the Mob look by purchasing porkpie hats at the Garden Wedding Chapel. Surrounding park area includes the Bugsy Siegel Memorial, complete with a bronze plaque referring to the founder's "preoccupation with safety," such as the casino's bulletproof windows and multiple exits.

The Flamingo Las Vegas shows how the city's skyline changes regularly. Few historic Mafia structures remain, a fact well researched by staff members at the Nevada Film Office. Only the courthouse where mobsters testified during the famous fifties hearings stands unscathed. Today, the former federal building houses an enlightening Mob Museum, but its existence on Stewart Avenue never much mattered to moviemakers. They wanted a forties-style Mob-run casino resembling the original Flamingo. By the mid-eighties, so many people called the Nevada Film Office asking for "something that looks like the old Flamingo" that it took no time to burst the bubble when the request came from the producers of *Bugsy*.

"It's just not economic to have a casino like the old Flamingo in the middle of nowhere," film commissioners explained, reminding producers that Las Vegas itself no longer claimed a location in the middle of nowhere.

These facts pained film commissioners because *Bugsy* boasted big, important elements headed by superstar Warren Beatty and *Rain Man*'s Oscar-winning director Barry Levinson. The production team explored the idea of building sets on empty desert land outside Las Vegas, but that failed when strict federal regulations protecting tortoises prohibited necessary construction.

Shifting to the San Diego area to re-create the original Flamingo Hotel, though, the set designers won Oscars. Going beyond such top production values, the movie resonates through strong characters. *Bugsy* explores the universal theme of a vision ultimately creating something bigger than imagined. By 1990, Bugsy's dream transformed to the glittery, neon-infused Las Vegas Strip, with towering casinos and playful architecture. A shot of the Strip remains on screen as end credits roll, the only scene from *Bugsy* actually filmed in Nevada.

Quality oozed from *Bugsy*, and it won a Golden Globe for Best Drama, later earning ten Oscar nominations. One nomination went to Beatty as Best Actor, playing Bugsy, a man whose gentle, sweet romantic hopes switched with hair-trigger speed to a nasty business temper.

An impressive cast, including Annette Bening, Joe Mantegna, Elliott Gould, and George Raft, provides strong backup. Harvey Keitel, as Mickey Cohen, and Ben Kingsley, as Meyer Lansky, earned supporting actor Oscar nominations.

Despite being "inspired by a true story," *Bugsy*'s dates, facts, and timelines weaken when compared to television documentaries, books, and articles. Most research credits William "Billy" Wilkerson as the real dreamer behind Las Vegas, a point outlined in the 1996 A & E *American Justice* episode "Vegas and the Mob."

Scrapping inconvenient factual details to heighten drama, *Bugsy* screenwriter James Toback condenses people and timelines. Still, truth shines in *Bugsy*'s basic conceit. As the movie shows, Las Vegas and Nevada needed audacious risk takers in order to evolve. While historians pick at the extent of his role in developing Las Vegas, Bugsy pushed the process forward, and his name infuses the city's Mob background.

Once Bugsy and his fictional prototypes made their dreams come true, they took time to appreciate Nevada's scenic wonders. Money allowed them to settle in Lake Tahoe's stunning natural beauty, where the 1974 sequel to *The Godfather* begins.

Part IV: Son of the Godfather

As *The Godfather Part II* opens, the iconic Corleone family conquered Nevada and maintain a palatial Tahoe estate. Much of the sequel involves a newly created story evolving from the first film's closing image of a mobster kissing Michael Corleone's hand as he takes over his father's leadership role in the Mob.

The sequel also includes the original novel's backstory of Vito Corleone's immigration and early rise to power. This portion uses the warm, orange tones from the first film and features Robert De Niro's Academy Award–winning performance as the young don. *People* magazine rated this section as one of the year's best films.

In an attempt at being cute, the magazine separated the colder, "modern" part of the movie and called it one of the year's worst films. This shortsighted view ignores that *The Godfather Part II* gets its impact from the contrast of Michael versus his father at similar stages in their lives. Rather than tell the two stories sequentially, the movie crosscuts between new and old approaches to leadership. *Godfather* producer Fred Roos insists this juxtaposition makes the second film stronger than the first.

The second *Godfather* movie starts in Nevada as Vito Corleone's grandson receives his first communion at Tahoe, followed by a celebration at the family's lakeside mansion. The real-life Sam Giancana/Frank Sinatra history at the Cal Neva Lodge gives Tahoe a historical connection with the Mob that made sense to audiences. Plus, gangsters have the aesthetics and funds to afford living at California's old Kaiser Estate, stepping in as Nevada.

Here, Nevada's US Senator Geary accepts an endowment check, distancing himself by purposely mispronouncing Vito Corleone's name. But Senator Geary hides his cards. He later meets with Michael and offers an outrageous price to get the family a gaming license. Michael rejects the opportunity.

"We're part of the same hypocrisy," Michael responds in actor Al Pacino's chilly tones.

This negative portrait of the Nevada politician continues when the senator visits a brothel and wakes up next to a bloody, dead prostitute. The Corleone family arranged the mess and quietly cleans it up—but not for free.

"Some of my very best friends are Italian Americans," the senator tells the world after blackmail reduces his proposed gaming license price.

Playing power games with politicians represents standard business, but Michael's life heads toward isolating extremes when he learns his brother Fredo betrayed him. This leads to the most striking Tahoe imagery ever put on film as Fredo takes a fishing trip in a small boat, heading to the middle of the massive alpine lake against a stormy backdrop.

Fredo describes how he says a Hail Mary every time he drops a line in the water; every time he says a Hail Mary, he catches a fish. But this time—silhouetted against an ominous, darkening sky—Fredo has other reasons to pray. The classic moment melds location with action to create unforgettable cinema. All of *Part II*'s visuals sear the story into memory, but the strongest images come from impressive use of Lake Tahoe. The major location, the Kaiser Estate, sold to private developers at Fleur du Lac, is easily viewed by boat from the north shore, near Homewood, California. Developers tore down the Godfather house and only the boathouse remains from filming days.

Despite the Nevada setting, California locations dominate. Although a July 1984 *Nevada Magazine* article mentions filming on the Nevada side of Tahoe, production designer Dean Tavoularis said the state was only used for Las Vegas scenes.

"I don't recall a tunnel near the Dreyfuss Estate or cabin near Crystal Bay," he said in response to rumored locations.

Years passed since *The Godfather Part II* filmed at Lake Tahoe, but put a toe in the water, and you find the temperature feels just like it did in when the crew arrived to shoot the movie's early scenes on a frigid autumn day.

Radio announcer Jock Scowcroft liked to tell stories about being an extra in the lake during that sequence. Tahoe waters resembled melted ice, and Jock claimed that everyone froze but did a great job frolicking in bathing suits.

"We deserved Oscars too, just like Robert De Niro," he said.

Years later, a third *Godfather* hit the big screen. The story pays heed to Nevada, as Michael Corleone searches for redemption by getting out of gambling and into the Catholic Church. Tahoe footage replays from the previous film, and while a scouting team scoured Las Vegas, casino scenes shot in Atlantic City. *The Godfather Part III* gets its biggest Nevada tie because Coppola and Puzo wrote much of the screenplay while staying at the Peppermill in Reno.

"Coppola told me, 'Whatever I lose on the casino floor, I just go upstairs and make it back by writing my screenplay,'" Peppermill's former general manager Phil Bryan recounted.

Part V: The Godfather's Evil Stepchildren Cross De Lena and Tony Soprano

The Godfather movies remain the most intense about mobsters. All three stories eclipse Puzo's next Nevada/Mafia project, *The Last Don*. The 1997 television movie replays a *Godfather*-style saga covering several generations of Family.

Interviewed for a DVD piece about making the three-part television miniseries, Puzo says the story's Mob element came accidentally.

"I was not writing a novel about the Mafia. I was writing about Hollywood. That landed me into Las Vegas, which I knew a lot about. Going to Las Vegas led me into the Mafia again."

It also allowed Puzo to explore new developments in casinos, as the title character decides to divest all major Mob activities except gaming, which the don wants to see legalized in every state.

Running a modern casino falls to Cross De Lena, played by Jason Gedrick, who told me on set he played a gangster with soul.

"He's a conciliator, more of a guy who would like to fix something."

Yet De Lena maintains the corrupt system, passing skimmed money to Mafia headquarters back east. He also uses a snowy mansion, representing a palatial estate in the Sierra Nevada, though the project mostly filmed in Canada.

Palm Springs provided many Las Vegas exteriors, with stock footage establishing the time frame when Elvis plays the Hilton in 1970. Each of the story's three parts features a Nevada setting, but the production company only came to the state for interiors at the fictitious Xanadu Casino. These shot at the Peppermill in Reno with its gaming tables rimmed in purple neon.

Top rated the week it aired, *The Last Don* earned an Emmy nomination for outstanding miniseries, plus supporting acting nominations for Joe Mantegna and Kirstie Alley. A prestige project for television, the picture's harsh lighting makes it look cheaper than *The Godfather* trio. It also reflects broadcast standards of its time, with action rehashed at commercial breaks. Mild language and no nudity contrast sharply with what television viewers heard and watched a few years later when HBO ran *The Sopranos* from 1999 to 2007.

Appropriately enough, the Soprano family enjoys Las Vegas. The final season includes a segment where taking peyote puts Godfather Tony Soprano in a mindset that lets him win big at Caesars Palace. Escaping from his East Coast burdens, the crime lord travels about a half hour outside Las Vegas to Red Rock Canyon, where he gets stoned and fully appreciates a glowing orange sunset.

Maerose Prizzi and Irene Walker

With most of its action in New York and Los Angeles, John Huston's *Prizzi's Honor* plays into the Las Vegas connection when professional hit woman Irene Walker conducts business there. Irene, played by Kathleen Turner, makes several mistakes. First, she keeps part of the money her Vegas victim scammed from the Mob. Next, she marries another hit man. Worse, that marriage enrages jealous Mob princess Maerose Prizzi, who travels to Vegas and learns about the theft.

Worst, Irene pits herself against Angelica Huston in her most intense, lethal mode, so effective she got the movie's best notice, an Oscar for Best Supporting Actress.

Ace Rothstein and Nicky Santoro

"Family films" include *The Sopranos* and Coppola and Puzo, but a complete list mandates Martin Scorsese. Most of Scorsese's Mob-related projects happen back east. In contrast, his *Casino* gamble involved extensive Las Vegas location shooting to tell a fictionalized account of mobsters Frank "Lefty" Rosenthal and Tony "The Ant" Spilatro.

Mobster Hall of Famers Robert De Niro and Joe Pesci play the duo bearing the fictionalized names Ace Rothstein and Nicky Santoro. *Casino* explores how easily they ran Mob money through Las Vegas operations, relaying basic principles about gambling, casino management, Nevada history, and organized crime. Author Nicholas Pileggi meticulously researched source material involving the Stardust Resort and Casino.

To avoid legal hassles, the Stardust shifts to a fictional Tangiers in the movie, a common name for projects needing to skirt lawsuits by existing properties. The movie team scouted many casinos, including vacant sites in Northern Nevada where production designer Dante Ferretti scouted Reno's Riverside Hotel Casino and the Ormsby House in Carson City.

Despite the ease of dressing empty space for the project's seventies look, he settled on two locations in Las Vegas. The Landmark serves as exterior. Interiors filmed in the Riviera.

"The first part of the Riviera with the slot machines, bingo, and keno was originally built in 1964," Ferretti explained.

"And then when they restored the other side of the casino in 1990, it was done in the same style."

To get the look of mechanical slots, Ferretti devised slipcovers to make existing machines look older. After dressing the machines, crew members removed the "costumes" each morning, allowing guests to gamble most of the month-long shoot. Likened to "a small-scale military invasion," the crew took over the casino from midnight to 10 a.m., sharing the floor with active gamblers. Though difficult, the effort proved worthwhile to producer Barbara De Fina.

"We never would have had the depth, we never would have been able to build something that big," she said in the *Casino* publicity packet.

"We had hundreds of real people, non-extras, in the deep background who were actually gambling in the fifth-largest casino in the world. There is no way you could have done that on a soundstage."

As in his brilliant *Goodfellas,* Scorsese used a Steadicam, mounting his camera on a person who moves smoothly without jitters to catch scenes showing Mob operations. Whizzing through narrow rows of slot machines and tables, a cacophony of shapes and colors fill the screen. Attention to detail provides the film's highlight.

One drawback comes from extreme violence and language. Joe Pesci uses the word "fuck" as a noun, verb, and dangling participle.

Curious about the word's frequency, Film Office staff spent some downtime comparing the script and final film, reading through the original screenplay and finding the word sixty-three times.

A DVD of the movie went well beyond the script's sixty-three-word "F-Count." No surprise, Pesci got the highest score, with a grand total of 208; after all, he specializes in improvisation.

Language issues aside, the film features top-notch production values, telling a fascinating story that minutely details casino operation by organized criminals. Its filming schedule of more than a hundred days in Las Vegas sunk millions into the community during one of the longest shoots on record.

Locals benefiting from production included the mobsters' real-life lawyer, Oscar Goodman, subject of the *Mob Law* documentary that premiered at the 1998 CineVegas Film Festival. In the documentary, extensive shots of the Vegas skyline accompany actor Anthony LaPaglia's narration and observations like "every great city in the world has a river running through it, and in Las Vegas, it's cash."

During the documentary, Goodman denies working with the Mafia.

"Over the years, my clients have never suggested to me that there's an organization called La Cosa Nostra," he insists.

The documentary's highlight comes when Goodman confronts an FBI nemesis after nearly twenty years, and the two refuse to back down on their version of what happened.

Later elected mayor of Las Vegas, Goodman discussed the films from his tenth-floor office. He said both films show a dramatic world.

"Every day—it was every day—was like being in a movie because you'd turn on the TV, and every day something was happening here regarding Spilatro or Rosenthal. I mean, every single day," said the mayor, dressed in a blue designer suit appropriate for a dignified politician or lawyer.

"There wasn't a day that went by that you couldn't turn on the TV and see a real-life soap opera. It was a real-life soap opera. You didn't need *The Sopranos* in those days. All you needed to do was turn on your local news."

Though Goodman resisted terms like *Mafia* back then, he eventually began using the word. The natural question arose:

"What made you change?"

His eyes twinkled as he responded.

"I saw the movie *Casino*," he quipped.

After watching it, he added, the FBI let him hear tapes detailed in the film, the ones where Goodman's clients detail atrocities they committed.

"I listened to them and then I realized . . ."

The former Mob attorney paused dramatically.

He waited another beat.

". . . I should have charged a lot more money."

Goodman goes along with the *Casino* proposition that big-scale organized crime in Las Vegas disappeared, though others might argue.

When asked if anything remains from the worlds displayed in *The Godfather* or *Casino*, the Las Vegas mayor shrugged and answered with a bit of a laugh as he gestured.

"I think the only vestige, the only remnant, the only remaining thing, is up here on the tenth floor," he said, pointing to himself.

Jane Austen and Tony Cortino

By 1998—three years after *Casino* hit theaters—a spoof seemed in order.

"See It Early. Avoid the Mob," urged the poster for *Jane Austen's Mafia!* a title making fun of the film industry penchant to spin out proper romances by England's literary queen.

Puzo's *The Last Don* inspired director Jim Abrahams to lampoon the Mafia genre with his own godfather named Tony Cortino. Ironically, coincidence brought him to the casino where *The Last Don* filmed, Reno's Peppermill. Abrahams and cowriters Greg Norberg and Michael McManus thought destiny insisted on the location because they already gave the name Pepper to their femme fatale. Better yet, they felt Reno interiors easily passed as their Las Vegas setting.

Abrahams earned his reputation for spoofs by nailing disaster films with *Airplane*. He went on to skewer genres like police films in *The Naked Gun*. A guy who likes to laugh, he requires three qualities for parody.

"First," he said, raising his index finger. "You need a genre."

"Second," he continued, bringing his middle finger into the mix. "The genre has to take itself seriously."

Both traits permeate most Mob films.

"There is a huge genre of Mafia-oriented films," said Abrahams. "With very few exceptions, these movies do not have any sense of humor about themselves at all."

But Abrahams needed one more dynamic to make his spoof work.

"Someone else has to pay for it," he said, raising a third finger.

This third piece fell into place when Touchstone Pictures stepped up and funded *Mafia!*

Researching *Mafia!* meant Abrahams and the screenwriters watched *The Godfather* trilogy and other Family films.

"It was interesting to us that in most of these movies the storylines are pretty similar," said screenwriter Michael McManus in cheery tones.

"They are always about honor, family, betrayal, and the stories are very Shakespearean and operatic."

He liked that *The Godfather* movies take a moral high ground.

"At least we weren't doing a movie about a bunch of unforgivable and morally corrupt scumbags," he said, eyes twinkling.

Throughout their research, the filmmakers looked for repeated imagery and clichés, so Nevada fit right in.

One joke follows the Mob movie idea that gang members often come to Nevada for meetings. *Mafia!* features a casino marquee with lighted letters reading "Welcome Mob Bosses." Peppermill computer operators programmed the message for their outdoor billboard, and it ran throughout an entire day's filming—with absolutely no comment from the general public.

Gino and David Mamet

The *Mafia!* concept that mobsters schedule meetings in Nevada propels *Things Change*. Played as warm character study, the farce comes from Pulitzer Prize–winning playwright David Mamet, who maintains no bigger goal than telling a story.

"I don't think I've ever sat down to write a message. Like Ziegfeld said, 'you can send a message by telegram.' I just sit down and write plays," smiled Mamet, sporting a casual look in Levi jacket and jeans.

Using the fish-out-of-water concept, he said the Mafia connection in *Things Change* draws from a plot device rooted in fairytales.

"The movie," continued Mamet on set at Harrah's Tahoe, "is a fable about mistaken identity. It's an age-old story. It's the same story as *The Prince and the Pauper* or anything where people exchange identities."

In this case, Don Ameche plays a shoeshine man named Gino who bears a remarkable resemblance to a Mafia don. The sweet and kind Gino agrees to switch places and serve a three-year prison sentence for the don.

Before getting locked up, Gino goes on holiday to one of those Tahoe estates where mobsters hang out. Applying all his shoeshine knowledge to the world he finds at Tahoe, Gino convinces everyone he's truly a wise guy.

Mamet maintained a lighthearted approach on set, playing practical jokes like sneaking up with a bear rug to surprise actor Robert Prosky during one take at the Ehrman Mansion. If Mamet had problems with dialogue, he quickly whipped out a different version, running into an office and rewriting a scene on a typewriter in the days before word processors.

Despite informal dress and a jokester attitude, Mamet focused on work as he walked around set to determine each character's movements, looking very much like a theatrical director blocking out scenes on a stage with limited space.

"The underlying philosophical and aesthetic concepts are the same, but the difference is that on stage you're working about 99 percent with script and 1 percent with the plastic or scenic elements, and when you work in a movie, you're working almost exclusively with the scenic elements."

These elements included the floor at Crystal Bay's Cal Neva casino, which closed in 2010. Other scenes use the Harrah's Tahoe showroom and high-rollers suite. California's Sugar Pine State Park offers a gorgeous Tahoe vista from the dock, while its Ehrman Mansion served as a home where the movie's mobsters meet.

"It was really exciting," Mamet said about using Tahoe locations. "It was fascinating working half in what was a working casino every day and half in what was a movie set every day, but it worked out fine," he said, noting that there were lessons that came from Nevada locations.

"We learned not to hit a soft eighteen," he joked.

As with most of Mamet's early movies, *Things Change* had a limited art house run for audiences who enjoy different approaches, like a stagy style and staccato delivery. The film's highlight comes from Ameche, seventy-nine at the time. Ameche enjoyed bonding with his little-known costar, Joe Mantegna. They spent hours together building rapport as they shared meals, chatted, and built a friendship.

"I love the picture," Ameche later told me at Harrah's. "I'm having as much fun on this picture as I've ever had on any picture in my life—as a matter of fact, more."

The experienced Ameche considered his director a newcomer and loved watching his style develop.

"Mamet doesn't know all of the subtleties of the motion picture business yet, but he knows he doesn't know them," said Ameche, as the director headed into his second film.

Ameche, who still sported his forties-era matinee idol mustache, originally signed on for a supporting role as a Tahoe don. After Giancarlo Giannini dropped from the lead, Mantegna suggested Ameche move into the top spot.

Director Mamet liked the change, saying of Ameche, "He has great simplicity and great depth and sincerity. And humor. All those things we've seen in his performances for fifty years."

Things Change not only gave Ameche a large and lovely role toward the end of his career, it reminded audiences of the connection between mobsters and Lake Tahoe.

Buddy "Aces" and the Jack Ryans

Things Change and *The Godfather* helped bring director Joe Carnahan to Lake Tahoe when he planned his Mob movie, *Smokin' Aces.*

"It seemed natural and sensible because Tahoe has a rich history of mobsters, going back to Frank Sinatra and the Cal Neva and all the wonderful things that went on there, and it has this kind of romantic, by-the-lake God's country and the gaming industry," he said during the October 2005 shoot at Stateline.

A Sacramento resident, Carnahan had visited the small lakeside community before.

"I'd been to Tahoe several times, and knew the layout and had actually written the script for the Horizon and knew Caesars across the street. . . . It was a huge part of the development because I rarely write a script for a location, and this is one of those instances where I did," said Carnahan, whose quick speaking pattern covers many subjects and mirrors his movie's jump-cut style.

Carnahan's script brings mobsters, cops, and miscellaneous killers to Lake Tahoe where they hope to "smoke" Aces, a magician with strange ties to a mobster named Primo. The location draws about a dozen different characters, including Alicia Keys in her screen debut, Ben Affleck in a superstar cameo, and Chris Pine in early work.

"It was really cool," Pine recounted at a party the evening he "killed" Ben Affleck at Cave Rock State Park.

The scene called for Pine to hold a postmortem conversation with Affleck by working the prone actor's mouth in puppet fashion.

"Ben just lay there and let me rehearse a bunch. He didn't have to." Affleck, who played Jack Ryan in the Tom Clancy series, boasted superstar status at the time. Pine went on to take the title role of Jack Ryan in the series reboot.

Carnahan figures distinct roles lured such big and upcoming talent.

"I think what people saw—established stars like Affleck, and Alicia Keys coming out of the music world—was the opportunity to see something utterly different. I think everybody's always looking for that, a chance to kind of change it up and alter their public persona and how they're perceived by an audience."

This helped put together what he calls a "very, very, very black comedy" with extreme violence in a scenic wonderland.

"Setting this kind of wild, surrealistic story against such unbelievable beauty amps it up a little bit," said Carnahan, a bundle of energy who shaved his head and thought nothing of wading out into Tahoe's frigid water to get the right shot of a floating body.

"It makes it that much more weird, that you would set something like that against such an extravagant natural location. I just love the lake. Tahoe I don't think has been shot nearly enough, and I think a lot of people, particularly on this film, really fell in love with this area and saw it for what I see it as. It's just this really unique kind of little spot that surprises a lot of people. It's so hip, and yet so kind of secret."

Epilogue

Smokin' Aces, like many Mob stories, emphasizes violence. It joins a long list of projects featuring Mob connections that show Nevada's dark side.

"Is this bad for Nevada?" I asked Las Vegas Mayor Oscar Goodman during our tenth-floor meeting.

The mayor recommended keeping an open mind.

"We have to talk about our past, because that's what got us to the present and will take us to the future," he told me.

"Anybody who apologizes for the days depicted in *Casino* and *Mob Law*, I think they make a terrible mistake because that's what differentiates us from everybody else. I think as soon as we homogenize, we're going to be like El Paso with a couple of casinos. We're not going to be anything special. For those who are the apologists, I think they make a big mistake."

5

Crime Scenes and Investigators

A casino loses its lion. An unidentified dancer floats dead in a pool. White rappers disturb the peace but worst of all, can't dance. Investigators solve these crimes in three of Nevada's most famous television series, *Vega$*, *CSI*, and *Reno 911!*. Driving a big cat down the Las Vegas Strip fixes one problem on *Vega$*. Crime-solving techniques include analyzing hair strands found at the Liberace Museum for *CSI*. Showing white boys how to get down and boogie keeps the peace in *Reno 911!*.

Rising to the top by spending all ten years of the new millennium's first decade as television's top-rated drama, *CSI* put Las Vegas back in the homes of viewers who began watching the city's weekly crimes on *Vega$* two decades earlier. Between broadcasts of new episodes plus multiple daily airings on Spike TV and other specialty networks, *CSI* grew into an icon itself, a franchise inspiring two other series that distinguished themselves from the original by specifying their locations in the title. But say *CSI*, and neon shines in mental images generated by the first and best of the shows, the one with a Las Vegas setting.

Anthony Zuiker, who moved to the city as a baby, created *CSI* after attending the University of Nevada, Las Vegas and supporting himself with jobs like running the Mirage tram. Throughout these jobs, Zuiker kept eyes glued to big and small screens, watching films and television shows incessantly. Calling himself "a frustrated movie writer who is having a love affair with television," Zuiker said both mediums inspired *CSI*.

From film, the Middle East war drama *Three Kings* startled Zuiker with graphic scenes of what guns really do to internal tissues. Extreme slow motion close-ups create their own shock and awe when a bullet rams into flesh, punching through a thick blockade as blood fans out in a series of elegantly dropping beads whose surrealistic beauty belie the wound's horrific meaning.

From television, Discovery Channel's *New Detectives* show fascinated Zuiker by looking at technology involved in solving crimes. Computers match fingerprint ridges in seconds. High-powered microscopes reveal details unimagined by previous generations of crime solvers.

"I wanted to show the science at a macro level," said Zuiker, sporting a trimmed beard and glasses on a face that occasionally showed up in cameos on the series.

Zuiker pursued his idea for a high-tech, detail-oriented crime program by conducting firsthand research. Going on twenty-four-hour "ride-alongs" with the Las Vegas forensics force called Field Services, he developed the idea of showing how an elite team of experts operates America's second-busiest crime lab.

The ride-alongs impressed him.

"It was really a culture shock," said Zuiker, a family man who frequently returned to his hometown to visit his mother during the height of *CSI* production.

"The Strip and Las Vegas are notoriously safe because of all the visitors. But I was seeing the other side of crime," he recalled.

"A lot of bad was happening that wasn't making it in the paper. If you really knew what was out there, you wouldn't leave your front door."

Despite this firsthand understanding of everyday dangers, Zuiker leaves home on business but takes precautions.

"I am a little more aware. Our door is locked. There are predators out there. Hopefully, our show communicates that, and lets audiences know our CSI people are helping."

The CSI people provide their useful services in an ideal setting—Las Vegas.

"When the show was first conceived, we wanted to be able to have Las Vegas as a backdrop based on the fact that it was a twenty-four-hour town."

Crimes take on different hues in Las Vegas, said Zuiker.

"There are lots of transients, and people come to Las Vegas to escape."

Another twist develops from a city that comes to life after dark.

"I wanted to do a crime drama in the graveyard shift—I thought that made it really exciting."

Along with these traits, Las Vegas provides sensory overload ideal for screen action.

For instance, investigators at Las Vegas Boulevard and Tropicana go up one of the Strip's escalators. For a second, Manhattan dominates the skyline, with views of the Statue of Liberty and skyscrapers of the New York, New York Casino. Turn slightly and a fantasy fairyland emerges with colorful castle peaks at Excalibur jutting into the sky. The scene shifts just as quickly to Hollywood, where a giant golden statue of the MGM lion looms on a nearby casino.

Farther north, in the first season's "To Halve and Hold" episode, Italian sights surround *CSI* team members as they pass through interiors featuring temple high ceilings decorated with ornate Renaissance paintings, a breathtaking welcome to the Venetian Resort Casino. The same episode features another Las Vegas contrast as team members head into a rugged outdoors reminiscent of the Old West. Their case involves a dog who chased a stick but brings back a human bone buried in sand around Red Rock Canyon. Among local settings, creator Zuiker likes the "Table Stakes" episode with the Liberace Museum and its "only in Vegas" motif.

"It's a classic example," he said.

The now-defunct museum housed costumes and props for the pompadoured entertainer, who based his piano-playing shows out of Las Vegas for decades. Liberace's artifacts include his signature candelabras and costumes decorated with enough rhinestones to dress every Elvis impersonator in Las Vegas. Looking for extra flair in the *CSI* episode, museum curators explored the collection and unearthed specialty items like a 1976 centennial outfit worn by Liberace—a red, white, and blue hot pants ensemble. Television fame put the once-forgotten back on display.

The Las Vegas propensity for roller coasters plays a role when the New York, New York ride provides a victim in one episode. More frequently, former *CSI* leader Gil Grissom rides because speed eases stress.

Besides roller-coasting stress therapy, Las Vegas provides distinct backgrounds and hobbies for *CSI* team members. Vegas girl Catherine Willows financed her education by dancing in strip clubs, giving her insight into the lifestyle influencing some crimes she investigates. Investigator Warrick Brown's gambling addiction put himself on the line during cases.

Using his local-boy knowledge, Zuiker wrote scripts dealing with casino heists and other regional crimes. The pilot includes a type of "trick roll" Zuiker witnessed on one of his ride-alongs, where he saw firsthand action involving a prostitute who drugged and robbed clients. While horrific crimes seem suited to a place of extremes, coproducer Josh Berman told *Entertainment Weekly* he scanned his hometown Los Angeles paper for ideas.

Though Vegas plays a major role in *CSI*, the series primarily filmed at Santa Clarita stages in California. Vegas appears in each episode during tracking shots filmed from a blimp, but a full-fledged production team kept Nevada location work down to a few visits a year.

"We would love to have a second stage in Vegas," Zuiker noted as the show started its fifth season. "If we had it our way, we would triple our budget and shoot outside on location 24/7."

Still, the real Vegas scene enhances the show, which introduced audiences to other original concepts. Sometimes more a "howdunit" than "whodunit," episodes often applied several possibilities to each crime.

Using an "imaginary flashback," a character says, in effect, "The evidence indicates it happened this way," narrating a scene revealing one scenario. But then a new piece of evidence arrives, disputing the previous scene and creating another imaginary flashback.

"It really violates every rule of television," Zuiker said, explaining that flashbacks "used to be considered a crutch."

Early on, some thought the back-and-forth approach too confusing for audiences who believed the first images they saw. Viewers proved the experts wrong.

"I think all those 'rules' are malarkey," said Zuiker. "I find what we do to be very entertaining television. It's very different, using highly complex scripts meant to challenge the viewer. It proves people don't just want to watch television to tune out."

Others agreed with Zuiker, including superstar director Quentin Tarantino, who put his *Pulp Fiction* touch to the fifth season, a two-part finale called "Grave Danger."

Along with drawing big-name talent behind the scenes, *CSI* benefits from careful casting. Attractive newcomers Jorja Fox, Gary Dourdan, and George Eads earned international stardom by the end of the show's first season.

Besides introducing new faces, *CSI* brought in experienced film actors like Marg Helgenberger, fresh off the Oscar-nominated *Erin Brockovich.* William Petersen seemed a natural leader for the group after his role chasing Hannibal Lecter in the movie that introduced the iconic serial killer, *Manhunter.*

"We love it here," Petersen said. "But you might be able to help us with something. We're having trouble getting permission to film at one of the casinos," he explained during a Nevada Film Office visit the first season.

He explained how casino management worried that serving as a crime site, even a fictional one, frightened guests. A few months later, *CSI* hit number one, and casinos vied for status as a crime site investigated—and watched—by millions.

Crime scene status turned properties into tourist destinations. Eventually, the MGM Grand charged thirty dollars admission to the $5 million

"CSI Experience," a 12,000-square-foot attraction that gives participants up to ninety minutes to solve three crimes presented in dioramas.

CSI shows crime solving at its best. Meanwhile, up north, from 2003–2009, law enforcement aimed to rise from the sewers in *Reno 911!!* If a guy ran down the street wearing a mask and carrying three flat-screen television sets, *Reno 911!* cops might stop to inquire if he noticed anything unusual in the neighborhood.

Inane crimes aside, ask viewers what they remember most about the show, and they offer a short answer: shorts. These shorts make Mickey Rooney look tall. They clamp so tightly onto Lt. Dangle that no body part imitates his name.

"Where are your shorts?" Reno visitors shout at local police, who often respond with irritated glowers.

Granted, some viewers fail to realize that any show airing on Comedy Central includes exaggerations—fashion and otherwise. Nor does accuracy truly matter, as *Reno 911!*'s frequent palm tree sightings demonstrate. In real life, Reno's mountain winters kill off anything tropical.

The city only inadvertently provided backdrop locations, shot when show creators worked in Reno on an earlier project. Later, creators hired area production companies to provide additional city views to intersperse with the bulk of action shots in Southern California.

Rather than focus on Reno, the series aimed at spoofing reality television programs embodied by *Cops* using shaky handheld camera work that follows daily, mundane operations like disturbing the peace.

The show also fosters the improvisational skills of Thomas Lennon as Lt. Dangle and Robert Ben Garant as redneck deputy Travis Junior. Off-the-cuff story development fit another *Reno 911!* goal, maintaining one of the lowest budgets on record. No scripts meant no screenwriting salary. The show relied on its skillful cast to move a basic setup in unpredictable, funny directions during ten-minute takes. Without network restrictions and censorship, cast members embraced fetishes, weird views, and general perversities. Insane, profane, warped, and proud of it, the *Reno 911!* team quickly found likeminded fans, and it proved an immediate hit to the chagrin of many locals comfortable with the official city slogan, "We Love This Place."

Other residents disputed dialogue.

"Reno is a lot like Mayberry on the TV except that everyone's on crystal meth and prostitution's legal," says one character in the *Reno 911!* movie spinoff.

"The program has too many things we've been working to prevent like racism and homophobia," Reno's police chief Jerry Hoover said before the first episode aired.

Southern California shooting meant no opportunity for his office to register protest by denying film permits. Also, a sneaky name change prevented lawsuits. The *911* team belongs to the nonexistent "Reno Sheriff's Department" rather than the region's real-life defenders in the Reno Police Department or the Washoe County Sheriff's Office.

While some residents flail over portrayal of obviously incompetent law enforcement officers, *Reno 911!* attracted local fans. University of Nevada, Reno students brought Thomas Lennon to the city as grand marshal of their annual homecoming parade in 2007, where he rode on top of a convertible in October. The season's chill fifty-degree weather provided Antarctic freeze for a Southern Californian in shorts.

As time passed, the program won over a few officials, and some at the Reno Sparks Convention and Visitors Authority led petitions to keep the show alive in 2009 when it was cancelled after its six-year run.

"The City It Mocks Tries to Save It," read a national headline in *USA Today*, recounting such efforts as a fundraising food fight featuring 50,000 pounds of tomatoes.

Operating someplace between *Reno 911!* inanity and *CSI* seriousness, a private investigator named Dan Tanna spent three seasons busting criminals in the series *Vega$*. Creator Aaron Spelling put his spell on the show, emulating *Charlie's Angels* and his other crowd-pleasing hits. Spelling never dug deeply into the reality of crime and detectives for any of his shows, instead taking an "eye candy" approach, emphasizing lighthearted humor and things that looked good.

Since Spelling adored Las Vegas, he found an excuse to spend time there by filming his program entirely on location, giving the show a colorful, light, and airy feel. Star Robert Urich recalled that the city's small size made it easy to film several locations in a single working day. As a result, *Vega$* provides a historic glimpse of the city from 1978 to 1981. It shows Fremont Street sans massive ceiling and light show. It features casinos separated by barren, undeveloped land on the Strip. The Frontier, Dunes, Maxim, and Desert Inn stand—not tall, but they stand. It recalls the time when players pulled handles on slot machines. They watched performers like Wayne Newton—oh wait, that part never changed.

Cancelled in 1982 after sixty-eight episodes, *Vega$* played well when the FX channel aired reruns in 1994, spawning DVDs of entire seasons.

Binge watching *Vega$* reminds viewers that the show never relied on good plotting. The jazzy *Vega$* theme plays ad nauseam, a common approach for the era. Repetition prevails—the same two officers exit the "Metropolitan Police" building whenever action moves to headquarters.

Since *Vega$* predates the chop-editing style popularized in music videos, pacing seems clunky. Actors telegraph movements and spend inordinate time walking in and out of buildings.

Yet a "guilty pleasure" charm suffuses *Vega$*. Producers milked Urich's eye-candy qualities, finding the vaguest excuse for him to take off his shirt and reveal a pleasantly muscled frame, predating body-builder cuts. With the broad shoulders of a swimmer, Dan Tanna keeps in shape at the Desert Inn pool. This provides dramatic justification to wear a skimpy bathing suit.

Urich's even-featured handsomeness survives the changing fads of various eras, despite sideburns. His tousled brown hair and engaging smile go beyond temporary tastes, and he wore the era's butt-hugging pants well. Still, his penchant for a blazer covering a suede vest seems impractical in the desert heat of Las Vegas.

Unlike classic film noir tough guys, Urich's Dan Tanna preferred a pleasant approach.

"It takes a lot to get me mad," he says in one episode.

And while he likes the ladies, Tanna avoids womanizing crassness. Earnest and forthright, he accepts offers to buy him his drink of choice—milk.

It took more than Urich's charms for *Vega$* to create nostalgic enthusiasm. The free-and-easy party lifestyle of Las Vegas contributes some appeal, allowing Tanna to live in the perfect man cave, a warehouse right in the heart of the Strip next to Circus Circus. Its privacy meant women visited discreetly but, most importantly, the giant living room featured enough space to park a car.

The car proved a centerpiece of both Tanna's home and the show. Tanna starts the pilot in a yellow Corvette but switches to a red 1957 Ford Thunderbird in following episodes. Urich joked the car got more fan mail than he did, and the car acted like a costar, enhancing atmosphere as the neon lights of Las Vegas reflect upon and dance along its hood. Now considered an icon in the history of television vehicles, toy versions remain popular collector items. The flashy car and the handsome Urich make an ideal match for the glitz and style of Las Vegas.

Glitz shone even brighter with an impressive roster of guest stars. The show lured the era's headliners, including Dean Martin, the Captain & Tennille, and Wayne Newton. One episode provided an early role for future Oscar winner Kim Basinger, sporting enough baby fat to make her appearance nearly unrecognizable today. Real-life Las Vegas resident Tony Curtis lent extra ease and charm in early episodes as Slick Roth, the Desert Inn owner. Curtis already proved his executive skills when he prevented Harrah's Tahoe from going under in the movie *Forty Pounds of Trouble*. The switch to *Vega$* let him show a tougher, edgier side of management.

For *Vega$*, Roth often needed extra muscle and kept Tanna on call, one time sending him out to recover a missing male lion named Lucille. Another scene shows Roth prancing on stage and punching his arms straight up in the air as he demonstrates how he wants his showgirls to dance. This makes Tanna laugh, and much of Urich's appeal involved his friendly demeanor in reacting to others. Urich often says his lines with a smile.

Aside from its likeability, *Vega$* offers a head-slapping look at technology. Light and color wizardry makes Las Vegas a magnet for new gadgets, and Dan Tanna used them the minute they came on the market. He stunned 1978 audiences with the amazing new ability to record phone messages on a machine, though he complained about its $400 price tag. Tanna talks on a newfangled car phone, about as convenient as a lumbering brontosaurus.

Combine a handsome man with techno-toys, a fun car, famous faces topped by a glittery city, and *Vega$* works as a tourism calling card. It's a point *CSI* creator Anthony Zuiker made when he first encouraged those in casino management to let their properties host heinous crimes.

"With reruns and syndication, *CSI* is going to give people the same type of nostalgia for Las Vegas as the show *Vega$*," he insisted.

Chronic reruns, streaming, and DVD sets prove him right. Similarly, *Reno 911!* airs frequently, with fans perusing a popular website and all six seasons available on DVD. These programs' continued popularity proves incongruous. Despite inane plots in *Vega$*, uniquely warped crimes in *CSI*, and ball-gripping shorts in *Reno 911!*, all three series raised public awareness—and fondness—for their respective Nevada cities.

You Work in Nuh-vaa-duh

Locals often ignore pronunciation guides, and Nevadans follow that pattern when it comes to the soft *a* that Spanish language roots require.

"You know," I often mentioned to *CSI* production staff members when they called the Nevada Film Office for help on various issues, "We pronounce the state Nevada with a flat *a* like *at* in the middle." Locals ignore any soft *a*, despite the name's heritage and relation to the Spanish word for snow.

I repeated the same thing to Gary Dourdan several times in 2003 when he worked at the Carson City prison on a feature film called *Black August*.

Dourdan, who played the crime scene investigator Warrick for seven seasons, smiled broadly.

"I know, and I'm okay with that."

We both knew *CSI* creator Anthony Zuiker grew up in Vegas and pronounced the state correctly.

Dourdan said the issue came from the guy who played investigator Nick Stokes, George Eads.

"George is from Texas. He'll never stop doing it his way."

The comment came several years before Dourdan's on-screen death, and the actor reveled in the *CSI* phenomenon. The show still topped television ratings.

Breaking into a big smile when the warden presented him with a Nevada license plate reading *CSI*, Dourdan posed for a photo and proudly held his index finger in the number one position.

6

Partiers and Las Vegas

Following the Nevada tradition of fostering the forbidden, the catchy slogan "What happens in Vegas stays in Vegas" solidified the city's reputation as America's party capital. No film better illustrates the idea than *The Hangover,* a blockbuster that turned Bradley Cooper into a superstar and won the 2009 Golden Globe for comedy. *The Hangover* shows Las Vegas as a bright place where you can stay in a beautiful room and find a sweet stripper, a cuddly tiger, or an annoyed Mike Tyson. It spurred calls to Caesars Palace from fans who loved the resort's suite shown on screen.

"I want to stay in the same suite in *The Hangover,*" went the mantra of inquiries, according to a Caesars desk clerk who called the Nevada Film Office to find out about location details.

Actually, the $4,200 a night Villa Suite from the movie stood on a soundstage, borrowing influences from the casino's Emperor Suite with marble, flat-screen televisions and floor-to-ceiling windows. Caesars' staff quickly accommodated movie fans, making the design-inspiring Emperor Suite part of an upscale Hangover Package. A less-expensive variation advertised on the casino's website promised, "A visit to Las Vegas is full of nights you'll never forget—and usually a few that you can't remember! Whether you prefer shenanigans straight out of *The Hangover* or a more laid-back night on the town, you can go over the top."

The Hangover's screen shenanigans start with a comic mystery. A bride gets a phone call: no one can find her fiancée. Flashbacks show the groom's bachelor-partying friends coming conscious in their Caesars suite. A baby sits in the closet. A tiger strolls through the bedroom. A chicken squawks. How did all this happen? Alcohol- and drug-induced fogs dissipate to reveal the way those weird things make total sense in Vegas, where everyone expects the unexpected. Emerging from hangover hazes and pursuing clues to the groom's whereabouts, each partier clearly sees problems in his or her own life.

When the film's producers chose Las Vegas as their setting, they played into an image everyone bought. By that time, even a blue-footed booby on an isolated Galapagos island knew about Las Vegas:

- Las Vegas gives its name to a James Caan television series where casino staff members all look like Hollywood stars.

Or:

- Las Vegas sends the original *CSI* team on adventures streamed daily with stunning aerial shots of the city's neon-glowing buildings.
- Las Vegas plays "Real World" for strangers living together in a multiroom suite at the Palms Resort and Casino.
- Las Vegas provides "Fear Factor," where bucket loads of money go to anyone successfully completing terrifying stunts off bizarre architecture.
- Las Vegas means "Dancing with the Stars" and their glittery costumes in an equally glittery setting.
- Las Vegas suits bachelor parties in 1998's *Very Bad Things,* 2001's *Tomcats,* and a 2006 feature that emphasizes the point, *Bachelor Party.*

Cementing that party hearty, free-for-all spirit, *The Hangover* made the city a natural setting for projects that followed:

- Las Vegas stock footage lures bachelor partiers for 2011's *Hostel: Part III.*
- Las Vegas hearkens to a colorful past in the 2012 series *Vegas* (even though it filmed in New Mexico).
- Las Vegas gives several young women a *Best Night Ever* during bachelorette festivities.
- Las Vegas lets experienced hell-raiser Michael Douglas say farewell to bachelorhood with Robert De Niro and Morgan Freeman for 2013's *Last Vegas.*
- Las Vegas brings back its iconic celebrants for 2013's *The Hangover Part III.*
- Las Vegas encourages women to *Think Like a Man Too* during pre-wedding parties.

- Las Vegas promises Paul Blart that "This Will be the Best Day of Your Life" at a security officers' convention in the 2015 sequel to 2009's *Paul Blart: Mall Cop,* featuring a Segway-riding mall cop.
- Las Vegas draws American Securitization Forum conventioneers, who seem more intrigued by skimpily dressed women at the Caesars Palace Garden of the Gods Oasis than the impending financial doom that Steve Carell spots in 2015's *The Big Short.*

Finding out more about this city where partying happens 24/7 requires simple button- or icon-clicking skills, followed by staring at a screen full of explosive, glittering images.

"Time and time again, I'm being interviewed by the Travel Channel, by Discovery, and others," former mayor Oscar Goodman said. "They're insatiable in their appetite for Las Vegas. In particular, the English folks are always over here, the French, the Germans, people from Holland. I mean one after another comes up here, and it's always the same questions with the Las Vegas background in the backdrop. They can't get enough of Las Vegas."

The Vegas appeal involves its colorful major streets with welcoming signs and statues. Elko's Commercial Hotel Casino boasts a polar bear, Wendover offers a big cowboy called Will, and a colorful arch proclaims "Reno the Biggest Little City in the World," all greetings shrinking to Tom Thumb proportions compared Vegas Vic and his worldwide fame.

"Howdy, Podner," calls Vegas Vic as visitors stroll along Fremont Street, but most people prefer the Strip's little "Welcome to Fabulous Las Vegas" sign, promising a universe of fun. A short walk north on Las Vegas Boulevard Strip takes you by Egypt, New York, Rome, Paris, dancing waterfalls, an exploding volcano, and a pirate battle. It calls to the dreamers of *Up in the Air,* a 2009 best picture nominee where George Clooney photographs a cardboard cutout in iconic locations throughout the world. Vegas makes the grade with a pyramid-shaped Luxor Casino in the background.

Well before all this international recognition, Las Vegas proved its fame and party status with *Bob & Carol & Ted & Alice,* one of 1969's most risqué movies. Bob and Carol go through early stages of the sixties' sexual revolution and free love, something they want to share with their best friends by escaping to Vegas at the Riviera Hotel Casino.

"Okay," says Ted shortly after admitting to a recent adulterous fling. "First we'll have an orgy. Then we'll see Tony Bennett."

The movie hit a nerve with audiences on release, earning Oscar nominations for writers Larry Tucker and Paul Mazursky plus actors Elliott

Gould and Dyan Cannon. Gould later said he thinks Las Vegas made the ideal location for the finale.

"Las Vegas, I think, represents a place that is wild, a place where you can go and gamble, especially in that time. There is no place else to the degree of Las Vegas."

One of the most controversial movies of its year, *Bob & Carol & Ted & Alice* nonetheless annoyed some critics who dinged it for a copout ending, something Gould influenced.

"I was way more inhibited and completely unwilling to participate in sexual interaction between the two couples," he recalled.

While an orgy seemed suitable during the Swinging Sixties, conservative new millennium viewers might find the group's decision easier to grasp. The conventional end also fits the story's main point, one encapsulated as the song "What the World Needs Now" plays.

"What's the key word in that song?" Gould asked. "The world is about love, not sex."

Groundbreaking for its day, the once-hip story and fresh dialogue now feels dated. The movie remains funny and works best as a criticism rather than a celebration of its times. Besides the importance of love over sex, the movie shows how Nehru jackets make a horrible fashion statement. Bob & Carol & Ted & Alice left Nevada with a better understanding of themselves—but not clothes.

Perhaps you can learn something about yourself in Las Vegas, but most people try to forget their problems once there. "Vegas, Baby, Vegas!" shouts a group of guys heading to the city in *Swingers*. One mopes over a breakup, and his buddies figure he should forget his girlfriend in a city where partying never ends. *Swingers* director Doug Limon liked the Vegas escape well enough to *Go* at it again. The 1999 comedy features a Los Angeles drug dealer visiting Las Vegas, where strip-club girls distract him from job duties.

Las Vegas makes it easy to ignore work. Vegas-induced delays prove a problem for several demigods in 2010's *Percy Jackson and the Olympians*. On a mission to protect humankind, Poseidon's half-human son faces Greek-inspired challenges at various locations. It turns out Las Vegas houses sirens, those seductive women who lure travelers to dire fates. With casino sets based on Caesars Palace, the heroic Percy Jackson and friends party so much they almost miss their deadline to save the world.

Comedian Jonah Hill nearly screws up his mission to make sure a rock star played by Russell Brand reaches his music gig in 2010's *Get Him to the Greek*. With an attitude that "life is one big party," the singer insists on a Las Vegas stop to visit his father, a bass player for The Pack Is Back tribute group at the Plaza Hotel. Back at his Planet Hollywood suite with fur-lined walls, the rock star looks like he may hang out too long and miss his concert date in Los Angeles. His producer, played by Sean "Diddy" Combs, devises the perfect strategy.

"We'll out-party him," he tells the beleaguered Hill. Sex, drugs, and rock 'n' roll proliferate to such extremes that the rocker decides on his own to flee Las Vegas, driving out of town via the scenic Red Rock Canyon.

Get Him to the Greek comes from the team that spent time at Treasure Island's *Mystère* stage show in *Knocked Up*, where Seth Rogen and Paul Rudd briefly escape the women in their lives.

"For one blissful night, gentlemen, we are free of all of our obligations, all of our responsibilities," summarizes Kevin Hart as he leads friends to bachelor party celebrations in *Think Like a Man Too*. Meanwhile, their partners head out with similar ideas.

"Las Vegas is the best place in the world for men and women to get their freak on," explains Hart in the trailer for the feature, which demonstrated both the comedian's and the city's popularity with a strong weekend performance of $30 million ticket sales in 2014.

The "You can do anything you want" concept works as a slogan for the Montecito Resort and Casino on the *Las Vegas* television show that ran from 2003–2008. Well, perhaps not *anything*, because the Montecito's security team keeps close tabs on you. James Caan's Ed Deline watches visitors, working as the head surveillance guy until promotion to president of operations. Caan left the series after eighty-eight episodes, and Tom Selleck moved in as the Montecito's new owner. An insider's look at casino management, it covered a variety of concerns, including preventing a rich gambler, aka "whale," from reaching another casino. For the most part, the show thrived on the interpersonal relationships of beautiful people like Josh Duhamel and Molly Sims.

Mandalay Bay served as the series' fictitious Montecito in the pilot, but most episodes filmed on two Culver City stages, avoiding time restrictions faced in an operating casino. Creators aimed for a realistic look at the casino lifestyle, though producers admitted they occasionally fantasized. One of their more intriguing inventions came at a breakfast restaurant, which Executive Producer Gardner Stern said emanated from his "twisted mind." At the restaurant, only the pancakes are flat, obvious because the waitresses go topless. The day after that episode aired, the Nevada Film Office received an e-mail from a viewer planning a Vegas trip and wondering where the topless pancake house stood because "it looks friendly."

It also looks fun, a major reason partiers, vacationers, and moviemakers keep visiting Vegas.

The Wedding Party

Once in a while, partiers and vacationers visit Nevada cities besides Las Vegas, often with marriage in mind.

This includes the impressive combination of Charlize Theron, Natasha Richardson, Patrick Swayze, and Billy Bob Thornton for *Waking Up in Reno*. The title's Reno location fits the characters. Director Jordan Brady explains that Las Vegas might be too daunting for a group from Arkansas, but Reno makes the travelers feel comfortable.

"I think it speaks to the characters and helps set the story in motion knowing that their dream is to come here because Vegas would be a bit overwhelming for these people," he said at the Reno premiere.

"This is a town where they feel like they could gamble, see a show, go see the monster truck show, and just relax on vacation," he continued. "This is still a little city, and I think that's important to the story."

He also liked the gag that eternally cheap Lonnie Earl, played by Thornton, chooses to vacation off-season.

"I thought it was funny they took their vacation in January. The cold, the sparkly lights on the street, the reflections on their car as they drive into town with all the craziness. It was the perfect blend of kitsch and big-time fun for these characters."

The story starts with a postcard of Reno, then sets up events in Arkansas (Southern California, really). Once on the road, the group makes numerous stops, partially because they drink one beer each for every mile covered. Nevada roads helped with this sequence.

"The stuff that we shot outside of town worked for part of the road movie—it took us out of Los Angeles, and it was different from the work we did in Texas. It was a different terrain here, with the evergreen trees and timberline," noted the director.

Part of *Waking Up in Reno*'s dialogue brings up another reason people celebrate in Nevada: marriage. When Swayze seems puzzled about renewing wedding vows, Theron offers a quick answer.

"I just think it would be romantic. And people are always getting married in places where gambling is legal," she observes.

"Yeah, one kinda goes with the other, don't it?" responds Swayze.

Theron's dialogue, written by Brent Briscoe and Mark Fauser, continues the marriage discussion by summarizing much of Nevada's appeal.

"It would be like a new start for us. Like if either one of us did anything we'd like to change in the past, it would just be erased. It wouldn't count no more."

But erasing *What Happens in Vegas* means work according to a judge who orders Cameron Diaz and Ashton Kutcher to take their wedding vows seriously. Like many, they discovered no one requires sobriety tests at Las Vegas wedding chapels.

While most hometown weddings involve big parties, Nevada nuptials often come as quick celebrations without major fanfare. Such anonymity works for a single woman suffering from spinsterhood in *Wedding Bell Blues*. She plans to find a guy, get married that night, and then annul everything the next day. The comedy suffers from dingy cinematography, though it highlights Vegas icons with an Elvis impersonator at the Graceland Wedding Chapel. Debbie Reynolds joins the mix, performing a show at her now-defunct casino.

Marriage brings Meg Ryan and Kiefer Sutherland together at the Reno Wedding Chapel in *Promised Land*, a feature film directed by Michael Hoffman. After drunkenly insulting a witness in the chapel, the newlyweds hit Interstate 80 on their way to Utah. Their trip meanders and shows poor map-reading skills. In catawampus order, they hit Utah's Bonneville Salt Flats, West Wendover's Silver Smith Casino, and the Toulon Mill near Lovelock.

Ryan's performance dominates the 1986 movie. Playing the free spirited Bev, she sports magenta hair and a wedding gown covered by a brown leather bomber's jacket. Best known at the time for a supporting role in *Top Gun*, Ryan earned good notices from *Promised Land*, including an acting nomination at the Independent Spirit Awards. Lacking big star status, she casually chatted and posed for snapshots on the Reno set.

Nevada's wedding motif showed up in *Surrender*, a 1987 film involving quick Tahoe nuptials. Currently getting laughs in Woody Allen's *Hannah and Her Sisters*, Michael Caine viewed *Surrender* as his first "truly American comedy."

"This is an out-and-out comedy. *Hannah* has something more in it."

Caine proved on target with his observations. *Surrender* flopped while *Hannah* earned him his first supporting actor Oscar. Still, Caine felt he played both roles similarly.

"It's not a lot different really, because the only way you can get laughs in movies is to be a real person and have funny things happen to you," he said, adding that many comedians fail on film because they do shtick.

"You need to be a person first, no matter what you do. Then you take care of the other stuff."

The comedy in *Surrender* sends its marriage-minded couple to Harvey's Casino Resort at Tahoe for their wedding, delayed when they fight about finances.

"It's a socio-screwball comedy," director Jerry Belson said. "It's about love and money and prenuptial agreements, and I hope it makes a social comment."

He originally planned for his couple to marry in Las Vegas, but decided the outdoor beauty of Tahoe better inspired personal insights for characters whose vision was clouded by material concerns.

Like *Surrender*, Joel and Ethan Cohen's *Intolerable Cruelty* combines screwball comedy with Nevada and prenuptial agreements. George Clooney plays a legal expert giving a keynote speech at a Las Vegas conference on weddings. His favorite example about the need for prenuptial agreements sits in the audience looking like Catherine Zeta-Jones. Fascinated by each other, the gold digger and lawyer succumb to the crazy, party atmosphere of Las Vegas and realize a truth other partiers sometimes find—what happens in Vegas doesn't always stay there.

Visiting Vegas

Las Vegas viewers and other trip planners rely on sources other than television shows and movies for itineraries. Still, *Vegas Vacation* provides useful guides as the famous Griswold family heads to the city and discovers its party lifestyle. Chevy Chase plays with Siegfried and Roy's tigers. Beverly D'Angelo flirts with Wayne Newton. The Griswold daughter learns important skills like pole dancing. With the series wearing thin, this fourth entry works best as a regional travelogue, plugging Newton, the Mirage casino, and tours at nearby Hoover Dam. The movie's hype worked when the Nevada Film Office arranged a Hoover Dam movie location tour as part of a convention for the Association of Film Commissioners International. Only a few people signed on until conventioneers saw a promo reel with a brief clip showing *Vacation*'s dam guide, Arnie.

"No one wander off the dam tour," he instructs. "And please, take all the dam pictures you want."

During a convention break, two pages filled up with names of film commissioners wanting to see the dam location.

7

Oceans in the Desert

Though landlocked, Nevada claims four Oceans, none with water. Featuring the most laid-back and stylish movie star combinations of their times, the four movie variations of *Ocean's Eleven* burst from Las Vegas like a sparkling fountain providing effervescent, refreshing fun under the sun.

The first *Ocean's 11*, from 1960, spent decades as the epitome of a casino heist story. Long an iconic Las Vegas movie, it captures a period when casinos operated compactly with intimate showrooms featuring swinging singers and cocky comedians. Superstars Frank Sinatra, Dean Martin, Sammy Davis, Jr., and Joey Bishop hit the Copa Room at the Sands performing their floor show for hundreds of lucky visitors. The entertainers sang, bantered, and goofed around before ambling across the street or some other nearby location to film *Ocean's* during the day. You get a sense of their shows in related documentaries, as well as a cable movie called *The Rat Pack*. Nowadays, various Rat Pack tributes with impersonators flit from casino to casino in Las Vegas, with one highlighted in 2010's *Get Him to the Greek*. Even better, you can easily find the original *Ocean's 11* movie and see the Pack at work—or is it play?

The Rat Pack comprised an informal group of superstars and moviemakers originally headed by Humphrey Bogart, with his wife Lauren Bacall as den mother. Frank Sinatra took over after Bogart's death; others moved in and out, but for screen purposes, Sinatra led the Pack, backed by Dean Martin, Sammy Davis, Jr., Joey Bishop, and Peter Lawford. Lawford served as straight man in the bunch, bringing extra credentials through his brother-in-law, President John F. Kennedy.

Lawford also alerted The Pack to *Ocean's 11* says Simon Levy's book *Rat Pack Confidential*. The actor pitched the idea to Sinatra after buying story rights from a gas station attendant named Jack Russell. Multiple characters provided the first opportunity to work together for all five packers—six if you count Shirley MacLaine in a cameo.

Falling squarely in the "caper" genre, *Ocean's* follows a blueprint showing three phases of a robbery planned by a team. The first section outlines preparation; the second act puts ideas in action, while the third portion complicates getaway plans.

Rather than rob a single casino, the *Ocean's 11* team distinguishes itself by aiming at five targets: the Flamingo, the Sahara, the Riviera, the Desert Inn, and the Sands.

Along with finding a place to rob, heist movies gather compelling thieves, a criterion met by the real Rat Pack. Rat Pack Chairman of the Board Frank Sinatra plays Danny Ocean and pulls together buddies from his World War II airborne unit. They use military organization for robberies and pay the same attention to detail they used in battle. Picking New Year's Eve as the perfect busy night for distracting regular casino operations, they blow out the city's electricity and rewire systems to unlock casino cages. Of course, a hitch sticks them; all caper movies require one. An ironic finale keeps the tone light and meets the era's standards of prohibiting crime from paying.

Two-time Oscar winner Lewis Milestone directed the action, milking Las Vegas for its bright lights and glitzy look. He let his cast members play it their way, suiting both Sinatra and Martin just fine. Known for giving their best "take" right away, without rehearsals that might kill the spark in their work, the actors show comfort and ease. The Sinatra/Martin approach extended to the costars, who seem more interested in hanging around with each other than working. This laissez-faire attitude fits the Rat Pack's off-screen image. Ultimately, *Ocean's* promotes panache, flair, and living high, just like the movie's stars.

Action meanders. This means Dean Martin needs no excuse to croon "Ain't That a Kick in the Head." Meandering allows Sammy Davis, Jr. to sing while driving a garbage truck with no attempt to explain lyrics in "Ee-oh-Leven". . . . Sure, it sounds like the movie's title, but really, "Ee-oh-Leven"? Perhaps a kick in the head puts sense in the lyrics. Still, Sammy's rich voice disarms musical questions.

After meeting characters and hearing what they think for about an hour, action moves to the Las Vegas Strip, adding colorful excitement to the visuals. Mostly though, there's Frank. And Dean. And Sammy. And Joey. And Peter. All having fun. And with that mix, so do viewers. The Rat Pack later made other movies together, but none captured their spirit as well as this sole Las Vegas project, where Packers thrive like sleek jungle cats prowling their natural habitat.

Years passed, and film theorists knew that *Ocean's 11*'s director's reputation lay in his more-respected *All Quiet on the Western Front*. Experts believed Sinatra never superseded the acting that won him an Oscar in *From Here to Eternity*. Dean Martin remained best loved for his television variety show. Sammy Davis, Jr. never topped his showroom performances of "Mr. Bojangles." Yet people still watched *Ocean's 11*. And that made the project an ideal candidate for one of the new century's favorite kind of movie, a remake with franchise potential.

But a couple of points needed consideration. For one thing, casino heists shown in the sixties seemed outdated jokes for the third millennium's Strip. The new team distinguishes itself by spelling out the title as *Ocean's Eleven* (not *11*) and tips its hat to the past in an early segment showing how badly most old casino heists failed. Each heist represents a different era, and the renewed *Ocean's* location manager Ken Lavett discovered how few circa 2000 casinos looked anything like their sixties selves. That old Las Vegas drew Elliott Gould to watch his fiancée Barbra Streisand open for Liberace. Nearly forty years later, Gould came back as one of the refurbished *Ocean's Eleven* gang members.

"It seems to be a changed and different place," he said.

"I think the energy is higher, the spirit is higher, and the illusion is broader," he noted, adding, "It's such a big business. Now, in terms of vertical integration and globalization, Las Vegas is an international Mecca."

By 2001, a single casino like the Bellagio overwhelmed all those shown in the original film, requiring expansion for the *Ocean's Eleven* heist. Corporate ownership of multiple properties meant one location held the proceeds from several. As a result, the new *Ocean's Eleven* robbers target only the Bellagio vault.

The elaborate robbery meant a bigger take in cash. Because the three target casinos sponsor a boxing match with heavy betting, they keep an extra $150 million on hand.

Staging a diversionary boxing match at the MGM meant bringing in about 2,000 extras for a fight between Lennox Lewis and Wladimir Klitschko. The crowd includes a tribute to the initial movie, with the first Mrs. Danny Ocean, Angie Dickinson, sitting near one of the original gang members, Henry Silva. Local celebrities appear as well, including singer Wayne Newton, comedian Danny Gans, plus resident singers Steve Lawrence and Edie Gorme. Las Vegas Mayor Oscar Goodman sat among them but ended up on the ever-dreaded cutting room floor.

"I was heartbroken," he said later, undaunted and plotting to find his way in front of other cameras.

Besides keeping the heist gimmick of a multi-casino mega robbery, the new *Ocean's Eleven* needed screen personalities to compare with the Rat Pack's insouciance. Relaxed swagger, confidence, charm, and drop-dead good looks overrode singing. George Clooney's mix of Cary Grant, Clark Gable, and his own personal style proved an ideal Danny Ocean.

Just as Dean Martin never seemed intimidated by Frank Sinatra, Clooney required a partner able to hold his own in looks and aplomb. Brad Pitt fits that bill. Not even Clooney makes Brad Pitt nervous or bland looking.

The revised "Pack" rounded out with Matt Damon, Don Cheadle, Bernie Mack, Carl Reiner, Elliott Gould, Scott Caan, and Casey Affleck. Julia Roberts, fresh off her Oscar for Best Actress for *Erin Brockovich,* stepped in as the estranged Mrs. Ocean.

The project lured the Oscar-winning director of *Traffic,* Steven Soderbergh, who acknowledged that the commercial packaging of *Ocean's Eleven* represented a major switch from his start in the low-budget critical pet *Sex, Lies, and Videotape.*

"It was scary because it was physically bigger than anything I'd ever attempted and, in my opinion, required a style of filmmaking that I hadn't employed before," he says in the film's publicity packet.

For one thing, he explained, "This film is exactly the opposite of *Traffic,* where we basically chose locations we could walk into and not have to dress much."

While *Ocean's Eleven* uses sections of the Bellagio and MGM Grand, sets stood in for hotel rooms and the casino vault.

"You really do just assume that we shot everything at the Bellagio. I kept forgetting that we had built the Mirador Suite on stage," he says. Constructed after extensive research on site, sets blend smoothly with real casino areas on screen, operating like a filmed postcard of the Bellagio. Real locations include the casino's Picasso restaurant, which *Wine Spectator* magazine once rated as Nevada's best. The property's conservatory and botanical gardens show up, along with the reception area and artist Dale Chihuly's glass-decorated ceiling. Outdoor dancing fountains get special play, reprogrammed with choreography for a shot near the end. Like its predecessor, this *Ocean's Eleven* puts a lot of money and talent toward giving its participants a hoot of a workday—and a good time for audiences, too.

Audiences liked the new *Ocean's Eleven* so well it made about $450 million worldwide, an amount beyond what the Rat Pack ever imagined. And while the original Rat Pack used *Ocean's 11* as a springboard for working together again in *Sergeant's 4* and unrelated projects, the new guys went straight for a sequel.

The group reteamed in Rome in 2004 for *Ocean's Twelve,* but the scheme and personalities flailed in Europe's old-world ambiance. Budget constraints shrank the sequel's Las Vegas connection to a small scene toward the end.

Despite weak reviews and a reduced audience, *Ocean's Twelve* made enough money to expand to franchise status. *Ocean's Thirteen* arrived in 2007 with a return to the gang's homeland, Las Vegas.

The plot begins as Oceanographers seek vengeance when a compatriot gets ripped off by investor Willy Bank, bearing a disconcerting resemblance to "Godfather" Al Pacino. Bank gives his casino an ideal name, especially if you need something to break.

Bank represents the new Las Vegas, one established after real-life entrepreneur Steve Wynn opened the Mirage and started a wave of themed mega-resorts, where gambling comprised just one facet of entertainment. In the old world, gamblers never cared about rooms they rarely saw, instead spending all their time on the casino floor. The new world insists on top quality amenities, from food to luxurious suites.

With this in mind, the *Ocean's* team steps in to nail this *Godfather* incarnation. Bank wants a prestigious "Five Diamond" rating for his new property. He leaps outside the box with design, a twisting orange and red abstract tower digitized on an aerial view of Las Vegas. An Asian theme inside lures gaming industry "whales," the word for customers who can afford $250,000 weekend losses.

The whales in this ocean swim through a casino blending movie fantasy and plausibility, an elaborate set built to gaming industry standards, with low ceilings and segmented floor space, where something around the corner lures players to keep exploring.

The casino and its operations aim to impress people who rate hotels and, as the plot progresses, the Oceanographers see to it that one reviewer goes through every childhood prank, from itching powder on toilet paper to laxatives and stinky incense in the room.

Oh, yes, and the gang members figure that Bank robbing requires more flair than masks and guns. One scheme fulfills every gambler's dream when the team reprograms all slot machines to hit winning combinations. Another scam involves stealing the diamonds Bank earned at other properties.

Taking a break from their manipulations, George Clooney and Brad Pitt stand outside by the Bellagio to breathe fresh air and reminisce about the old Las Vegas, the one with the Sands and the Desert Inn.

"They built them a lot smaller then," notes Clooney wistfully.

"They seemed pretty big," puts in Pitt.

"Town's changed," sighs Clooney.

They talk wistfully of their predecessor, the town where Sinatra and the original *Ocean's 11* team played. The singer's name comes up several times as a sacred icon.

"There's a code amongst guys who shook Sinatra's hand," insists a shocked Elliott Gould as he's being ripped off.

Sinatra's voice sings "This Town" during the several layers of scams and heists, lending tacit approval to his *Ocean's* followers "taking on the world today."

Thirteen proved a luckier number than Twelve, with better reviews and more enthusiastic box office attendance. None of this fazed the stars, who always seem to have a good time regardless of their project's quality or reception.

The *Ocean's* robbers prove more effective than any others to hit Nevada. Vast amounts of cash make the state a natural setting for heist projects, but few get the right mix of personalities and schemes. One of the better variations came much earlier, before the original *Ocean's 11.*

5 Against the House benefits from an intelligent plot crafted by Jack Finney, a well-regarded author famous for the science fiction classic *Invasion of the Body Snatchers.* His *5 Against the House* title tells the basics—five people fight the odds. The quintuplet challenging the house for this 1955 release use the G.I. Bill after returning from the Korean War, making them senior citizens among other students at "Midwestern University." The lovely, leafy grounds with classical brick buildings display a wonderful Ivy League look still found at the real location, University of Nevada, Reno's quad.

Besides hanging out with a nightclub singer played by Kim Novak, the antique students enjoy adult activities like gambling, which leads to the title plot against Harolds Club in Reno. The location choice made sense to fifties audiences when Reno eclipsed Las Vegas in size and fame. The casino's nationwide marketing program, with signs crying "Harolds Club or Bust," set the destination as a goal for millions. Now a plaza for Harrah's, Harolds left behind little, other than a building-sized western mural now displayed at Reno's Livestock Events Center. The mural appears in the movie when a chatting cop insists nobody can successfully rob Harolds Club. Overhearing the remark, an intelligent, antique student jokingly enlists friends to design a feasible robbery. They take it a step further by attempting the robbery as a prank, planning to return the loot after proving their brilliance.

The *5 Against the House* theft takes only about fifteen minutes to show, reflecting its outdated simplicity, which includes a parking garage system where elevators transported cars to various floors. Reissued on DVD in a package of three Noir Classics from Columbia, the film shows director Phil Karlson's compact style in presenting crime thrillers. Besides effective direction and a good cast, *5 Against the House* supplies intriguing character interactions, making it a remake contender in the early nineties when director Stephen Kay joined me in Reno to seek locations for a new version starring Leonardo DiCaprio. Kay scouted University of Nevada, Reno's older classrooms, also checking out the Bonanza just north of town on Virginia Street for its retro casino look. Around that time, DiCaprio signed on for *Titanic* and plans for the *5 Against the House* remake sank.

Other heist projects sink without using a ship. Case in point: *Paul Blart: Mall Cop 2.* The 2015 comedy boasts two impressive firsts. It took advantage of Nevada's short-lived film incentive program before anyone else and received $4.3 million from the state, which helped with a $30 million budget. The feature also beat out others who wanted to initiate Steve Wynn's self-named casino as a location, the owner's blessing indicated by appearing in a briefer than brief cameo. With Adam Sandler among the producers and a previously popular film featuring the title security officer, the sequel held promise it never actually reached.

The sequel brings its dedicated but klutzy title character to a security officers convention at the Wynn, where he inadvertently discovers a heist involving art pieces hanging throughout the casino. The heist serves as a plot device rather than a format for the film, while the movie's slapstick humor relies on too many tasteless food jokes about fat people. Looked at another way, the film creators pulled off a big heist, since their project made more than $100 million at the box office despite getting one of the lowest scores possible on the Rotten Tomatoes reviews website.

Other heist projects show their own weaknesses, going back to Stella Stevens as a *Las Vegas Lady*, severely constrained by 1975's television movie-of-the-week format. Held in check by tight, low-cut dresses, the actress offered the project's only suspense by providing hope that a nipple might pop out. Tension failed because every viewer knew such things never happened on television in those days.

Lacking nudity, *Las Vegas Lady* followed a predictable path, with Stella's breasts covering a heart of gold as she joins a shadowy figure in a plot to steal skimmed funds. Headquartered at a nearby tourist cowboy town called Bonnie Springs, the robbers send a black-dressed acrobatic thief to scale up the hot pink and white walls of Circus Circus, with no one noticing.

Years later, the lack of Sherlock Holmes observation skills seemed equally absent among casino crowds as bad guys ran through the Desert Inn with brick-sized cellphones, an odd sight for 1994, when *MacShayne: Winner Takes All* filmed. The inane plot highlighted singer Kenny Rogers' charm, with high enough ratings to inspire a sequel that few viewers wanted, needed, or watched.

Whether Kenny Rogers and Stella Stevens on television or Frank Sinatra, George Clooney—and even Paul Blart—in movies, Nevada's caper stories play on people's mixed feelings about casinos. Millions love them. At the same time, the big, flashy designer towers visually symbolize the real winners; a typical player's take represents only a fraction of casino earnings. In contrast, the robber risks more than the gambler hitting a twenty in the game of blackjack. On screen, a robber's daring goes beyond the expected and earns oceans of admiration—and money.

8

Gamblers and Casinos

Money pours down on you.

A game, a fantasy—or a nightmare? Sally Field faces that dilemma in the little-known movie *Surrender* when she wins the "Blizzard of Bucks" and feels $120,000 worth of bills falling over her in a shower promising a bright, clean, debt-free world. One little coin slips in a slot; suddenly lights flash in a hallucinatory burst while bells ring with the insistence of a pinball game on steroids. All that money can chomp up problems with the quick, methodical accuracy of a voracious yellow Pac-Man.

While *Surrender* filmmakers created the "Blizzard of Bucks" game as a prop at Harveys Lake Tahoe, they used real money. After the first take, piles of bills remained on the floor, awaiting retrieval by Designated Money Counters.

"I'll help!" Sally Field cried enthusiastically, joining a team assembled to pick up each and every $5 bill and assure full return. The two-time Oscar-winning actress grabbed a pile of green with a smile on her face. But money counting features major drawbacks. Even perfectly legitimate dollars get dirty.

"It's icky," the future Mrs. Lincoln said, after retrieving all those portraits of her 2012 movie husband. She stared in dismay at hands so black that one swipe would turn the Flying Nun's white hat gray.

And as it turns out in *Surrender*, and similar stories where someone wins big, money often causes more problems than it solves.

A byproduct of betting, money usually functions as little more than a prop in gambling stories. The best tales go deeper and look at fate, chance, and luck. *The Cooler* mixes those traits, with William H. Macy playing a man so unlucky his mere presence makes things go wrong for everyone around him. He works off his own gambling debt by hiring out as a walking jinx who simply passes a "hot" winning table and immediately cools it with his bad aura. Do coolers really exist?

"I get asked that all the time," screenwriter Frank Hannah said on set at the former Golden Phoenix in Reno, a casino standing in as an old school Fremont Street operation in Las Vegas.

"I think the way it's dramatized in the film," Hannah explained, "It's an invention. But if you go to a casino, you would find people that are having a hot streak where they seem to just be winning all the time, and so the casino sends in someone else to kind of cool it off, but that person may change from day to day."

Hannah got the idea from Las Vegas craps tables.

"I always kind of felt like craps was the game where everyone's betting on the same thing, so if it becomes unlucky because somebody walks up, it's a collective type of karma."

The notion that one person changes the game "snowballed from there."

Hannah also uses the story to vent frustration with early millennium trends to convert the Las Vegas Strip into a family theme park owned by big corporations.

"It's just not my idea of what Vegas is or should be, and even my vision of Vegas is a bit seedier than it is. There's a romanticized idea about Vegas and the Mob, and it's just become this overblown amusement park instead of a gambling hall, which is a bit more serious and dark and shady."

As a result of Hannah's desire for a dingier, older Las Vegas setting, *The Cooler* needed a straightforward, basic casino. Scouts found most Las Vegas casinos already remodeled, transforming into the venues Hannah criticizes. But an hour's flight north, Reno's Flamingo Hilton closed, partly because its seventies-style casino floor looked old, just like the movie needed. Sealing the deal, a two-week gap before new owners took over provided a fully dressed, empty casino available as a film location.

Director and cowriter Wayne Kramer moved across the casino floor unimpeded, free from gamblers and machines making distracting noises. He never worried about kicking anyone out of the casino's large theater. Empty hotel rooms provided cost-effective lodging, allowing more production dollars for a high quality cast.

William H. Macy's slight physique and hangdog expression fit the authors' vision of a downtrodden "cooler," backed by acting chops strong enough to earn Emmy Awards and an Oscar nomination for *Fargo*. Beefy and truculent, Alec Baldwin came on board as the domineering casino manager and earned an Oscar nomination for his performance. Meanwhile, Macy's *E.R.* television costar Maria Bello earned a best dramatic actress Golden Globe nomination playing a love interest.

A casino cocktail waitress available to please men, Bello distracts the cooler romantically to prevent him from quitting his job. This led to an

NC-17 rating for an explicit oral sex scene that director Kramer repeatedly defended. He told me the sexual bluntness suits the story's rough elements and shows why a beautiful woman falls for a nebbish gambler. Love improves luck.

"We wanted to talk about how luck changes and some of the superstitions people have about luck, and specifically how it relates to gambling," elaborated screenwriter Hannah.

He and the rest of *The Cooler* team succeeded well enough to put the 2003 release on a number of "ten best" lists for movies about gambling.

Luck, chance, and coincidence show up frequently in Nevada casinos, and they all blossom briefly in the feature film *Magnolia*. During an opening series of bizarre coincidences, a narrator describes one at the "Nugget Hotel and Casino in Reno," an inaccuracy that writer/director Paul Thomas Anderson grasped since he filmed his gambling scenes at John Ascuaga's operation in nearby Sparks. The scene derives from a tale easily found on urban legend sites by Googling "dead diver found in tree." *Magnolia* shows a firefighter in a plane scooping up water from a lake to drop on a burning forest, little realizing he also picks up a scuba diver. The movie takes it a step further, saying the diver and pilot previously met and fought over the numbers *eight* and *two*. The diver dealt cards at the Nugget. Playing those cards, the pilot asks for a lucky *eight*, gets an unlucky *two*, and barrels over the twenty-one table, attacking the dealer. Overcome by the "measure of coincidence" in his connection with the dealer, the player kills himself in a motel room, wondering if the whole scenario was "all only a matter of chance." Given the meticulous attention to detail that screenwriter/director Anderson pays to every nanosecond of his movies, each image shown on screen entails long ponderings rather than chance.

He shot at least twenty retakes of the pilot, asking for that *eight* over and over and over again. During a brief break between deals, the obvious question came up.

"So what is it about the *eight* and *two*?

Paul, thin and looking like a teenager just out of high school, gave a perfect example of a cryptic smile, barely moving his mouth upwards.

"It's from the Bible," he answered as if that explained everything. "Exodus," he continued, a slight twinkle in his eyes.

Several variations of the verse give a vague idea.

"If you refuse to let them go, behold, I will plague all your borders with frogs," reads a typical version.

Sure enough, Anderson brought down frogs as the climax for a truly unusual script that earned him an Oscar nomination in 2000. His screenplay also put *Magnolia* on the list of movies filmed in Nevada, though the state's role lasts barely a minute. *Magnolia* didn't need Reno.

So why shoot there? Well, despite his fame for tough and edgy projects like *Boogie Nights* and *There Will Be Blood,* Anderson carries a soft little nostalgic part in his personality. On one level, he wanted to pay homage to his favorite Nevada movie, *Melvin and Howard.* That took him across from a former bus station to a seedy motel on Second Street to stage the gambler's suicide. As for the Nugget and Reno in general, Anderson wanted to return to the area where he filmed his first movie.

Anderson initially experienced Reno in the early nineties as a production assistant on a Robert Conrad television movie called *Sworn to Vengeance,* where the crew stayed at Reno's Peppermill. Rather than show good-boy wisdom by going right to bed when each long workday finished, he night-owled in the casino, absorbing characters he met and forming a story about people who live the gambling life. More than compulsive gambling, these folks love casino ambiance and choose to make a hand-to-mouth living there. Anderson's idea earned him Sundance Institute support to shoot the script's opening sequence of an old-school gambler showing the ropes to a young guy. Called *Cigarettes and Coffee,* the short film inspired further financial backing, and Anderson returned to Reno in 1994 with a script called *Sidney,* after the story's older, main character.

Since Anderson wrote the script with Reno's Peppermill in mind, he wanted management approval for filming his story showing people who milk the "comp" system for free rooms and food. Sidney only pretends to spend money, afterwards collecting rewards and freebies. Luckily, newly installed monitoring systems made Sidney's specific methods impossible to imitate, so management accepted the project and appreciated the love it shows for casinos. When it comes to public relations, casinos and love provide just the image needed, the kind that might inspire movie viewers to check out the Peppermill in person.

Casino approval came without the promise of famous names to guarantee big movie audiences. Leading man John C. Reilly had years to go before his Oscar nomination for *Chicago.* For that matter, no one on site had heard of the leading lady Anderson wanted so badly that he delayed the project a whole year until she finished a distracting movie called *Jefferson in Paris.* Anderson thought little-known Gwyneth Paltrow warranted the wait, and time proved his faith in her talent when she took home an Oscar for Best Actress for *Shakespeare in Love.* A tiny part also went to Philip Seymour Hoffman, later an Oscar winner for *Capote.*

The delay in filming *Sidney* meant Anderson switched out a bad guy role planned for John Travolta and gave it to Samuel L. Jackson. Jackson got to Reno in March 1995, just as the Academy nominated Travolta and him for Oscars in *Pulp Fiction*. Despite sharing the same amount of screen time, Travolta got the Best Actor nod while Jackson landed in the Supporting category. Jackson faced a particularly competitive field, with Martin Landau favored to win for *Ed Wood*.

Attending a preproduction party in Reno, Jackson got the expected "Congratulations on the Oscar nomination" niceties, even though he really deserved recognition in the lead actor category. Jackson growled unquotable sounds.

"Yeah, but isn't it a good thing to at least get in the race?" I asked. Jackson's growl grew fiercer.

With a barely noticeable nod, Jackson answered in a tough-guy snarl.

"Yeah, except for Martin fuckin' Landau." (Landau went on to win.)

Jackson and the rest of the cast made *Sidney* a dream for a first-time director, and Anderson enhanced acting opportunities by hiring Peppermill employees to play workers in the movie.

"This kind of real function is hard to get from an extra, and I think it makes our film more authentic," he said.

As for Reno, he noted, "It has the feeling of a real city—it's like an Old West town."

Though he still smarts from memories of movie executives switching his title from *Sidney* to *Hard Eight* and changing his original downbeat ending, Anderson retains fond memories of location filming in Reno.

"I think shooting *Hard Eight* in Reno enabled me to capture a state of mind that I wanted for this film," he said.

"It was a great time here," he said years later when he and his future wife Maya Rudolph scouted the Nevada desert for *There Will Be Blood*.

Hard Eight premiered at Sundance but, despite good response, played few theaters. Nonetheless, it earned positive reviews and makes many "Ten Best Gambling Movies" lists. An impressive first film, *Hard Eight* proves value in gambling on newcomers like Anderson, now a multiple Oscar nominee with the clout to assure his own director's cut whenever making a movie.

Gambling on unknown names worked a decade earlier in 1984 when Reno's Peppermill provided interiors for *Stacy's Knights*. The film's finale involves an intricate blackjack scam, allowing a woman to get revenge for her lover's murder. Director Jim Wilson developed the movie's concept while studying a few hours away from Reno at the University of California, Berkeley.

While in class, Wilson decided to switch the usual conceit of men as professional gamblers. "I was in acting class at the time," he said, "and I thought, 'OK, maybe I don't want it to be a male lead. Maybe it would be fun if it was a young female who was a bit of a mousey, bespectacled gal, who had trouble in her shell, and give her some psychological problems that she would take on the big boys of the gambling world in Reno."

He specifically chose Reno rather than Las Vegas for his story.

"It adds a ton to it, 'cause Reno at that point in time, and maybe it's still true, parts of it were wild. It's the biggest little city in the world, so it was a place where you could dream then. I mean you could go up and you could take your couple of hundred bucks and, wow, who knows, you could have a lot of fun up there."

Though the film struggled to get an audience, Wilson says making it proved valuable on many levels.

"Look, I was all of twenty-four when we wrote it and twenty-five when we made it. The greatest schooling is going out and making something and learning from your mistakes. I'm real proud of the movie," he said in 2014.

"I do think for me the only way was not to necessarily take another four years of schooling. I think the twenty-some-odd days of shooting, and the editing and the release and the friendships and the way you learn the business—the best way for me to learn obviously was that. Just getting out and doing it.

"I'm still a proponent of gathering up a camera and friends and putting pen to paper and get it done rather than sit around and commiserating about how to do it. The best thing is to go out and to shoot it and cut it, make it, and feel it and put it up there and get critiques and make a better piece that way."

Of course, having talented friends helps. Wilson's inexperienced co-workers for *Stacy's Knights* included Michael Blake and Kevin Costner.

The three worked together so well they decided to gamble on another project. *Dances with Wolves* hit the jackpot with both profits and Oscars for the trio.

Screenwriter Anthony Zuiker found a similar happy ending following his first project, 1999's *The Runner*. Perfectly manicured and looking like a production executive in a well-tailored grey suit, Zuiker said low production values sabotaged his *Runner* script.

"They did the movie for no money. It was sort of like, maybe a C-plus at most."

Lacking enough money to shoot in Las Vegas, producers filmed at the little eastern Nevada border town of West Wendover, a place no one confuses for a giant gambling Mecca.

The story features a compulsive gambler hired as a "runner," someone who places other people's cash bets at sports books. With insightfully phrased narration, Zuiker says hiring a gambler as a runner resembles allowing an alcoholic to tend bar. Zuiker saw and heard enough about sports books to draw a believable portrait of the life.

"As kids, we always hung out at sports bars," recalls the man who once paid his bills from a job running the Mirage tram.

Zuiker peppered the plot with local stories. One has a player hit cards eleven times before getting twenty-one. Think about it. Four deuces, four aces, and a trio of threes. Zuiker told me someone really played the hand downtown in 1979, a legend cemented into his background growing up in a casino town.

"I saw a lot of gamblers and their antics. My buddy was a real-life runner. But that's all gone now because of Internet betting."

Still, gambling addiction and its dynamics cross timelines. The runner, like many gamblers, breaks all the rules of his job. Money burns his pocket. He blows it all, piling on a huge debt. The solution? Gamble again. He wins more than needed to pay back what he stole. But the runner is a gambler. So . . .

. . . So, that's the point where the majority of non-compulsive viewers need writing, acting, and directing to help them comprehend why the gambler keeps going. Despite the talent involved, *The Runner* failed to create sympathy for its troubled protagonist and went directly to video at a $10 price tag. Later, Zuiker found it floating around town for $2.99. Pretty soon, he saw it in the 99-cent bin.

"It's a heck of a bargain in Las Vegas," he laughed.

He gets the last laugh, too. Key people for Jerry Bruckheimer's production company saw *The Runner* on video and let Zuiker in the door to pitch his idea to set a television series in Las Vegas. He thought the show should be called *CSI: Crime Scene Investigations.*

As Zuiker found with *The Runner,* audiences resist selfish, compulsive gamblers. A long list of films proves the point, epitomized by *Fever Pitch.* Often referred to as the worst exploration of compulsive gambling ever made, the movie's pitch probably sounded promising. *In Cold Blood* director Richard Brooks, *Love Story* actor Ryan O'Neal, and *Heaven Can Wait* cinematographer William A. Fraker shared many Oscar nominations between them, credentials that inspired publisher Hank Greenspun to appear in the film and provide an authentic atmosphere at his *Las Vegas Sun* offices. But *Fever Pitch* crapped out. Celebrating bad work, the Razzies singled out *Fever Pitch* with multiple nominations, including Worst Picture, plus writing and directing nods to Brooks. Meanwhile, viewers of the Poker Forum website voted *Fever Pitch* as "turkey of the past two decades," partly because of its inane dialogue.

"Live and suffer!" growls a cartoonish thug after pounding O'Neal as punishment for failing to pay gambling debts.

O'Neal suffers enough to end up in a trashcan full of mustard, a fate milder than deserved given the film's subversive finale, which undermines every anti-addiction program ever developed.

The purposefully comic *Honeymoon in Vegas* seems more realistic in its look at the crazy behaviors compulsions inspire. Nicolas Cage runs loose as an addict willing to gamble his fiancée. Bug-eyed and frenetic, Cage earns sympathy and laughs with the extremes he takes to fix his mistake, including dressing up as his (real-life) former father-in-law in a sequined-laden white jumpsuit. The 1992 comedy foreshadowed events the following year when Robert Redford makes an *Indecent Proposal*, and where Demi Moore is substituted as cash in compulsive gambler Woody Harrelson's next bet. Sleep with Robert Redford? Make that "Really Decent Proposal."

Under Adrian Lyne's slick direction, *Indecent Proposal* turned the Las Vegas Hilton into delicious eye candy, from low-level views of rolling dice to a luxurious suite that inspired viewers to request the same room on their next visit.

Beyond eye candy, Las Vegas and Nevada casinos link the strange connections between the luck or bad choices that lead to winning and losing.

Damage caused by compulsive behavior envelops 1994's *The Gambler*, featuring a Las Vegas segment at Caesars and the defunct Mint and Dunes casinos. (That segment switched to a Palm Springs casino in the 2014 remake, which only features verbal reference to Las Vegas.) Screenwriter James Toback drew on his own gambling experiences, adding an intellectual spin by quoting Fyodor Dostoevsky. Lecturing on the Russian novelist, James Caan plays a literature professor explaining the gambler's mindset.

Most people, he tells his students, stay trapped in a rut believing that two and two always equal four. Dostoevsky and the gambler expand their minds and reserve "the sacred right" to believe that someday two and two will equal five—that possibility makes the future intriguing. The average person's difficulty following such logic explains why compulsive behavior mystifies by-the-book Dudley Do-Rights.

Gamblers love the philosophy that absolute truth mutates. Gamblers realize casino buildings grow huge and luxurious because the owners usually win, but they wear armor to prevent the realization from sinking in. Playing *Beautiful Joe*, Billy Connelly asks Sharon Stone's gambler a key question in West Wendover, Nevada

"Do you think these lights go blinkety-blink because people like you win?"

For a compulsive gambler, losing offers a different thrill. Caan's gambler bypasses a surefire move to easily clear his $40,000 debt, proclaiming playing it safe means no "juice." Risk spikes energy and excitement.

Heading to Las Vegas, he deflects his girlfriend's concerns about losing money by making a distinction.

"I'm not going to lose it; I'm going to gamble it."

Tension heightens as he plays the twenty-one tables at Caesars and wants another card on his eighteen.

"You're crazy," says an onlooker who knows all those rules about staying with an eighteen.

Caan throws in more money to double down.

"I'm blessed," he insists before the dealer throws the final card.

That's the gambler's mindset.

Caan delivers insightful, often witty lines with conviction, earning him a Golden Globe nomination as best dramatic actor. His confidence attracts admiration, despite such cringe-inducing behavior as risking his mother's life savings and destroying the career of a promising college athlete. Toback's screenplay makes it possible to get into this gambler's soul; liking it is another matter.

Around the same time Caan hit Las Vegas, Robert Altman made *California Split* with a gambling scene in Reno. Like *The Gambler*, *California Split* often shows up on those "ten best" lists of movies about gambling. George Segal and Elliott Gould play compulsive gamblers who bet on anything, from illegal poker to horses. The top-billed Segal plays a rigid businessman named Bill, while Gould embodies the lackadaisical, optimistic Charlie.

Reflecting on Bill and Charlie a couple of decades later, Gould said he helped inspire the story.

"*California Split* was semiautobiographical about Joey Walsh and me," he explained.

California Split screenwriter Walsh called himself Charlie in the story, a happy-go-lucky, freewheeling guy. More reserved than comedies like *M.A.S.H.* indicate, Gould inspired Charlie's neurotic friend Bill. As *California Split* developed, the legendary Steve McQueen signed on as Charlie.

When McQueen dropped from the film, director Robert Altman changed things around.

"Altman said to me, 'I know if I give you a nickel, you'll stretch it further than anybody else is willing to; will you play the other guy?'"

Gould hesitated, worrying about his friend's reaction.

"What does Joey think?" he asked the director, continuing, "It's his picture."

Altman knew a gambler's soul.

"Joey doesn't care," he told Gould. "Joey's playing poker."

Gould took the role, responding, "I was thrilled to play that part."

Though he shaved his famous drooping mustache for the part, Gould's unruly mop of curly dark hair, plus a Band-Aid on his nose, made him look like an offbeat free spirit, and he worked comfortably with Altman's famous technique fostering improvisation and developing scenes naturally.

"On films with Robert Altman, he would always give you the opportunity to live within your role," said Gould about the discovery process that improvisation provides.

"I think that in life we don't know necessarily what we're going to say next, or do next, or what's going to happen. Like the joke, if you want to make God laugh, tell him your plans."

The movie's improvised scenes include a finale at the now-defunct Mapes in Reno, where the gamblers arrived on a glum winter day. Footage provides a nostalgic memory of low-ceilinged casinos with red-flocked bordello wallpaper. The look continues to the Mapes' famous Sky Room restaurant, which art director Leon Erikson transformed into a poker room. The extensive space allowed Altman to stage an elaborate game featuring Reno Mayor Sam Dibitonto.

While *M*A*S*H* remains Altman's most popular film, *California Split* highlights the director's style featuring meandering, leisurely pacing. Altman's penchant for overlapping dialogue and improvised lines gives a "slice of life" feel, capturing the world created during a hot streak at the tables. Throughout the film, Gould's engaging humor as Charlie generates laughs even as he and Bill lose themselves in a rootless, self-centered, and nearly functionless lifestyle fueled by gambling.

Altman claimed the movie celebrates gambling, despite Bill and Charlie's long faces at the end. The two realize winning feels just as depressing as losing and gambling lacks the clear-cut rewards they wanted. They discover gambling resembles taking the famous Road to Hana in Maui where "it's the journey, not the destination" that counts.

"The picture is a metaphor about survival, about keeping the spirit alive. The picture is about staying in action. It's about staying alive," said Gould, reflecting on why the movie still resounds with viewers. "Gambling is not about winning, it's about playing."

Both on screen and in real life, money often serves as little more than a prop.

The Other Compulsive Behavior

Leaving Las Vegas nods at the gambling genre even though its main character only hits the tables briefly—and literally. Nicolas Cage won an Oscar for Best Actor for playing Ben, a compulsive drinker who knows all about losing and feels at home in a city where luck and winners change course instantly. Ben joins his amour on a gambling fling, pleased that casinos give players free drinks. A time bomb, Ben explodes easily and upends a blackjack table at what is now the River Palms in Laughlin, a nearby gambling town whose flashy casino interiors pass for some in Las Vegas. Las Vegas exteriors, including aerials of the Strip, lend the film its location atmosphere, sneaked without permits as director Mike Figgis ran unobtrusively through the city, his tiny crew using high definition 16-millimeter film later blown up to 35 millimeter. This technique, plus cinematographer Declan Quinn's keen technical sense, contribute to an appropriately dark look for a difficult, compelling tale about finding a final way out of compulsive, losing behavior. Fine acting and creative technique make the film rewarding despite its downbeat tone. Importantly, Las Vegas provides the perfect symbolic setting; most locations fail to promote the right mental image. "Leaving Punxsutawney?" "Leaving Lake Placid?" Las Vegas wins.

9

Rocky and the Fighters

Destiny sent Rocky Balboa to Nevada since all great boxers fight in Las Vegas. The state thrives on promoting the forbidden, and in 1897 it became the first to allow real boxing matches. Since then, Las Vegas fine-tuned the art of providing the sport's best arenas.

But when Rocky first fought in 1976, his Philadelphia roots dominated the story. Before *Rocky*, Sylvester Stallone bummed around movies with minimal success, including a 1970 softcore project renamed *The Italian Stallion* after *Rocky*'s success. With *Rocky*, Stallone envisioned revving up the sport, portraying an underdog playing into a heavyweight champion's scheme to give an unknown a shot at the title. The champ resembles Muhammad Ali in many ways, while the contender calls himself the Italian Stallion and shares traits with Stallone.

Coming in the middle of a decade with brilliant but downbeat movies ranging from Martin Scorsese's *Taxi Driver* to Roman Polanski's *Chinatown* and Bob Fosse's *Cabaret*, *Rocky* swept through theaters with refreshing joy and excitement. The script plays a neat trick in its final match. Rocky winning outright stretches believability but losing opens depressing doors. By hanging in fifteen rounds with the champ, Rocky goes the distance and feels like a winner.

Audiences loved cheering with *Rocky*, making the movie tops at the box office in 1976. Award attention showed up with ten Oscar nominations. *Rocky*'s wins included best director for John Avildsen and best picture, beating *Taxi Driver*. The mix of prizes and money meant more movies as the franchise traveled a rocky road, passing through Nevada several times.

It took until *Rocky III* before mention was made of Nevada and Caesars Palace. *Rocky IV* ups Nevada's role in 1985. Years turn Rocky and his old nemesis Apollo Creed into best buds, a tie explored decades later in 2015's non-Nevada series entry, *Creed*. Though retired, the senior Creed decides to get back in the ring with a Soviet Olympic titleholder bearing the ominous name Ivan Drago. The Cold War fight boasts production show quality at the former MGM (now Bally's) in Las Vegas. The event opens in red, white, and blue glitz as James Brown sings the rousing "Living in America." Thousands of extras filled stands and watched the show, imitating audiences at real Las Vegas fights.

The Vegas fight looms significantly. Creed vastly misjudges Drago, who uses his superior size to pummel the former champ. Creed makes a fatal move when he insists on staying in after round one.

Fueled by anger and guilt, Rocky leaves Las Vegas on a trail of vengeance, forfeiting his own title to fight Drago in the Soviet Union.

"I gotta do what I gotta do," says Rocky in his guttural slur.

Stallone won Oscar nominations for acting and writing the first *Rocky* and another as supporting actor for *Creed*, but he reduces emoting challenges during the fourth by keeping words and sentences short and simplistic.

"We can't change who we are," claims the boxer in early scenes.

This means Rocky once again hits the road for musical montages, running in striking locations, backed by "Hearts on fire/strong desire" lyrics pounding the soundtrack.

As Rocky enters the ring in Russia, he absorbs new sensations. The crowd hates him. They love Drago. Rocky faces his hardest fight ever—no change from the climax of his earlier films. Rocky feels like stopping but formulates his deepest thought.

"Going in one more round when you don't think you can—that's what makes all the difference in your life."

Change, Rocky realizes, has positive points.

Ultimately, *Rocky IV* proves the drawbacks of change. Sincere, honest emotions from the original *Rocky* changed into bombastic platitudes. The gritty little fight from the first movie expanded to a glittery showcase. Truly inspirational music pumped into empty power rock. Even awards changed. The first *Rocky* won the Oscar for Best Picture. The fourth *Rocky* ran away with multiple prizes at the Academy Awards' antithesis, the Razzies.

Despite the inevitability of change, Stallone and his creation found pleasure by going back to the old style in 2006 with *Rocky Balboa*. Written and directed by Stallone, the movie plays in a much lower key than the *Rocky Roman Numeral* franchise movies. As in his original, Stallone writes from the heart. Hungry again, after seeing his movies open in the denigrated direct-to-video market, he reevaluated trends. Sure, everyone knows Stallone and wants his autograph or the chance to join him for a photo. But respect? Try Hilary Swank and her Oscar for Best Actress as a boxer.

With his professional highs behind him, Rocky changes careers and operates a restaurant. Still mentioned in boxing history, Rocky sparks interest when sports analysts computerize a fantasy bout pitting the old guy against current world champion Mason Dixon. The imaginary match inspires Rocky to apply for his fighting license. Hearing this, Dixon's promoters suggest a charity exhibition between the older and younger champs in the place with the most potential to raise money, Las Vegas.

For this sequence, Stallone wanted reaction from a real audience. He chose Bernard Hopkins' middleweight title fight at the Mandalay Bay where 12,000 people sat. Without telling the audience, Stallone entered the arena. Puzzled, the crowd nonetheless cheered. Of course, they knew—and loved—the iconic boxer Rocky. Stallone left, and the crowd watched the Hopkins fight with the option to stay afterwards for the fake Rocky Balboa match. Thousands did. They behaved like a real audience, heckling Rocky and eventually chanting his name. The resulting authenticity mitigated doubters questioning a 60-plus-year-old man surviving in the ring with a 30-year-old. The potential Rocky horror show transformed to a sweet piece of genuine nostalgia for the man rated by the American Film Institute as the fourth greatest hero in movies, a true cinematic icon.

The *Rocky* image affected real-life boxer Ray "Boom Boom" Mancini when he brought his HBO version of *Body and Soul* to Reno. Mancini, the World Boxing Association (WBA) lightweight champion two years running during the eighties, put his own stamp on the boxing genre. On set, Mancini avoided what he called "Rocky punches."

"You know, where you pull the hand back from one end of the coast to the other end of the coast."

He also hoped to elevate boxing dialogue.

"In movies, the fight guys speak out of the side of their mouths. I hate the idea of fighters as uneducated stumblebums, pugs with flat noses and scar tissue all over their eyes," he said, emphasizing that massive boxing payoffs mean fighters need intelligence.

"They have to be a little more sophisticated and knowledgeable about business."

Mancini's costar, Rod Steiger, agreed about the importance of changing Rocky clichés despite their iconic status.

"I don't want to do a *Rocky* trainer. I mean every time they do a trainer, they kind of insult the intelligence of people involved in boxing," he said, proceeding into an Academy Award winner's imitation of Burgess Meredith slurring dialogue as the coach in *Rocky*.

"They talk like this—'hit him, hit him'—and that's not true. I've met some trainers who speak rather well. And some who were well-read. I made my whole living by going against counterpoint," said Steiger, explaining, "I try to get around clichés."

With both actors looking for something different, the tough 1947 *Body and Soul* offered promising source material.

"*Body and Soul* to me is the greatest fight movie ever made," said Mancini, adding, "and John Garfield is my favorite actor of all time. The reason I think that it's the best fight film ever made is because it's about the business side of boxing."

Mancini, speaking at a dingy little Reno gym on Fourth Street, dispensed more praise for the original movie.

"It's film noir, a real dark piece that hit all the right points at that time."

By 1998, mega-media broadcasts and the power of networks changed a few elements in the sport, raising payoffs to Jack and the Beanstalk proportions for boxers and promoters.

Yet many aspects remain.

"Boxing is the one sport that has not sophisticated through the years. It's basically the same backroom scene, a little more upscale, but the same ol' same ol'. This can be contemporized easily, and that's what we did."

Mancini's background provides an insider's view of boxing.

"We take the audience in the backrooms and let them see why deals are made and the reasoning going on."

With a WBA championship at age twenty-one, Mancini deeply grasps the qualities needed for a boxer and showman to win millions of fans.

"What I do is bring some authenticity to this film. You know, I lived it, I hope I'm the real deal."

Though retired from the ring, he put his compact, muscled body through tough rehearsals. Sweat glistened during filming and he never pulled a punch.

"There's nothing worse than seeing a guy try to fake hitting a bag. You have to actually do it so the public sees me panting, and they see me sweating, and they know that I'm actually doing it, and I'm not trying to create anything that's not real."

Reno and its surroundings filled in for all *Body and Soul* locations, including early scenes in Ohio and cross-country driving shots. The Eldorado Hotel Casino served as a prime location, with key matches on the convention floor. Smaller bouts staged in upstairs storage space, while parties shot in luxury suites and gaming action filmed on the casino floor. Mancini switched plans for Las Vegas filming, though the 1947 original set scenes there.

"Reno's been good to me," Mancini explained.

Mancini fought well in Reno. In contrast, Vegas sent him his most intense career moment when a match with Duk Koo Kim ended with the Korean's death (covered in a 2002 Korean movie called *Champion,* featuring Nevada location filming).

Shifting discussion from boxing to acting, Mancini recognized overlap in the two fields.

"Both acting and boxing are being in the moment," he said.

"You hear about thinking fighters. No, fighters are trained to react. Same thing with acting. You free up the lines so it becomes second nature, so you're not acting, you're creating. Subconsciously, you're just reacting. So they are very similar, and I hope that having the mindset and being trained as a fighter has helped me as an actor."

Then he paused, and said with a wry smile, "The bottom line, though, is that the camera doesn't punch back."

Parallel thoughts about similarities between sports and acting came from a director who loves the competitive arena, Ron Shelton. A professional athlete turned moviemaker, Shelton brought two boxing movies to Nevada, *Play It to the Bone* and *The Great White Hype,* which join 2015's *Southpaw* and many other films by staging a key fight in Las Vegas. Claiming "a jock's view of the universe," the onetime minor league baseball player said his attitude affects how he makes movies.

"In a sense, it's based on discipline and enormous preparation and the kind of old-fashioned commitment to practice and craft, all of which is a way of freeing you up creatively. In other words, all the preparation an athlete does is so that he is free on the athletic field, and all the writer-director-storyteller's preparation is to become free in the storytelling, and that's a real athlete's view of the world."

A huge boxing fan, Shelton speed-lists movies about the sport and aimed at a finale more complicated than outright victory or loss. *Play It to the Bone* pits two boxing buddies against each other in a Las Vegas fight at Mandalay Bay. Which actor wins—Woody Harrelson or Antonio Banderas—matters less than the intensity of their fighting. Fed up with lightweight elements in heavyweight matches, they complain how fighters barely take a lick for a single round. Placed in a killer showdown, Shelton's fighters slug it out in a boxing bloodbath. Hugely violent, *Play It to the Bone* got knocked down at the box office. Like an unfazed champion, Shelton rose for another round of movie boxing with his script for *The Great White Hype.*

Directed by Reginald Hudlin, the resulting film, 1996's *The Great White Hype,* lets Samuel L. Jackson channel real-life boxing promoter Don King with a character named Fred Sultan. Called a "con man, hustler and perhaps [the] devil incarnate" in the 20th Century Fox promotional packet,

Sultan "rules over the modern-day Sodom and Gomorrah better known as Las Vegas." Concerned about shrinking boxing crowds, Sultan promotes a new Great White Hope to spur racial strife and raise attendance.

The production filmed in what publicists called Sin City a few days before the Mike Tyson/Peter McNeeley fight, also featuring a Great White Hope. The *Hype* version seeks a humorous, cynical, and intentionally politically incorrect tone. But it pulls punches and funny men Jamie Foxx, Cheech Marin, Damon Wayans, and Jon Lovitz generate smirks rather than belly laughs. As usual, Las Vegas looks like a natural setting for these flashy players at MGM Grand.

The title *Great White Hype* plays on a Nevada reality, the famous Johnson-Jeffries fight of 1910 pitting African American Jack Johnson against Anglo James Jeffries. Filmmakers captured the actual 1910 Johnson-Jeffries Fight when it happened, and documentarian Ken Burns repeats portions in his 2005 PBS documentary *Unforgivable Blackness: The Rise and Fall of Jack Johnson*. A 2013 *American Experience* segment looks at the fight with much better quality than clips found on YouTube. Film viewers back in the days just after the fight rioted and caused a ban on documenting future bouts.

Jackson also inspired a play turned into a 1970s Great White Hope movie. Flamboyantly portrayed by a trim James Earl Jones before anyone heard of Darth Vader, the fighter faces racism, exacerbated by his relationship with a white woman. Writers changed many details, referring to the "Jefferson-Brady" fight. Yet the location stays the same in dialogue as several organizers determine where to hold the fight, looking for a region with a small black population.

"What about Tulsa?" asks one. "Denver? Reno?"

"Hey Reno!" says another enthusiastically.

"Why not?" puts in a businessman, adding inaccurately, "The good ol' Rockies." He calls "white man's country" perfect for the fight.

"Yes, but who lives there?" asks Jackson's manager.

"It's on the mainline now," the conversation continues, with the observation, "and it's high and dry."

"The higher the better," observes another. Reno wins.

Reno remained part of the movie in name only since director Martin Ritt filmed the fight near his other production locations in Arizona.

The Johnson-Jeffries fight joins a string of well-known matches benefitting from Nevada's openness to the so-called vice of boxing. The first filmed match came with 1897's Corbett-Fitzsimmons world championship fight in Nevada's capital, Carson City. One of those true "greatest stories ever told," the landmark match represents both Nevada's initial legal prizefight and the state's first screen presence. The fight's movie version places in record books for technical advancement.

One of *The Corbett-Fitzsimmons Fight* innovations involved recording footage with three cameras to crosscut scenes. Producers used 70-millimeter film, allowing huge projection, similar to *Lawrence of Arabia* and later epics. Emotion made the project a sentimental favorite, as title defender James Corbett (played by Errol Flynn in 1942's *Gentleman Jim*) went fourteen rounds against Robert Fitzsimmons, with a surprise ending. The excitement of *seeing* rather than reading about the fight compelled nickelodeon audiences for years, creating a blockbuster for its time.

Modern viewers find footage bright, faded, and grainy, whether in 16-millimeter versions or on YouTube. Still, the footage retains tremendous historical significance, preserved in national film archives. The Corbett fight sustained public awareness through 1953 when *The City of Bad Men* producers made it part of their heist film starring Dale Robertson and Lloyd Bridges. Another historical boxing match, the 1906 Gans-Nelson fight in the old Nevada mining town of Goldfield, also plays in archives, with Gene Hackman commenting about it in a Nevada-filmed feature, 1975's western *Bite the Bullet*.

Boxers fighting historic matches show up in documentaries and biopics with Nevada ties. Muhammad Ali includes Las Vegas scenes with clips from real bouts when he starred in *The Greatest* from 1976. Several fighters pass through the 1997 biopic *Don King: Only in America* with a Golden Globe–winning performance from Ving Rhames as the legendary promoter. The HBO movie uses Las Vegas stock footage for Ali versus Spinks and Ali versus Holmes at Caesars with the Las Vegas Hilton banner easy to read in the background. The Don King biopic re-creates a highly significant Las Vegas fight, one billed as "The Sound and the Fury" at the MGM Garden Arena in June 1997.

The fight features Evander Holyfield and Mike Tyson, an icon who eventually moved to Nevada. The most promising boxer of his era, Tyson blew it on several levels, first going to prison for rape and then biting off his opponent's ear during a 1997 comeback fight. He tattooed his face like a Maori warrior from New Zealand and eventually talked about all of it in the fascinating 2009 documentary, *Tyson*.

Tyson's career put him in contact with filmmaker James Toback, whose fictional movie *The Gambler* explores a risk-taker's mindset. Toback sees similar fearlessness in Tyson, letting him explain his actions without analysis or contradiction from other sources.

Technically, Toback's format traps him into the often-static talking head shot. But what a talking head! No one else comes close to Tyson's past and memories. Computer editing programs let Toback use multiple images, fading various views with overlapping talk and preserving Tyson's meaning so the boxer gives his side of events without distortion. Toback intersperses images from key boxing matches and various interviews conducted by ESPN and Barbara Walters, but Tyson dominates with his own illuminating and often stunning interpretations.

As a boxing icon, Tyson played archetype for other movies. He bookended the *Tyson* documentary with hilarious interludes in *The Hangover,* showing his love for music by air drumming a Phil Collins song, finishing with a pounding punch to a bystander's face. Tyson inspires *Undisputed,* a 2002 fiction film featuring a world heavyweight titleholder incarcerated for rape. The "undisputed" world champ ends up in a Nevada prison with its own boxing king, one obsessively aiming for a shot at the official titleholder.

Wesley Snipes plays the prison champ, an arrogantly aloof man guilty of murder. During filming, Snipes gained unwanted attention with an altercation at the Mandalay Bay Hotel Casino and later made headlines protesting that *Undisputed* scenes softened his movie character by adding sympathetic traits. To Snipes' credit, his undisputed prison champ never asks for empathy. Similarly, his opponent shares a mix of good and bad qualities. Ving Rhames shows his Tyson offshoot as a tough guy, always looking for a fight.

Director Walter Hill quickly establishes these details, repeating the flair for high testosterone action movies he began in 1975 with a well-liked fight film, *Hard Times. Undisputed* action heads single-mindedly to the illegal fight that everyone expects from the moment the world champ arrives at Sweetwater Prison in what passes as the Mojave Desert. Nevada's newly built High Desert Prison steps in as location, nearly empty during production. Hill takes full advantage of the freedom to move unimpeded around prison facilities, emphasizing the climactic fight. The movie audience—both on screen and in theaters—grunts along with the boxers, who tear into one another with wild fury.

Those seeking a direct contrast to the rough-and-tumble world of man against man in the boxing ring find it in *Matilda,* a 1978 movie showcasing a championship fight between a guy and a kangaroo in Nevada. The story stars Elliott Gould promoting a kangaroo who gets his name from the Australian song "Waltzing Matilda." Gary Morgan played Matilda, disguised in a furry suit.

In person, the suit looked stiff and bulky, qualities magnified on screen. Kids might accept the movie if Matilda appeared soft, cuddly, and cute, but this 'roo bore a hard, tough frame that looked kind of scary. Instead of large, liquid, soulful eyes that made the ugly E.T. lovable, Matilda saw the world through beady little orbs lacking expression. Matilda hardly ever blinks, a trait more common to serial killers than adorable animals. Worse yet, Matilda threatens with his size. The six-foot-three Gould stands taller, but the kangaroo goes face to face with other performers.

A phony-looking kangaroo heightens the ridiculous notion of an animal challenging a human world heavyweight. With a ludicrous premise and no heartwarming main character, a simple question arises.

"What *were* they thinking?"

They thought they could make a lot of money. Everyone associated with the project boasted impressive credentials, and Reno buzzed with excitement when the crew arrived to take advantage of the city's record-hosting prizefights. The Washoe County Fairgrounds' interior quickly transformed to a stadium for Matilda's first East Coast match, while surrounding highway made it look like promoters covered many miles of cross-country travel. Though relatively small, the real-life Harrah's passed as a glamorous casino suited to handling big events. The convention center south of town offered spacious interiors for the final match.

Locals enjoyed stargazing, with Gould still hot from *M*A*S*H* and other seventies adult hits. He chose *Matilda* because he took his real-life role as a father seriously and felt ready for a change.

"It feels good to be making a picture that my young children can watch," he said at the time.

Decades later, he expressed doubts about whether they ever saw *Matilda*.

"I don't know. I subsequently made *The Last Flight of Noah's Ark*. That's a picture my children watched and my children's children watch. It has a very good shelf life. I didn't think *Matilda* fulfilled or lived up to its potential from the Paul Gallico book."

Yet *Matilda* misses the full definition of "flop." Even before release, McDonald's joined in with product placement including a burger for the boxer.

"He deserves it," says Gould, playing on the fast-food chain's period "You Deserve a Break Today" motto.

Mark Damon, who negotiated advance guarantees with distributors for the Producers Sales Organization, said in *The Movie Business Book* that *Matilda*'s McDonald's connection pushed the movie into the profit zone before release. That made a difference since few paid to watch the film in theaters.

Matilda disappeared in any serious boxing fan's movie memories, but one name hung in for that final knockout. Twenty-six years later, *Matilda* producer Al Ruddy bounded on stage at the Oscars to accept his award for producing yet another boxing movie, which blended an unusual contender and a scene set in Nevada: *Million Dollar Baby*. Screenwriter Paul Haggis originally intended to direct the movie himself, with Sandra Bullock starring as a woman determined to become a professional boxer. Directing duties shifted to Clint Eastwood once the actor took the role of boxing trainer. Another change came when Bullock headed to Las Vegas to film the sequel to her huge hit *Miss Congeniality*. Hilary Swank stepped in as the boxing hopeful and went on to win her second Oscar for Best Actress. The plot includes a final fight in Las Vegas, a site familiar to the director from *The Gauntlet*.

Eastwood made several other films, including *Honkytonk Man*, in Nevada and said he likes working in the state.

"It's always been terrific. Being brought up in California, I spent a lot of time in Nevada and made a lot of films here. I keep coming back."

He also values working outside a studio.

"I guess maybe because I started my career on the plains of Spain years ago, I just always liked being on location, and especially if you can go on location in a modern-day setting where there are real places, not sets," Eastwood said in Reno, promoting a movie he shot there, *Pink Cadillac*.

However, he decided to stay in Los Angeles for *Million Dollar Baby*, partly because the script's Las Vegas Arena did not need the scale and glitz of flashy places where men fight.

"We always knew we could do this scene in Los Angeles," location manager Kokayi Ampah told me. "We knew the Hollywood Palladium was a real location that had the darker, less-fancy look we needed."

Signs and banners reading "Las Vegas Arena" gave *Million Dollar Baby* its Nevada connection.

Like most fictional boxing stories, *Million Dollar Baby* uses Nevada as a classroom in the school of boxing. Fighters pass through for the lessons learned on their way up, often finding the biggest match of their lives. A Nevada boxing match might result in the boxing equivalent of a PhD. What a concept—party central in Las Vegas functions as an Ivy League school, at least when it comes to fighters and movies.

Kangaroo Kissing in Reno

Given a choice of rooting for a man or a kangaroo, I chose the 'roo.

Moviemakers gave me more freedom than the typical extra because I provided publicity by writing a piece on their project, *Matilda*, for a local paper. Still, I followed instructions from director Daniel Mann.

Like most people associated with *Matilda*, he brought notable credentials; in his case, guiding Elizabeth Taylor to her first Oscar for Best Actress in 1960's *Butterfield 8*. Part of Mann's job with *Matilda* involved eliciting loud response from a crowd of kangaroo fans who booed their hearts out whenever the human boxer landed a punch.

"This does make one feel a bit ridiculous, doesn't it?" asked a person booing beside me.

Ridiculous, yes. But it provided the chance to see screen legend Robert Mitchum playing a sportswriter. Later, Mitchum walked by and sneered, "Kangaroo kissers!"

"We're men kissers," I corrected him.

"Speak for yourself," said a guy next to me.

Mitchum eventually forgave me. Without realizing it, we both aimed at walking through the same small space. Facing each other, we stepped forward simultaneously with the unintentional result that neither of us could move. We retreated in unison. We moved forward again. Finally, Mitchum just grabbed my hands and waltzed through a set's arched doorway as he headed toward his mark for action.

Like many reporters who write about the "extra experience," I discovered moviemaking involved a lot of hurry-up-and-wait spread out over a twelve-hour workday. By the end of my shift, I developed three new favorite words.

"Cut! Print it!"

The Sound and the Fury in Nevada

The Sound and the Fury fight stunned the world when World Boxing Association Heavyweight Champion Mike Tyson bit off part of Evander Holyfield's ear. The amazing image plays in multiple forms on YouTube where, yes, Tyson really bites down on that ear. Next, he spits it out across the ring, one of those scenes that feels invented for a fictional movie, not real life. The incident resulted in Tyson losing his boxing license, catapulting referee Mills Lane to international attention.

Three Sound and Fury participants spent time in Nevada. One, Tyson, eventually moved to Las Vegas and got laughs playing himself in *The Hangover*.

I saw another during a jog around Reno's one-mile course at a popular local park known as Virginia Lake.

"Isn't that Evander Holyfield?" my partner asked, nodding to a tall man preparing to hit the track.

Compared to the park's typical lanky runners, this guy's muscles loomed big despite the sweatshirt covering his broad chest. We tried to act discreet but gave up when he smiled at us.

"Good luck," we said and he grinned more broadly.

The Sound and Fury referee, Mills Lane, worked in Reno as a district attorney and later, judge. Our paths crossed occasionally when I worked for the Nevada

Film Office and he pushed a *Judge Mills Lane* television show. Bumping into him at McCarran International Airport in Las Vegas, Mills asked if he could tag along when my friend drove my husband and me into town.

No problem normally, plus we looked forward to bragging about helping out a world famous figure. Except...

"Uh, my little convertible barely holds two grocery bags," my friend Julie Wilcox said to Mills. "But..."

"Great!" said Mills.

Julie took the driver's seat, Fred got front, I sat behind, and Mills propped himself on the back ledge, enjoying a full-body breeze as we whizzed from the airport onto the downtown Strip, breaking seatbelt and safety rules.

As Mills noticed my suitcase in the tiny car, he admired its tag promoting Nevada.

"Where'd you get that?" he demanded.

"We have a machine to laminate business cards at our office," I responded.

"Can you get me one?" he asked me excitedly.

"Sure," I said, since promoting Nevada's name on luggage tags represented a win-win situation for the state Commission on Economic Development and its Film Office.

Mills gave me his business card. Once back in the office, I made the tag and sent it to him. He called the day it arrived at his Reno office.

"You're a woman of your word," he said. "I like that."

From that moment on, he always greeted me the same way.

"Robin, you're a woman of your word. Great to see you!"

That kind of friendly magnetism—plus the Tyson/Holyfield fight's spotlight—paid off for Mills with a reality television program based in New York.

10

Big Things at the Atomic Test Site

Size matters, and Nevada claims big movies, even those with little budgets. As home to the atomic test site in Mercury, Nevada proves a place to grow massively without eating a thing. Just apply radiation.

It works for *The Amazing Colossal Man*. As the title implies, the story features a really big guy. But that term "Amazing" happens because people still watch the film more than fifty years after it was released in 1957. With dozens of user comments on the Internet Movie Database and its own *Amazing Colossal Man* page on Facebook, the movie boasts fans, surprising director Bert I. Gordon, who realizes people must take extra steps to watch his opus since it lies outside normal distribution channels.

"The film has been out of circulation because the film is owned by the ex-wife of one of the distributor partners and she hasn't released it," he said in an e-mail.

Gordon takes the nickname "Mr. B.I.G." from his initials and a propensity for sci-fi projects featuring giant ants and other large characters. He made movies for the drive-in circuit with American International Pictures and Samuel Arkoff, a producer known for his passion to make a quick buck rather than a great film. No one expected to find American International's pictures in classic film archives.

So why pay tribute to "*The Amazing Colossal Man*"? One explanation: A kitschy old one-sheet ad for *The Amazing Colossal Man* helps keep the movie alive, popping up quickly and easily online. Against a striking yellow-orange background, the titular Colossal Man dominates the page by forming an arc reaching from right to left. Tanks and soldiers charge him from the bottom. His right arm swats away attacking planes like a horsetail on flies, while his left hand grasps a tiny woman in a blue dress. Bald and grimacing, the Colossal Man's choice of attire startles—he wears what initially passes for a humongous diaper.

Sadly, this poster uses only a generic city site in its art instead of playing up the movie's Las Vegas setting. Other movie art corrects this. The Spanish-language one-sheet for *El Gigante Ataca* adds Hoover (formerly Boulder) Dam into the mix.

Another promotional sheet makes the Nevada connection clear, showing a black-and-white photo of the Colossal Man to the left, with green writing at the right proclaiming, "A 70-foot giant is terrorizing Las Vegas!" A logo for the Sands Hotel represents the city in the bottom left, with a marquee for entertainer Danny Thomas incorrectly linking a star with the movie.

None of the posters emphasize the Nevada Test Site, the movie's key setting and one of the state's most significant locations. Because the test site, Las Vegas, and the renamed Hoover Dam remain recognizable decades later, though, iconic locations draw people to the story.

Director Gordon came to Nevada to shoot part of the movie.

"The Boulder Dam scenes in the movie were filmed at the dam. Of course, some of the shots were composites with the Colossal Man, et cetera, thanks to the optical printer."

Besides iconic locations, Gordon mines classic horror themes, pulling the Frankenstein edict, "You Can't Fool Mother Nature." Peril magnifies when science goes to extremes.

In Gordon's script, fooling with Big Mama starts at the Nevada Test Site, where scientists expand their limits by exploding a plutonium bomb. Accidentally exposed to excessive radiation, a military officer faces the *Frankenstein* link as he transforms into a sympathetic monster who never asked to be created.

True, the Frankenstein monster's bad habits include killing people, but only out of frustration when everyone treats him badly. Similarly, Col. Glenn Manning of *The Amazing Colossal Man* wants to live a normal life but ends up qualifying for a Mr. Clean commercial by growing tall, going bald, and wearing a wraparound swaddling cloth.

Like *Frankenstein, The Amazing Colossal Man* appeals to conflicting emotions: we want what science provides but, at the same time, we fear it might turn around and bite us in the butt. The atomic bomb represents this double-edged sword. It pulled the United States and its allies out of World War II, but then sent leaders into a Cold War of hot fear that someone else would develop and use the weapon.

The Amazing Colossal Man draws on fears and fascination surrounding experiments during the fifties when atomic bombs regularly exploded

Mercury, Nevada, sixty-five miles north of Las Vegas. Often announced, the tests inspired Las Vegas residents to put on sunglasses and have a blast holding "explosive" parties as they watched mushroom-shaped clouds spread across the horizon.

The Amazing Colossal Man reflects the general public's blasé attitude about aftereffects, as Col. Manning feels protected by hiding behind a barricade during the explosion a few feet away. He triple ensures his safety by wearing a military helmet and big, dark glasses.

Col. Manning leaves his protective barricade for noble reasons, running out to rescue a crash-landed pilot, hitting the desert floor just in time to get the full force of the blast. Unfortunately for Col. Manning, the bomb's side effects prove enormous. As one poster says in lettering that keeps getting bigger, he's

"Growing
Growing
Growing
Growing
To a Giant!
To a Monster!"

Pretty soon, the colonel stands 70 feet tall, annoyed about losing his hair, and realizing none of the Big and Tall stores carry clothes his size.

"Who but a clown would have an expandable sarong like this," he asks one of the soldiers, who shows up with supplies.

Sitting scrunched in a huge tent erected as shelter for him, Col. Manning elaborates on his clothing.

"It's adjustable. I can grow to be one hundred feet tall, and I don't need a change of wardrobe," he says, pausing with a sneer.

"Army ingenuity," he concludes with disgust.

Col. Manning faces other problems, according to his physicians, who are befuddled by the bomb's side effects.

"Something out there is beyond the limits of our knowledge," one medical expert concludes.

Apparently, their own limits exceed blue whale proportions. One doctor analyzes impacts from the stress of unimpeded growth, leading to dialogue that still makes fans of bad movies chortle with glee.

"It might be explained that, since the heart is made up of a 'single' cell for all practical purposes, instead of millions of cells like the rest of the organs of the body, it's reacting in an entirely different manner to this unknown stimulus or forces behind this whole thing."

Yes, the expert says that: the heart has one cell.

Besides a crazy ticker, Col. Manning develops mental issues. Bitterness grows along with his body parts, and he suggests his tent should have a sign reading, "See the Amazing Colossal Man."

Snapping in frustration, Col. Manning escapes the military compound and zigzags across Southern Nevada, startling drivers on U.S. Highway 93. He eventually makes it to Las Vegas, established by stock footage of Fremont Street and its iconic waving cowboy sign known as Vegas Vic. He first passes the Dunes, where he takes an eye-level look at the three-dimensional figure standing atop the multistoried hotel.

Next, he lumbers to a hotel window where he plays a King Kong Peeping Tom routine by peering through a window at a woman taking a bath. He moves on to a hotel decorated by a huge crown and removes the headgear. Since his bald head already gives him Yul Brynner's *The King and I* look, he puts the crown down and lumbers forward.

This takes him to the Last Frontier Village and the Silver Slipper Casino with a glittery giant shoe circling its top. But the single shoe seems too small and feminine for a heterosexual, 18,000-pound giant man to wear, so he still faces difficulties walking barefoot in the desert.

Reporting events, local newscaster H. Wells serves as tribute to one of Mr. B.I.G.'s favorite writers, whose work he later mined for the movie *Food of the Gods*. H—not H. G.—Wells eventually opens a studio window to reveal a view of the totally irate Colossal Man venting his anger on poor Vegas Vic, breaking the sign to bits.

Leaving Las Vegas, the Colossal Man's barefoot journey continues toward Lake Mead, where a helicopter carrying his fiancée and two doctors intervene by bringing a cure. Of course, complications arise, leaving the Colossal Man to his final rendezvous at Hoover Dam.

By current standards, the scariest thing about the movie comes from outdated special effects. With no access to computer-generated graphics, director Gordon took separate shots of the dam and Glenn Langan, then combined the images, superimposing an enlarged version of the actor stalking through the location.

Lighting differences show, even in black and white. With an inherently fake look, the shots shock anyone weaned on today's computer graphic effects.

Those original 1957 viewers who looked up from whatever drive-in activity preoccupied them saw images mining their memories of atomic bomb explosions at Hiroshima and Nagasaki a decade earlier. These memories and the frequently visible nuclear tests near Las Vegas tapped into Cold War paranoia and inspired a spate of science fiction films, including an amazing colossal sequel called *War of the Colossal Man* set in Mexico.

The ability to inspire a sequel makes *The Amazing Colossal Man* a success, though the movie never aimed at being a cinematic masterpiece. Other films easily eclipse it in the bad movie genre, a field luring fans who love to ridicule cheesy production values and silly ideas.

While *The Amazing Colossal Man* never competed for the title of Worst Film of All Time,, its inadvertent humor drew the attention of *Mystery Science Theater 3000,* a cult comedy series featuring a man trapped on a space station with nothing to do but watch bad movies. He and his robot companions survive by making fun of whatever screens.

Mr. B.I.G. views his *Mystery Science Theater* connection with disdain.

"I've never seen it."

He remains proud of the movies he made. And for those who laugh that *The Amazing Colossal Man* was no *Citizen Kane,* and that Bert I. Gordon never belongs in a sentence with Orson Welles, think again. Gordon eventually directed the creator of *Citizen Kane* in a movie called *Necromancy.*

Besides failing to compete in the Worst Movie of All Time sweepstakes, *The Amazing Colossal Man* also misses the mark as top terrible film about nuclear-induced monsters at the Nevada Test Site. *The Beast of Yucca Flats* takes that title hands down. Possibly inspired by *The Amazing Colossal Man, The Beast* assumes its audience knows about the Nevada Test Site, where Yucca Flats houses one of the facility's four major drainage basins.

Like *The Amazing Colossal Man, The Beast of Yucca Flats* shows its protagonist catching the full wave of a nuclear blast. Rather than burn to a crisp, scientist Joseph Javorsky mutates into The Beast.

Except his new form barely differs from the old since Tor Johnson plays Javorsky. A former Swedish wrestler, Johnson's giant frame and bald head inspired director Ed Wood to cast him in the project winning the Medved Brothers' Golden Turkey Award for Worst Film of All Time, *Plan 9 from Outer Space.*

Johnson's screen presence rarely changed, and The Beast let him do his usual hulking chase after potential victims. At six-foot-three, Johnson lacked massive height, but his 54-inch waist, 62-inch chest, and 367-pound frame made him intimidating.

It also made it hard to fit him into the business suit required for his first scenes as "a noted scientist who dedicated his life to the betterment of mankind." The bomb created by scientists burns and tears Tor's suit, ripping away his jacket and causing skin warbles on his face. Despite looking nearly the same as before the blast, he loses his mind and turns into "a fiend prowling the wastelands, a prehistoric beast in the nuclear age."

Or something like that. Tor, also known as Javorsky, goes after highway travelers, including two young boys separated from their parents. They escape and hide in a cave as a narrator explains the action.

"The Beast, finding his victims gone, unleashes his fury."

Tor picks up a rock the size of a soccer ball and throws it to the ground while crying "Eyah! Eah!"

Fury let loose, Tor finds the cave and. . . well, how could any audience be ready for what happens next.

Overwhelmed by fury, the Beast. . .

. . . lies down and takes a nap.

If this scene demonstrates questions about director Coleman Francis's sense of action and pacing, the whole movie shows an amazingly colossal lack of skill. Francis shot it as a silent film to avoid paying for sound equipment and an operator. He dubbed limited dialogue over images, avoiding angles showing moving mouths. Endless establishing shots remain static. Words qualify as bombastic, appropriate for the setting.

Director Francis saved money on sound and continued pinching pennies by avoiding location filming. As a result, the movie never shot a frame in Nevada. And, of course, neither *The Beast of Yucca Flats* nor *The Amazing Colossal Man* ever had a chance at filming the real Nevada Test Site, since the Nevada Department of Energy controls all access and forbids any project that puts it in a negative light.

Feds allowed only a specific type of filming at the location. The department used its own cameras on site to document explosions and now sells many of these films. The films provide a general idea of the area's appearance, a valuable tool for movie and television producers replicating the site in their projects. YouTube, the *The Atomic Cafe* documentary, and a brief sequence of *The Amazing Colossal Man* feature some of the footage.

Those with time can see (but not photograph) the real location firsthand by signing up with the Department of Energy website at www.nv.doe.gov/nts/tours.aspx#Registration. A bus takes visitors a little more than an hour outside Las Vegas, not quite "the middle of nowhere" anymore. Still, lack of development on more than 1,000 miles of territory makes the test site seem like another world. Visitors pass remnants of "doom towns" that bring to mind the television series *Crime Story* and the blockbuster theatrical release *Indiana Jones and the Kingdom of the Crystal Skull.*

The bomb fit into the 1986 season of *Crime Story* because of its early sixties Las Vegas setting, where a cop tenaciously chases a crime lord. Bad guy Ray Luca, played by Anthony Denison, escapes to one of those doom towns, created for researchers to study the effects of an atomic blast on a typical community. Though the series filmed on location in Las Vegas, the Nevada Test Site remained closed to producers.

Facing NBC cancellation, producer Michael Mann took a "Why not go out with a bang" attitude and let a test site explosion kill off the series as well as its criminals.

But then the network reversed course and decided to renew the series. Fans loved Luca and wanted him back. This resulted in an amazing colossal cure with a second season, episode titles including "Blast from the Past," "Atomic Fallout," and "Shockwaves."

The idea of someone surviving a Nevada Test Site doom town goes back to 1957's *The Atomic Kid* with Mickey Rooney. Wandering into an empty building, Rooney's uranium prospector munches a peanut butter sandwich when a bomb goes off. Writer-director Blake Edwards, who later became famous for *The Pink Panther* series, spreads the idea that people survive close contact with atomic bombs.

Such survival fills action at the beginning of 2008's *Indiana Jones and the Kingdom of the Crystal Skull* from Oscar-winning director Steven Spielberg. The fourth in a series inspired by Saturday afternoon serials, the film followed its predecessor by nearly twenty years. Rather than pretend star Harrison Ford looked the same as his first incarnation in the role, producers aged him by setting the story decades later in the fifties.

As a result, the movie begins with a series of icons, as teenagers race across a desert to the sounds of Elvis Presley singing "Hound Dog." Titles label the place and time: Nevada, 1957.

Encompassing the first twenty-four minutes of the movie, the segment filmed in New Mexico—not just because the state's undeveloped desert easily passes for test site terrain, but due to an incentive program providing money to production companies using its locations. The narrow two-lane highway opening the movie resembles many in Nevada. The car full of teens joins a flock of military vehicles that turn off at a crossroads, where a lone building called the Atomic Café offers breakfast, lunch, and dinner. The vehicles continue until they reach entry gates marked "Hangar 51," a "classified facility."

Denied access because of "weapons testing for the next 24 hours," soldiers shoot guards and reveal themselves as the great nemesis of the fifties, Russians. They also remove a prisoner from the truck, the iconic Indiana Jones, nicknamed Indy and rated as the second-greatest hero in movies by a 2003 American Film Institute poll.

True to action hero form, Indy escapes Hangar 51, crossing desert all night long until he spots the twinkling reflections of a small housing development. He arrives in the neighborhood, full of small houses in garish yellows, blues, and oranges. Clothes hang on a line as he looks for some sign of life, eventually wandering into one of the homes.

Hearing music from *Howdy Doody*, Jones walks into the living room and spots a family of four in front of a television set. None of them see the show—they can't because they're plastic.

"This can't be good," says Indy.

He stumbles out and sees a plastic newsboy as sirens and speakers blare.

"One minute to zero time."

Running back to the kitchen, Indy quickly surveys the room and empties a refrigerator, which includes a product description.

"Lead lined" reads the convenient label.

Sprung from its location as the bomb explodes, the refrigerator bounces through the desert until the door springs open and Indy rolls out, eye to eye with a prairie dog. A mushroom cloud recedes as Indy walks away, shadowed against a dusty, smoky horizon, the kind of striking special effects possible when a movie has an amazing, colossal budget.

A quick cut puts Indy naked in a shower as men in hazardous materials suits scrub him down to the sounds of a clicking Geiger counter.

"Don't you know it's dangerous to climb into a refrigerator?" jokes a general during Indy's debriefing. "Those things can be death traps."

Almost as credible as the "one cell" heart theory in *The Amazing Colossal Man*, Indy survives the nuclear blast without a scratch, ready to pursue the rest of the story's action-packed adventures.

Millions of dollars and more than fifty years separate *Indiana Jones* and *The Amazing Colossal Man*. Yet despite all that time and money, writers fail to advance the science or believability of atomic action on screen.

Giants and the Worms

Nevada growth spurts generate from causes other than atomic testing. Go back in time to the first *One Million B.C.* movie from 1940, and large dinosaurs mix with relatively small cavemen who roam the Valley of Fire. The area's emptiness and striking, jutting rocks look appropriately prehistoric, accompanied by equally primitive special effects.

State-of-the-art effects help giants terrorize the Strip in 2014's *Godzilla*. Escaping a holding facility in Utah, a MUTO (Massive Unidentified Terrestrial Organism) descends on Las Vegas. Television station KYPN covers the breaking news on screen with a "Live—Terror in Vegas" scroll totally ignored by gamblers in the Flamingo until the pinheaded MUTO smashes into the building and squashes players. The camera pulls to computer-generated shots of a demolished Strip where towering hotels-casinos like Treasure Island look like something took a bite out of the roof, all to the sounds of Elvis singing "Devil in Disguise."

Predating the MUTO attack, scientist Rick Moranis reverses his *Honey, I Shrunk the Kids* gimmick from 1989 and turns his toddler into a giant for *Honey, I Blew Up the Kid*. Like the guy in the famous *Amazing Colossal Man* poster, this 112-foot giant wears diapers—but the two-year-old really needs them. Following the pattern set by his amazing, colossal predecessor, the baby makes a mess of Las Vegas icons, in one instance grabbing the Hard Rock Hotel's huge neon sign and playing air guitar.

While science run amok explains colossal men and big babies, the original *Tremors* never clarifies why an imaginary town called Perfection, Nevada houses giant worms that cause earth-shattering tremors before bursting out from the ground to eat human residents. The *Tremors* production team scouted Bureau of Land Management property for the 1991 feature film's Southern Nevada setting. Problems arose when environmentalists realized that visually creating the worms' underground lair meant blasting trenches and disrupting homes of the federally protected desert tortoise. Chased away by small reptiles, the worms found dirt near Lone Pine, California, free from federal restrictions.

Nevada remained the story's setting because of the state's reputation for undeveloped land in the middle of nowhere. The story needs a place where help takes a long time coming, without access to phone lines, cell towers, and other standard city services. The first *Tremors* set the stage, with no outside resources to protect a town with a welcoming sign boasting "Population: 14." First-timer Ron Underwood bypasses the story's questionable plausibility through slick direction. He maximizes tension, aided by a tongue-in-cheek script plus a fun bunch of actors. Kevin Bacon increases his six degrees of movie connections, heading a cast that includes Fred Ward, Michael Gross (who continues in the sequels), and country singer Reba McEntire.

The middle-of-nowhere setting moved to Mexico for 1995's *Tremors 2: Aftershocks* but returned to Nevada in name only for *Tremors 3: Back to Perfection* in 2001. The franchise then backtracked with a prequel called *Tremors: The Legend Begins*, which starts in 1889 when silver miners discover Graboid worms in Rejection, Nevada. Stories continued when *Tremors* became a series on the Sci-Fi Channel for thirteen episodes. The four movies comprise a "Tremors Attack Pack" set of DVDs, and Universal Home Entertainment presented the television series on DVD in 2010.

For giant worm stories, the first *Tremors* rates among the best. That means *something*; the movie works better than David Lynch's screen interpretation of Frank Herbert's classic, *Dune*, which gets a 55 percent positive rating on Rotten Tomatoes compared to 84 percent for *Tremors*. Flip touches make *Tremors* a hoot, like McEntire as a redneck. Casually, she notes she *might* have something to help fight worms and reveals a weapons collection capable of arming an entire war.

Bacon teams well with Ward as grumbling handymen who want to get out of town even before they discover infestation by creatures they dub "Graboids."

While enough giant worms populate the film world to nearly create a genre, Nevada stands alone when it comes to oversized mutant sheep. *The Godmonster of Indian Flats* looks *baaahhd*, as expected for an eight-foot sheep walking upright on two legs. Such a sight "must have given brain seizures to those who saw it on the big screen," enthuses the back cover for the release from Something Weird Video. Yet the movie rewards Nevada fans looking for readily recognizable or iconic locations and landmarks—some long gone. Reno's Primadonna Casino, with its own giant showgirl statues, vanished in 1978 but relives its glory in *The Godmonster*, along with casino interiors and outside street shots featuring "The Biggest Little City in the World" variation of the Reno Arch, which now resides in Willits, California.

The *Godmonster* story takes place around Virginia City, clearly shown in several establishing shots. A Virginia and Truckee Railway engine and its cars chug by, while interiors at the Crystal Bar, Chollar Mine, and St. Paul's Episcopal Church add atmosphere to other scenes. The dilapidated mining mill ruins found at American Flats today look far healthier in their title role as Indian Flats.

These locations match writer-director Fredric Hobbs' look at Nevada's mining history and environmental perils. Well, sort of. Hobbs provides some accurate facts about the Comstock Lode's mines. But history lacks cases where a newborn lamb breathes noxious mine gases and mutates into a carnivorous threat to nearby residents. The movie issues a warning to sheep ranchers: keep stock away from mine sites or ewe too may find a godmonster!

Watching movies like *The Godmonster of Indian Flats* and the *Tremors* series takes dedication. Get the right mindset, and Nevada's giant movies provide enormous entertainment. Still, watching these giants of cinema requires help: lots of friends, a working barbeque to grill a leg of lamb, and perhaps a case of beer . . . or something a whole lot more mind-bending.

Serious Issues at the Nevada Test Site

Ignoring fantasy, action, and amazingly colossal survival skills, some films take a serious look at atomic bomb impacts. *Desert Bloom* touches on symbolism with its portrait of a nuclear family in fifties Las Vegas. Just as narrator Rose blooms into her teenage years, atomic energy enters adolescence in Nevada. Rose's optimistic mother repeats clichés like the one about clouds and silver linings. However, the cloud about to bloom over the Nevada desert needs lead lining.

The low-key movie used minimal Las Vegas locations during its eighties shoot.

"It's nothing but a small desert town," says Rose about fifties Las Vegas, bemoaning that it boasts "nothing but a few casinos and the air force base." Far too big to fit that description during the movie's eighties production, Las Vegas gave way to Arizona for the film's town shots.

Though curiosity about military plans runs throughout the story, the movie gains most of its impact from family dynamics, with good performances from Jon Voight, Ellen Barkin, and Annabeth Gish in her first starring role. The acting team works well, playing a nuclear family finding harmony as the first of Nevada's nuclear bombs detonates in the background.

"It's beautiful," notes one without any irony.

Explosiveness works as a metaphor for *Blue Sky*'s focus on the relationship between Tommy Lee Jones' military man and his fiery wife, played by Jessica Lange. In a vibrant performance that won her the 1994 Oscar for Best Actress, Lange displays personal nuclear meltdowns that almost destroy her husband's career as he heads to Nevada's Test Site—played by Texas.

His job involves overseeing studies of atomic testing residue of the Blue Sky program, described in the film.

"You can't see radiation or feel it or smell it," says one character about the exciting bombs that millions watched explode.

"For all they know, the sky is just as blue as ever."

Nuclear risks stay in the forefront with *Nightbreaker*, based on Howard L. Rosenberg's book *Atomic Soldiers*. Given content criticizing the government's role in testing, no one expected Atomic Energy Commission approval for filming at the test site. Any other hope for support exploded when actor Martin Sheen signed on. Sheen's public and sincere opposition to testing got him arrested outside the gates of Mercury, Nevada in 1987.

Sheen plays a medical researcher whose return to Las Vegas sends him down memory lane to the fifties and his experiences interviewing soldiers about their exposure to radiation. Played by Emilio Estevez, the young researcher bears a reasonable resemblance to Sheen (his real-life father). The project shifts back and forth in time, as the researcher faces ethical challenges about publicly revealing his discovery that the government's nuclear research hurts its own people. Though denied Mercury access, the film shot at Jean Dry Lake and used other Nevada sites.

Nightbreaker joins *Blue Sky* in raising questions and contributing to controversy surrounding atomic bombs. Serious projects set at the iconic test site mine fears, promising dangers far more threatening than colossal men and beasts on Yucca Flats.

11

Stephen King and the Monsters

Horror's ruling author, Stephen King, sees Nevada as part of his realm. It started in 1978 when he set part of his fourth novel, *The Stand*, in Las Vegas. Nearly twenty years later, the book turned into a television miniseries shot on location.

"It's amazing what a long life that show has," director Mick Garris said while scouting for another King project.

Long life—and long running time. Television's miniseries format of four installments took nearly eight hours to unfold *The Stand*, an appropriate length for a novel running more than 1,100 pages. Commercials interrupted the viewing process, but DVD and Blu-ray discs erase that problem.

Still, the network television format suffers, which puts the story in line for a feature remake, associated with such directors as Josh Boone, Ben Affleck, and David Yates. Time, attitudes, and venue offer beneficial changes for a remake. The original aired when network broadcasts toned down sex and violence, long before families considered *The Walking Dead* a bonding experience to watch together. While true horror fans revel in gore, outdated network restraint makes the old *Stand* watchable for a squeamish audience.

Focusing on horror's human edge, shocks come from a slime factor as the world's population faces quick, messy deaths from a virus inadvertently released by a military facility. Survivors break off by inherent nature, heading in different directions.

Perhaps because of King's pleasant memories staying in the Rockies, decent, family-oriented survivors heed mysterious thoughts calling them to Colorado. Gorgeous, with towering mountains and sturdy trees, the state provides peaceful colors for Molly Ringwald, Gary Sinese, Rob Lowe, and Stephen King.

So what lures bad guys? A war-ravaged region? A politically corrupt capital city? Nope. Cut to: the neon of Fremont Street in Las Vegas, where signs blare for "Topless Girls of Glitter Gulch."

"There was no real intention on my part to suggest that Las Vegas is the center of evil in the U.S.," says King in commentary for the DVD release. "Everybody knows that's really Secaucus, New Jersey."

Joking aside, he adds, "It seemed to me that Vegas with its brightness, with all the neon, would be the perfect place for the evil forces to congregate. I love that."

The evil forces he talks about go all the way to the top in the demon world's chain of bureaucracy.

"Pleased to meet you, hope you know my name," says Randall Flagg, introducing himself. "It's a classical reference," he adds.

For those missing Flagg's red eyes and horns, he quotes the Rolling Stones' song "Sympathy for the Devil." Taking human form, the friendly Flagg smiles a killer grin, dressed for Western adventures in Levi jeans and jacket. Special morphing effects provide occasional demonic faces, but for the most part Flagg looks like actor Jamey Sheridan.

As another cowboy waves a neon-outlined hand and calls out "Howdy, Podner" on a casino building, director Garris takes advantage of Fremont Street's classic Vegas ambiance. Much more contained than the Strip's isolated bastions of themed architecture, Fremont Street's lights burn garishly with leering excess. A looming Union Plaza Hotel serves as Evil Headquarters.

"As glamorous as this looks, it is the seedier part of Las Vegas," recalls Garris on the DVD.

Garris spent two weeks filming in the Las Vegas area and appreciated the enthusiasm shown by 600 extras playing bad guys.

"I loved it," Las Vegas resident Jeremy Settles said while scouting locations for his own Nevada-King project, *Lucky Quarter.*

"It was my first experience on a movie. I got to walk around carrying dead bodies and acting like a zombie."

It seems everybody loves zombies and no one—even image-conscious civic leaders—questioned content in *The Stand.* Where else should the heart of evil go?

Well, perhaps a place called Desperation. King gives that name to his fictional town in a novel playing on fears generated by isolation. Horror intensifies when an officer stops the few travelers he finds along the Loneliest Highway in America, harassing them before locking them in jail on false charges. Terror increases with participation from an ancient evil spirit, but the biggest horror for Nevadans comes from the use of Arizona locations when the book turned into a television movie.

The long path to that location choice began in 1991 when King took a road trip and stayed in Ely.

"He's writing a book about it," reported excited residents during multiple rounds of wishful thinking.

Rumors proved true.

"I got out on Highway 50 and there's nothing, then you go by the open-pit mines and it's like somebody buried this ancient god there," King recalls in a DVD feature called "The Making of Desperation."

"The whole book just sort of came to me there."

Still, five years passed before publication. Film Commission–style wishful thinking hoped Nevada specifics like the Loneliest Highway guaranteed filming in the state. Some locals feared that a story about an evil spirit slaughtering travelers passing through town might deter tourists, but location filming brings big bucks to small communities regardless of content.

Eventually, producers asked the Nevada Film Office to send location photos for *Desperation*'s feature film version. Pictures of pits in Battle Mountain, Virginia City, and Elko County joined shots of Ruth, the mine King saw during his Ely stay. The project, however, went into turnaround, another way of saying, "It's dead."

But horror specializes in waking the dead. When growls of revival snarled, director Mick Garris once again received those old location photos from the Reno-Tahoe branch of the Nevada Film Office.

He responded quickly and enthusiastically, wanting more. But then he was sent a photo of the Lavender Pit outside Bisbee, Arizona.

"Do you have anything that looks like this?"

The dramatic view of a huge open-pit mine with an easily accessible road right by its edge looked more enticing than Nevada mines. The in-your-face establishing shot provides an instant, visceral understanding of the setting. Ruth, Nevada inspired *Desperation*, but Bisbee looked more dramatic, giving it the edge.

"No hard feelings," seemed a generous response from Nevadans as the program aired on network television in one three-hour presentation.

Desperation opens with a Nevada icon—a Loneliest Highway in America sign—decorated by a dead cat tied to it. Locals might grumble how roadside vegetation looks wrong and characters pronounce the state's name incorrectly. Even so, many viewers enjoyed the movie's spooky beginnings, as Garris heightens the Arizona/Nevada sense of isolation and creepiness by using low, wide-angle shots.

What comes around goes around, and *Desperation*'s Arizona setting represented payback for *Misery*, where Nevada played Colorado.

Usually located in the horror section of rental outlets, *Misery* feels more like a character study featuring a psychotic, human criminal. The role of number one fan Annie Wilkes provides depth for good actors to turn into awards.

"She'll win the Oscar for this," director Rob Reiner insisted during his Nevada scout, months before he started cameras rolling on the face of Kathy Bates.

Lacking typical movie star glamor, Bates had never starred in a film before, but Reiner loved her work on Broadway in *Frankie and Johnny*.

He boasted experience in recognizing talent. Son of beloved comedian Carl Reiner and a familiar face in his own right from the classic *All in the Family* television series, the tall, friendly-featured Rob knew a lot about how Hollywood and movies work.

Directing *The Princess Bride* took him to Ireland's famous Cliffs of Moher, teaching him about complicated outdoor locations, and he wanted to remove the misery from this new project's wilderness mountain and snow settings. Harsh, unfriendly faces of gray, granite cliffs make the Sierra Nevada near Reno look implacable and threatening, yet convenient city services lay within easy reach for cast and crew.

Reiner applied his moviemaker's magic to making conditions look insurmountable. For instance, in real life anyone could take a simple drive up the South Tahoe side of Highway 50 and arrive at the Round Hill Forest Service facility where protagonist Paul Shelton checks in. But *Misery* shows it as a massive undertaking involving snowy curves on narrow Old Donner Pass fifty miles away. There, a bestselling author crashes his car. His number one fan, Annie Wilkes, spots the wreck and rescues him.

In another instance of movie magic, Annie takes the writer Shelton a short way to her home—a set built some eighty-five miles south on tribal land near Carson City. Looming mountains surround the Clear Creek Road location, serving as prison walls for the author, whose number one fan forces him to rewrite his next book.

Easily rating in the top-ranked film interpretations of a King novel, the movie features brilliant work by Kathy Bates in a role originally slated for Bette Midler. Bates ignores glamour touches, wearing dowdy clothes and downplaying makeup. Her emotional intensity and variety make the performance work as she morphs from a sweet, cheery caretaker into an erratic, demanding force. Her innate likability quickly turns into frightening fury.

King's novel and William Goldman's original screenplay let Annie use an axe and lawnmower to bloody extreme. Reiner reduces the violence, replacing Annie's original weapons with sledgehammer and shotgun. Playing down gore, Reiner trades on Alfred Hitchcock moments, with *Psycho* high-angle shots from above that include a cellar scene. Like Hitchcock with *Rear Window*, Reiner works around a character whose injuries restrict his movements to a single room. Overall, Reiner creates a study in nightmare and personality that highlights how effectively King develops characters. *Misery* shows that whether in Nevada, Colorado, or anywhere else, human beings challenge the frightening qualities of vampires, werewolves, and other monsters.

King's use of Nevada continues as Dolan's Cadillac rides the highway between Las Vegas and Los Angeles. The project started preproduction in 2001 with Kevin Bacon and Sylvester Stallone attached. After running out of gas and losing those stars, *Dolan's Cadillac* rose from Production Hell a few years later for a ninety-minute feature that went directly to DVD release. Based on a short story inspired by an Edgar Allan Poe fear of premature burial, *Dolan's Cadillac* feels padded despite its brief running time. It finally catches on toward the end when the half-crazed hero realizes his acts turn him into the thing he despises.

Though lacking box office draw, Will Bentley and Christian Slater give good performances. Quick establishing shots of the Las Vegas Strip at night add minimal flash. Otherwise, low production values undermine literary quality and Saskatchewan locations make a poor Nevada substitute. Long credited as a great place to hide bodies, Nevada's desert suits the story, while Las Vegas and its sin city image make it a believable home for a crime lord who traffics in human lives.

Others beside Stephen King noticed Nevada's scary qualities. Las Vegas provides colorful surroundings for Warwick Davis doing a *Leprechaun 3* jig as a nasty Irish monster terrorizing the fictional Lucky Shamrock Hotel. He fits right in and no one notices him walking down gaudy Fremont Street in full leprechaun regalia—stovepipe hat, green suit, striped tights, and pilgrim shoes. Well, one person takes heed: an Elvis impersonator who likes the shoes.

A key element to the story, Las Vegas features on the movie's poster in a picture using the tagline, "Welcome to Vegas. The odds are you won't get out alive."

Throwaway lines and sick humor make the project funnier and better than its predecessors, "better" being a loose term in a cheesy series whose success might very well come from a deal with the devil or the luck of the Irish.

Besides the oddball leprechaun, Las Vegas and vicinity offer an ideal nightlife for day-fearing vampires. One, *Vampirella*, arrives from outer space to get revenge on a fellow alien, posing as a rock star played by The Who's Roger Daltrey. This project's biggest horror involved numerous unpaid bills to local crew workers.

The scariest and best Las Vegas vampire showed up in 1972 as *The Night Stalker*. The ABC television movie shows its age with blaring music, glary lighting, and shots of a barren Strip lacking hotels and inventive architecture. Still, *The Night Stalker* remains innovative in many ways. Promoted as a straightforward serial killer procedural in television previews, the story surprised first-time viewers with its take on how the traditional monster might function in modern society. The teleplay, by horror expert Richard Matheson, draws from Jeffrey Grant Rice's novel *The Kolchak Papers* and avoids later trends toward namby-pamby vegetarian vampires.

The project introduces Darren McGavin as investigative reporter Carl Kolchak, covering a series of deaths. Everyone thinks the killer falls into a recognizable Jack the Ripper pattern as a man who hates the many prostitutes frequenting Las Vegas.

A straight-out monster story, *The Night Stalker* features a genuinely frightening vampire more prone to growling than talking. With no mitigating background excuses for violent behavior, this vampire enjoys kidnap, torture, and killing (well, he calls it dining). Of course, no police or newspaper execs believe Kolchak when he fingers a vampire, and the show ends with the reporter banned from Las Vegas. This prohibition continued in a follow-up movie called *The Night Strangler* set in Seattle.

Afterwards, *The Night Stalker* became Kolchak himself, as he evolved into an obsessive Chicago reporter chasing a variety of monsters for twenty episodes that *X-Files* creator Chris Carter cited as inspiration for his own spooky programming. One episode, "The Vampire," takes up right after the first television movie, starting south of Las Vegas when highway construction work unearths one of the original vampire victims. The 2005 series reboot also scuttled Las Vegas.

A failed move to remake the original television movie in the mid-nineties planned a Las Vegas setting, validating claims that the location contributes to the first *Night Stalker*'s top ranking. The Las Vegas location adds color, excitement, and life for the undead. Plus, a vampire makes sense in a state that hosts psycho book fans, devils, and evil leprechauns. In Nevada, demons, aliens, vampires, and their friends roam comfortably with cowboys, dancers, and Elvis impersonators. And no one notices.

Enjoying *Misery*

Despite its creepy story, *Misery* set visits proved anything but scary. Rather than use a "method" approach by staying in character the whole time, Kathy Bates easily turned her psycho character on and off. Ranting and stomping one moment, she switched gears the minute someone called "Cut!," losing the glower, shotgun, sledgehammer, and other tools of her trade as a whacked-out killer. Easily breaking into belly laughs, she enjoyed fellow actor Richard Farnsworth's stories ranging back to his days as a stuntman and extra. The actor deepened his fan base by chatting with locals and joining extras as they waited for their brief moments of screen glory.

Meanwhile, cast and crew members joked about seeing star James Caan find love at first sight. The heartthrob actor fell hard for the big brown eyes and soft loving features of an Akita-husky mix puppy he spotted in the arms of a woman at the Peppermill Hotel-Casino. Promptly applying movie star charm (and cash), Caan acquired Reno the Wonder Dog and brought him on set where I waited with several visitors hanging out in his trailer.

One by one, people left. Just as I set out for my own vanishing act, the remaining production assistant asked me to stay behind and watch the dog. Well, sure. Film commissioners do whatever it takes to help on set, including dog sitting. Reno approved as he mouthed the leather shoe on my foot.

A few minutes later, another assistant and Caan bolted in for a quick costume change. Pulling off his shirt and revealing a nicely muscled chest, Caan reached for his pants without noticing me.

"Uh, I can leave?" I asked—hesitantly, since I felt perfectly inclined to stay and admire Caan's strip show.

"Oh, no problem, I'm leaving now," he replied and bolted out the door.

Damn!

Clint Eastwood pays attention to detail on the Fuji Park set of *Pink Cadillac* in Carson City, Nevada.

Randa Haines directs *The Doctor* at Pyramid Lake.

At his Las Vegas home in his late eighties, director George Sidney loved recalling his projects like *Viva Las Vegas*.

The Making of the Misfits documentary returns key crew members to the original filming location in Lyon County, Nevada.

As a key setting in *Independence Day*, Rachel, Nevada earns a special plaque from the moviemakers.

An Area 51 hangout.

Actor Jason Gedrick fights mob rule in *The Last Don* at Reno's Peppermill Casino.

Gary Dourdan gets a special gift from prisoners during the filming of *Black August* at the Nevada State Prison in Carson City.

Actress Sally Field enjoys cleaning up the results of her gambling win for *Surrender* at Harvey's Lake Tahoe.

Million Dollar Baby producer Al Ruddy advises a different boxer in *Matilda*.

Rob Reiner and Richard Farnsworth discuss a scene for *Misery* in Genoa, Nevada.

Tommy Lee Jones joins his screen son Nik Kosach on set in Carson City for *Cobb*.

Mark Twain impersonator MacAvoy Layne receives direction for an episode of *History's Detectives* in Virginia City, Nevada.

Jenny McCarthy enjoys her role as a working girl, with Kirk Douglas, in *Diamonds* at a private home in Reno.

Helen Mirren waits for her *Love Ranch* scene outside the now-defunct Fitzgerald's Club in Reno.

Whoopi's *Sister Act* singers the Ronelles needed their Nevada Club billboard changed.

John Ireland leads a new group of family members by Spooner Lake, near Tahoe, for *Bonanza: The Next Generation*.

Director Christopher Coppola plays a cameo in *The Gunfighter* near Lovelock, Nevada.

A display at Fallon's Naval Air Station includes the kind of F14 Tomcat flown in *Top Gun*.

A Darwin Award cameo came with Mythbusters Jaimie Hyneman and Adam Savage in Reno.

Far from Home moviemakers emphasize their title with a set on Nevada's isolated Black Rock Desert, home to the annual Burning Man art celebration.

Former Lt. Gov. Loraine Hunt shows support for the state's film industry by visiting sets and meeting stars like Patrick Swayze during the production of *Waking Up in Reno*.

Director Paul Thomas Anderson celebrates the Reno premiere of *Hard Eight* at the Peppermill.

Maggie Smith's *Sister Act* experience includes a visit with author Leo Buscaglia.

Rural filming of *Sin*, with Ving Rhames and Gary Oldman, at Misfits Flat.

12

Melvin and the Really Famous People

Most people want to tell their Nevada story this way: "I was just sort of hanging out, doing my thing, and all the sudden I became a millionaire."

For a minute, Nevadan Melvin Dummar told that story. The Oscar-winning movie *Melvin and Howard* gives Dummar's version of how an act of kindness almost made him rich. Though his story earned worldwide media coverage and serious treatment by the courts, most people just shook their heads when they heard it.

But when two young filmmakers learned that same story, they envisioned a movie, using what the director called "imaginative interpretation." The director and screenwriter already showed Oscar-winning promise, and they later put statues on their shelves—Jonathan Demme for *The Silence of the Lambs* and Bo Goldman for writing his then-current project, *Melvin and Howard*.

Despite preposterous content, "We just did it like it was a true story," says the man who played Melvin, Paul Le Mat.

In Melvin's version, billionaire Howard Hughes left him a fortune. It makes no sense. Why would the famously reclusive inventor, aviator, and empire builder will millions to a former milkman from Gabbs, Nevada? Of course, that's the ingeniousness of Melvin's claim—it was so outrageous that it might actually be true.

The movie replays Melvin's version of meeting Howard in a way believable to anyone traveling Nevada back roads. Driving alone one night in 1967, Melvin steered his truck along U.S. Highway 95 near the Lida Junction, about 150 miles north of Las Vegas. His headlights dimly illuminated massive expanses of undeveloped land. In a flash, he saw someone lying at the side of the road, apparently the victim of a motorcycle accident.

Despite the possibility of tricks played by a psycho killer or modern highway bandit, Melvin put fear aside and followed Good Samaritan "do unto others" karma. He loaded the man and bike into his truck. Breaking through his grumpy passenger's crustiness, Melvin's genuine warmth charmed the man and the two lived in a very fine moment as they headed into Las Vegas singing "Bye, Bye Blackbird."

Without getting his passenger's name, Melvin drops the dude at the Sands Hotel Casino, owned by a worldwide icon for wealth and ingenuity, Howard Hughes. Hughes retired to Las Vegas and used an entire hotel as a fortress to protect him from the legions who wanted to pollute him with their greed, demands, and germs. And Hughes, according to Melvin, liked to escape the city and an entourage to feel the wind in his face as his motorcycle zoomed across a Nevada dry lakebed. Jason Robards earned an Oscar nomination playing the reclusive Hughes as a longhaired, scraggly old geezer who took a ride from Melvin.

Slipping into high gear, the movie shows Melvin leaving the injured man in Las Vegas, heading back to his own messed up life and crumbling marriage. Melvin hates that his wife Lynda works at a Reno strip club, leading to the movie's highlight comic moment and a scene earning Mary Steenburgen a Best Supporting Actress Oscar. Furious with Melvin, Lynda rips off her skimpy outfit and stomps out buck-naked.

Years pass and Melvin struggles. Things look promising when Lynda competes on a Southern California game show, but like Nevada casinos, the gamble offers only fleeting hope. Melvin eventually moves to Utah with a new, Mormon wife. Life improves in 1976 when word comes from the Mormon Church: someone delivered a will at headquarters granting Melvin Dummar $156 million of Howard Hughes' fortune.

"The script was basically taking Melvin Dummar's version of events and making a movie out of it," said Le Mat. "There wasn't a question as far as our storytelling was concerned as to whether it was really Howard Hughes that he picked up and whether Howard Hughes really wrote his name in his will. That was our take, so we just did it like it was a true story."

"It may well have been true," he said at a Reno Film Festival screening of one of his other key movies, *American Graffiti.*

"As the years have gone by, I've learned more and more about the incident itself and the surrounding circumstances, and I'm more than half convinced that it's true," he continued, age and experience dappling his still-boyish face.

Fiction or not, *Melvin and Howard* tells truths about people and attitudes. Its effectiveness comes from defying standard movie hero qualities. People step on Melvin frequently, but he remains sweet, polite, and always hopeful, looking like a casual Everyman in Levis. If anyone deserves a lucky break, it's Melvin.

Playing Melvin as a simple, non-manipulative type, Le Mat initially avoided meeting the real deal, who shows up in the movie as counterman at Reno's Greyhound depot.

"At first I stayed away from him because I felt that if I thought he was lying," explained Le Mat, "and if I thought he was a shyster and a con artist, then it would hurt my performance, it would interfere with my acting because I was going in the direction that he was totally sincere. But then I did meet him. I liked him a lot, and he was more sincere than I played him. And he was more guileless than I played him."

Le Mat's approach gives *Melvin and Howard* a fairytale's appeal, and in many ways it represents the quintessential Nevada film. The movie covers all ends of Nevada, from a glimpse of Las Vegas to downtown Reno. Sets include strip clubs, the bus station, and funky wedding chapels. Demme reveals striking highway imagery and no other famous director before or after worked in Gabbs, a community so small it lost its official ranking as a city. *Melvin and Howard* moves all over the Nevada map and provides an effective screen portrait of the state's visual diversity.

More significantly, *Melvin and Howard* explores the hopes that built Nevada and affect the rest of the nation. Edgy and self-consciously off the wall, it beautifully captures one essence of the American dream.

"Melvin almost got rich quick, so it represents that ideal or goal that a lot of people have," noted Le Mat.

The Nevada dream of quick wealth goes backto the 1800s when Sam Clemens left his home to head west and join the territory's treasurer, his brother Orion. Leaving Orion in Carson City, Sam took the dramatic stage ride twenty miles up steep trails to Virginia City. Like many, Sam hoped to strike it rich, trying his hand at mining the city's famous silver ore. Hunting ore proved slower and harder than he wanted, so Sam mined his mind, writing a column for the local Virginia City *Territorial Enterprise* newspaper. Hoping not to embarrass Orion, Sam devised a pen name, Mark Twain. Nevadans stake claim on the name, and many prefer the version repeated in a television movie called *Mark Twain's Roughing It*. Ordering two drinks at a Virginia City bar, Sam asks the proprietor to "mark twain." Some storytellers feel the version about "marking twain" from his Mississippi River boating period protected Mrs. Clemens from recalling her husband's early days as a Nevada hellion and drinker.

Twain went on to write one of the great American novels, *The Adventures of Huckleberry Finn*, filmed first in 1920 and several times afterwards. In contrast, *Mark Twain's Roughing It* filmed for the first time in 2002, reaching screens as a four-hour, two-part show broadcast on the Hallmark Channel.

"I think maybe it took a long time to arrive on screen because the plot is kind of long and rambling and no one had ever figured out how to convert it into a filmable story," notes director Charles Martin Smith, with features familiar from his stint playing nerdy Terry the Toad in *American Graffiti* alongside Paul Le Mat.

"Our writer, Steven Berman, did a very good job of it. It's all done in flashback as an elderly Mark Twain, played by James Garner, tells the story of his childhood to a graduating college class, so you get the feeling, since it's all told in flashback, that a lot of it is true, but it also is Mark Twain stretching the truth and telling a tall tale. It gives it a nice, whimsical feel to the whole show."

Mark Twain's Roughing It covers a wide range of terrain as Sam travels across country by stage in his early days. Producers shot in Alberta, Canada, resulting in Kelly green backdrops for the high desert reds and pastels for Virginia City and Carson City. Director Smith, who visited Virginia City as a kid, grasped the visual disparity between the reel and real places compared to his Canadian locations.

"Obviously, Twain's connection to Virginia City is legendary," he said, adding that this made the town's appearance "really important to us" and caused him to reject a convenient set.

"It was a Western town that had been built and used for a number of Westerns, and on a nice, flat meadow of green grass," recalled Smith.

Childhood memories told him the set felt wrong.

"I've been to Virginia City, it doesn't look like that," he told his production team, urging them to find a better-suited spot.

"We actually ended up building kind of a tent city on a sloping hillside, trying as much as we could to duplicate the region."

The project gives viewers a sense of Twain's audacity in Nevada, and it shows him formally starting his writing career at the Virginia City *Territorial Enterprise*. The piece also soothes a sore spot for Nevadans because characters pronounce the state's name with a flat *a* in the middle, an *a* that rhymes with *add*. Smith takes credit for that accuracy.

"My mother was from Missoura, and I grew up knowing how to pronounce all the states."

Virginia City, which brags about being the biggest official National Landmark in America, frequently capitalizes on its Twain ties. The makers of an IMAX feature called *Mark Twain's America* followed the connection in their 1998 documentary for the giant screen. The project's huge 3-D camera photographed the Virginia & Truckee Railroad, with moving wheels symbolizing Twain's travels. The period engine fit the era for many of the author's trips, though ironically he never rode the V & T line since it came after his Nevada stay.

Still, Virginia City famously preserves its past and easily replicates the community where Sam Clemens learned so much. Virginia City and the Mark Twain Museum lured an episode of *History's Detectives* in 2003, as investigators sought to determine if a family souvenir really came from Twain. Local Mark Twain impersonator McAvoy Layne appears in scenes, walking along preserved boardwalks with wooden buildings in the background. Wearing a white suit and spraying his hair and mustache gray, Layne takes on the persona of the author in his later years, after he had left Nevada. One of about a dozen working Twain impersonators (quite shy of the Elvis stats), Layne boasts a distinction.

"I'm known as the Nevada Mark Twain, and I'm very proud of that," says Layne.

While many people like Sam Clemens came to Nevada hoping to get rich, baseball icon Ty Cobb spent some of his millions at Cave Rock, a Tahoe enclave for the wealthy. Cobb's many records include the highest batting average in Major League Baseball at .367. He impressively stole home thirty-five times, demonstrating key personality traits—he never stopped testing limits and going over the edge.

Off the field, Cobb knew how to play the money game. A Georgia native, he invested early in his native state's homegrown product, Coca-Cola. Tight and shrewd about financial matters, he easily afforded a ten-room lakeside lodge that seemed perfect for the big-game trophies and bearskin rugs he took home from hunting. Nevada property also made it easier to claim residency and get a quick divorce in the forties. Cobb spent more time at Tahoe as he got older. Known as "the meanest man in baseball," Cobb battled alcoholism, diabetes, and prostate cancer. Nearing death, Cobb hired the era's best sportswriter to produce a sanitized biography. Al Stump wrote that nice version, but many years later detailed his real experiences working for the pain-addled, drug-abusing baseball legend. Director Ron Shelton turned the 1994 book into the movie *Cobb*, with Tommy Lee Jones in the title role and Robert Wuhl as the abused author. Shelton shows Cobb as a dark man who took too much medication and treated everyone badly.

"This may be a controversial portrayal," Shelton said on set at Crystal Bay's Cal Neva Lodge. "I don't think it's an unsympathetic one in the sense that we don't romanticize Cobb; neither do we show him to be a sort of one-note monster."

Saying Cobb "could charm you to death and seduce you," Shelton noted how the baseball legend befriended presidents, invested in Wall Street, presided over banks, and sat on boards of major corporations.

"Cobb had all of that in one raging athletic kind of demon."

A minor league baseball player before turning to movies, Shelton understood Cobb's need to turn every aspect of life and death into major competition.

"I'm also interested in Cobb because he just refused to die. And that's sort of what the movie's about," said Shelton. "To his last breath he was placing buy-and-sell orders on Wall Street, though he knew he would never see the benefit of them. It was part of that, that love and passion of competition and for pushing yourself as far as you could go that draws me to him."

Cobb achieved success by staying tougher than anyone else, an alpha dog who instinctively sized up anyone he met. He chomped Stump's jugular, terrorizing him by insisting they drive from Tahoe to Reno at 3 a.m. in a miserable blizzard.

"Anything that smacked of the apparently impossible brought an unholy gleam to his eye," recalls Stump in his book, *Cobb: The Life and Times of the Meanest Man Who Ever Played Baseball.*

Driving old U.S. Highway 50 fit this "impossible" description, with 200-foot drops and a record eighty people dying there. The hair-raising trip in blinding snow from Tahoe to Reno defined the relationship between Cobb and Stump, and director Shelton wanted to film the drive realistically, preferably in the real location.

But dangers shut down the old U.S. 50 decades before Shelton started preproduction. Visually, California's Old Donner Pass, about thirty miles west of Reno, provided a much scarier look than the new U.S. 50. Sharp, steep turns on a narrow, two-lane stretch of asphalt bring back memories of the old U.S. 50.

Despite its appropriate appearance, Old Donner Pass threw a curveball at the director. Snow usually dumps all over the road and closes it in winter, but Shelton arrived during a seven-year drought.

"If you can forgive me a sports metaphor, that's a tough pitch to hit," said the director. "But your job is to hit it, and so every day and every night we figured out how to make snow, how to find a shady ravine so we can put fake snow on the ground, and we're just going along trying to hit whatever pitches they throw out. We never in our life believed we'd come up here and get no snow. I was here the year before and it seemed like there was forty feet of snow on the ground."

Solutions included making snow, plus hauling the real stuff from other locations and supplementing it with mashed potato flakes, an approach that likely pleased squirrels emerging from hibernation when spring arrived.

Just as Highway 50 changed in the thirty years between the real event and its filming, downtown Reno looked different. A new arch stood over widened streets where casinos experienced face-lifts and growth spurts. Director Shelton wanted the old Reno icon in his film to establish the location and era. His need resulted in a long-term filming souvenir.

It started when Shelton sent his production team after an arch once spanning Virginia Street from 1935 to 1963, the second of four variations to grace the city. The original showed up in 1927 and celebrated the Transcontinental Highway. Locals grew fond of it and asked the city fathers keep some variation of it, adding the phrase "The Biggest Little City in the World" in 1934. Replaced again in 1963, the old arch found homes in various local parks until disappearing into a city maintenance yard. Years of extreme weather and hazardous pigeons damaged the icon, whose lights no longer functioned. *Cobb*'s set design team calculated the price to make a new version, but chose the more cost-effective route of fixing the real one. They painted, they polished, they pounded one side for the movie cameras. Since Virginia Street lacked period buildings and stretched too wide for the old arch, they hauled it to a time-warp zone on East Fourth Street, where the Fifties remain in small, brick buildings. Homeless people, streetwalkers, and others hung out and watched curiously as the arch arose by the Morris Hotel, now a base for Burning Man artists. Word got out about the newly returned arch, and locals who never ventured near rundown Fourth Street arrived, popping into the middle of the road to take pictures under their favorite old icon.

The *Cobb* team left, but a groundswell grew to save the refurbished arch. Fans raised funds to fix its other side and found it a new home by the National Automobile Museum on Lake Street, a perfect place to parade older cars by as part of the area's annual special event, "Hot August Nights."

Production team members also spent time and money re-creating a Fifties casino interior full of mechanical slot machines and one-armed bandits. They rented historic equipment, hauling it to the rustic, wood-lined Indian Room of the Cal Neva Lodge at Crystal Bay on the north shore of Lake Tahoe. In addition, a Victorian-era neighborhood in Carson City provided one of Cobb's Georgia residences.

With attention to period detail plus fine performances by Tommy Lee Jones and Robert Wuhl, Shelton succeeds in his goal.

"I want to show a more complex view of who and what legends are and what sports heroes are and what role models are or are not," he said.

The conundrum comes because such accuracy makes *Cobb* difficult to watch; most of us go out of our way to avoid hanging out with selfish, bombastic, psychotic personalities, even if they are icons.

Famous people like Ty Cobb, Mark Twain, and Howard Hughes claim distinct Nevada connections, but the biggest name in the state's biopics never set foot in the state. A grand, sweeping epic, *The Greatest Story Ever Told*, recounts the life of Jesus Christ. A massive budget allowed director George Stevens to shoot anywhere in the world, so he spent six weeks scouting the Middle East where Jesus lived. He found the region too developed and lacking drama. Stevens envisioned land shaping the people, with locations vital to the piece. For his vistas, Stevens chose what he called "the excitement" of the American Southwest, primarily Arizona, Utah, and Nevada. About thirty miles north of Reno, Nevada's Pyramid Lake lies far from the movie's other locations, but its desert look fit right in. Even Nevadans familiar with Pyramid may find themselves gasping at its grandeur on screen, highlighted with Oscar-winning cinematography. Still, Pyramid Lake misses perfection in one respect. Those who know the Sea of Galilee never saw a large, tufa rock pyramid formation on its far end. Like the spectacularly gorgeous star who refuses to cut her long hair or try a new accent, Pyramid maintains her defining image and proves an inflexible performer—but a breathtakingly beautiful one.

Using United States locations meant bigger wages for the crew, plus increased costs for a project already promising huge expenses from an A-list director. Taking a recognizable title from a radio series that started in 1947 and presented more than 500 half-hour episodes about Jesus Christ, the movie starred Max von Sydow. To sweeten the package and generate box office interest, director Stevens hooked a who's who of famous faces from 1965: Carroll Baker, José Ferrer, Van Heflen, Sidney Poitier, Angela Lansbury, David McCallum, Sal Mineo, and Pat Boone among them. As a Biblical epic, it practically mandated Charlton Heston, who shows up as John the Baptist wearing a fuzzy fur costume that would embarrass Fred Flintstone.

John Wayne gets bigger laughs with a single stilted observation as the Centurion, a Roman soldier overcome by the death of Jesus. Wayne's one line makes for a greatest story in itself, retold on the project's video package and the respectful MGM website. According to those sources, Stevens disliked Wayne's delivery of eight simple words.

"Truly, this man was the son of God," Wayne repeated in take after take.

Stevens wanted more oomph, something he usually got from actors. He guided Alan Ladd to his best performance in *Shane*. Stevens inspired a memorable Elizabeth Taylor with *A Place in the Sun*. Stevens led Rock

Hudson to his only Oscar nomination for *Giant*. Stevens worked his magic on Wayne.

"Give us some awe," he directed.

Following instructions, Wayne paused before getting into the cowboy mode that made him such a natural actor.

"Awwww, truly, this man was the son of God."

Ultimately, *The Greatest Story Ever Told* needed a miracle, one big enough to recoup its $20 million budget. Bad reviews and a sarcastic renaming as *The Longest Story Ever Told* scared audiences away from theaters. Though the movie gained respect over the years and annual Easter broadcasts earned profits, it never lived up to its hype or title. *The Greatest Story Ever Told* remains beautiful to look at, but fails as either the best film ever made or one that provides a definitive look at Nevada. To date, Nevada awaits its own *Greatest Story Ever Told*.

13

Mustang and the Ranches

My first week working for the Nevada Film Office brought one of those "Toto, we're not in Kansas anymore" moments. Someone called asking for agricultural spreads, the kind Nevada made famous with the Ponderosa Ranch in the iconic television series *Bonanza*.

"Of course we have ranches," I said, and quickly pulled out a phonebook to scan the yellow pages—the step we film commissioners took in the days before the web led us everywhere.

"*R*," I said aloud, as I hit the section marked "Ranches."

"Uh," I paused.

The category's many listings included "Chicken Ranch," "Cottontail Ranch," and "Mustang Ranch."

By then, I had lived in Nevada long enough to know these places did not raise birdies, bunnies, or horsies.

These were legal brothels, Nevada's last bastion for fostering the forbidden. Nevada once stood apart from the rest of the nation as the only state allowing boxing, quick divorce, spur-of-the-moment marriage, and gambling, though by the eighties most permitted these so-called vices. But as various prohibitions tumbled elsewhere, Nevada remained the only state in the union licensing prostitution inside highly regulated legal brothels. That creates a specialized, iconic location for movies and television.

"When you think of Nevada, you think of four things," retired state archivist Guy Rocha said in 2010.

"You think of Las Vegas," he ticked off.

Next, he added, "You think of Lake Tahoe."

Then, comes number three.

"You think of Hoover Dam."

And to round out the list?

"You think of Mustang Ranch."

If legal brothels represent an iconic Nevada location, then Mustang

Ranch rates as an icon among icons. Sure, the HBO reality television series *Cathouse* let the Moonlite Bunny Ranch hop on the trail to massive international exposure. But Rocha felt Mustang rules as an icon.

"It has the history, it has the drama, and it's had it for forty years," he explained. "It's been on the national radar for all that time."

Rocha traced Mustang's initial major exposure to 1971 when it took title as the first legal brothel in the United States. Various incarnations survived before that, but its status as a law abiding, taxpaying entity catapulted it to international attention.

Joe Conforte cultivated such publicity, showing up in the feature film *Charley Varrick* and the *Mustang: House of Pleasure* documentary, where he described himself as a public relations man.

He also hit the world's screens with national news coverage of events he failed to control, like the time a bullet killed a heavyweight-boxing contender training at the ranch.

Receiving worldwide coverage, the case later brought the movie industry's biggest names to Nevada for a feature film called *Love Ranch.*

Hot off his Oscar nomination for *Ray*, director Taylor Hackford juggled high-level Directors Guild of America (DGA) politics while developing *Love Ranch.*

A big, self-assured guy with an Oscar and hits like *An Officer and a Gentleman*, Hackford exuded confidence about his upcoming project.

His idea for a movie inspired by the Mustang Ranch and its owners involved signing highly recognizable, top quality stars to play roles some might consider sleazy. This included a grandiose brothel promoter and the madam who ran what the script described as a bunch of "psychotic whores." The world knew them as Joe and Sally Conforte; the script called them Charlie and Grace Bontempo.

"Joe always told me there were only three guys who could play him," brothel lobbyist George Flint recalled.

"De Niro," he said, pausing to pull the name of another *Godfather* actor. "Al Pacino. And Joe Pesci."

Of the three, Pesci looked right, tightly bundled and radiating raw energy.

It made sense to locals who saw the real Conforte in action. With a similar broad frame but less hair than Pesci, Conforte dominated any room, including his restaurant, where he liked to stride in wearing a dark suit and narrow tie, a half-smoked cigar jutting out of his mouth.

He both literally and figuratively owned the room, a dinner house called Cabin in the Sky just outside the historic mining town of Virginia City in Storey County. Like any owner, he came by for a good meal on the house, but with his ranch making him the biggest contributor to local coffers, he preferred making an entrance. He strutted into the main dining room, each arm adorned by a tall and leggy, drop-dead gorgeous working girl outfitted in brightly colored, skin-tight glittery dresses, shining as much as any showgirl on stage. Shortly after one of these entrances, a waitress came by my table and seemed surprised when no one took her up on an offer for drinks.

"Mr. Conforte is buying a round for everyone in the house," she elaborated. "What would you like?" Her tone indicated we better like something. We ordered another round.

So that's how Joe *C* treated locals, and Joe *P* seemed a good match, carrying both smiley- and frowny-face qualities. Pesci won an Oscar as a vicious SOB in *Goodfellas*, but everyone loves him for *My Cousin Vinny*.

As for "Mrs. C," Sally? In real life, she kept a low profile in the community. Director Hackford envisioned a stronger, more influential woman. He thought the role of madam for the first legal United States brothel should go to a phenomenal actress, the Dame who just won an Oscar for *The Queen* and an Emmy as *Elizabeth I* during the same awards season.

Helen Mirren's regal stature might intimidate some, but Hackford used influence when asking her to play royalty at a brothel. Mirren is his wife.

"I didn't have one moment of trepidation saying, 'Baby, I've got a great role for you,' 'cause I do," he said during the filming of *Love Ranch* in Reno.

He continued, "And she read the script and immediately knew it. I could describe the role to her and she knew it," he said enthusiastically.

"So, yes, there's a little joke, 'I played two queens and what does my husband do? He makes me the madam of a brothel,'" Hackford recalled, adding, "But I responded, 'Hey, it's a queen of a different type.'"

That regal imagery made it into the film when Mirren annoys Pesci with one of her demands.

"Who do ya think you are?" he asks. "The queen of fuckin' England?"

Besides gathering a great cast, Hackford prepared for the film by exploring his setting. A thorough filmmaker, he immersed himself in the subject matter. Using an incentive program and therefore shooting most of the movie in New Mexico, he came to Reno to learn the business behind running a brothel, contacting Nevada's Film Commission for ideas.

"Can you help us with an itinerary and take us to all the Northern Nevada brothels?" he asked after the Reno-Tahoe Branch—me—provided detailed advance information.

Of course. Film commissioners share traits with travel agents, so I do itineraries in my sleep, with triple backflips and any other special skills required.

Setting up this travel plan meant calling brothel managers in the area. All signed on to meet with such a high profile, respected director. Since Hackford and I communicated frequently and shared ideas by e-mail, he asked me to join the investigation in person, a prospect I relished.

Though I visited a couple of "ranches" during familiarization tours of rural counties in the past, this represented a more extensive, focused look at the region around Northern Nevada. Locals tolerated brothels as far back as the mining rush of the 1800s, but more widespread acceptability took nearly a hundred years, when Mustang Ranch owner Joe Conforte pushed through legislation making them legal in counties of fewer than 400,000 residents (which excludes Las Vegas and Reno). Despite mass media images of prostitution as legal all over the state, it takes a countywide vote to permit the business. That business encompasses more than sex according to the people we met on our scout.

"It's not just the sex," says Susan Austin, madam at both the Wild Horse Adult Resort and World Famous Mustang Ranch. "It's the fantasy."

Or from Dennis Hof at the Moonlite Bunny Ranch: "It's not just the sex. It's the adventure."

Adventures, according to "Pleasure Menus" available at most brothels, include whipped cream, liquor, and much more. Despite similarities, each features different ambiance. Management styles vary too. Every stop fascinated us in some way, though much of our focus came at the place that inspired *Love Ranch.*

Possibly the most famous legal brothel in the world, the Mustang Ranch experienced many forms, ranging from trailers off Interstate 80's Mustang exit to the mid-seventies buildings sold on eBay and helicoptered at great expense to a new location four-and-a-half miles east at the Patrick exit. Located on the same property as the Wild Horse Adult Resort & Spa, the buildings fell under the purview of Lance Gilman and Susan Austin.

Austin designed the Wild Horse as a bright, airy place with working girls' needs in mind. In contrast, Conforte's original buildings feel narrow and confined, fitting the *Reno Gazette-Journal* description as "The Love Fortress." Conforte surrounded the octagonal complex with a twelve-foot-tall metal fence, overlooked by an intimidating gun tower rising from the surrounding desert.

The octagonal building with its pink stucco façade takes on a more welcoming look in its new location, with a redecorated interior featuring a painted ceiling for an Italian theme honoring Conforte's heritage. Wings with hallways of rooms jut out from the main octagon, with one section preserved as the Joe Conforte Suite. A small display of Mustang memorabilia lines the walls, and Conforte's portrait hangs over the fireplace.

"It's unusual," explained Susan. "It was painted when he was in prison so he doesn't have a cigar."

The room serves as the World Famous Mustang Ranch Museum, a carefully chosen description. Though Nevada allows brothels, it forbids advertising them. By law, no Reno cab promotes the World Famous Mustang Ranch Brothel. But plenty feature plastic signs pushing the museum. That means you can tour the museum. Owners advise making reservations since a guard gate limits access.

"Usually, one of the girls takes guests to the museum," said Susan.

The cost?

"Oh, a $5 tip is fine," Susan answered.

Of course, the price rises for those using the museum's "Joe Conforte Suite," complete with its own bondage room.

"It starts at $10,000," Susan told the production team.

This new Millennium Mustang differs from Conforte's style and the bygone era he represents. In the decades since the action depicted in *Love Ranch,* a law mandates that clients must use condoms. Women show up as customers, both solo and with partners. Women also get their own officially marked restrooms.

Conforte's penchant for stark, plain decor was transformed into Austin's preference for themes and colors. Some rooms come with rails to help the elderly and handicapped. At the Wild Horse, a huge tiled shower fosters food parties with easy cleanup.

The new Mustang puts tantric chairs in most rooms to let users explore the many positions of Kama Sutra. In another room, one bed easily fits six people. Overall, the Mustang reflects Susan's taste and experience, going back to her first days as a working girl at age forty-two.

"I love sex," she told the *Love Ranch* scouting group, pursing her lips.

Her passion gave the onetime Army brat an idea for a job when her military husband left her with five children. She put her kids through school; she says the older ones handled it well while the younger ones took time getting used to her new job. Susan and a former brothel client, Lance Gilman, partnered for both the $12 million investment to retrofit the Mustang and to build its neighbor across the way.

Before retiring from brothel duties, Susan served as official advisor for the *Love Ranch* movie, showing actresses how to stand and move in their roles as working girls, while giving Helen Mirren insight into the complications of being a madam. Mirren shadowed Austin for a night at the brothels.

"She was kind of hesitant to go," recalled Hackford. "Then, around 3 a.m., I'm saying 'come on baby, let's get back to Reno.'"

Mirren herself used British reserve in calling the evening "very interesting" and noting how older, more experienced women often targeted clients more effectively than young newcomers. Mirren added that Madam Susan impressed her and influenced the movie's performance.

Susan makes an ideal role model for a madam, though different from the real Sally Conforte. Stylishly dressed and favoring Native American motifs, Susan bears a slight resemblance to Debbie Reynolds. But the movie image of America's sweetheart quickly explodes.

Susan comfortably goes into details about sex. After all, the best in any business usually understand their subject well. Technical ability helps too. But most of all?

"It's people skills."

The scouting team saw these skills in action while a worker called "Love" dealt with the bar crowd during lunch. Nearly six feet tall and willowy thin with a generous chest, she got no argument from any man she approached, simply grabbing a guy by the hand and taking him to a negotiating room to make a deal.

She passed the scouting group several times during a question-and-answer lunch session with owners. She first wore a bright tropical dress with a floral design, slit so low that most of her ample breasts slipped away from the fabric. She next arrived in a schoolgirl uniform featuring a plaid skirt and bobby socks. Two other outfits appeared—four clients and four costume changes in just over an hour.

After lunch, Susan continued as tour guide, pointing to a bed with a tilted mirror above it.

"No one looks good on a flat mirrored ceiling," she explained, putting her hands on the far edge of the bed. "Now look," she directed.

"The mirror shows off my cleavage, and see how it reflects the other mirror on the wall over there?"

Yes, we saw.

"I got that idea from Versailles," she continued, adding "That mirror shows off my ass. This is perfect for doggie style."

The reference to Marie Antoinette's French castle mirrors Susan's aim for class and elegance, something well beyond what Joe and Sally Conforte managed when they refurbished the brothel portrayed in *Love Ranch*.

Back then, the brothel looked more like the Old Bridge Ranch, located at the original site Sally ran before marrying Joe.

Described by an online guide as one of the most laid-back brothels in the state, the Old Bridge Ranch featured strong ties to original Mustang history.

Appropriately enough, a band of wild horses grazed in a corner field near the sign, past cement pads and remnants of Conforte's original Mustang site. Conforte in-law Troy greeted the scouting team in the bar. Wearing a denim jacket, with sandy hair in a ponytail, Troy resembled a modern day farmer, a partially accurate conclusion since he grew alfalfa on the property. He happily received a report that workers ran off the herd of horses, which eat through newly laid sod in a couple of hours.

Before moving our discussion into the kitchen, Troy scowled at all the Nikons and Canons carried by scouting team members. Production designer Bruno Rubeo loved the retro seventies look of the bar and clicked away like crazy.

"Those cameras are scaring the girls," Troy said.

Everyone stopped snapping and sat around a table in a simple kitchen area, where other topics came up, including Troy's involvement with the Nomads, Northern Nevada's Hells Angels chapter. He frowned when someone referred to the Hells Angels as "outlaws."

"I've never been convicted of a crime," he said, flinty eyes glaring. "You saying I'm a criminal?"

"No!" the group almost shouted. That outlaw reference relates to the admirable qualities of living on the edge and being a rebel, director Taylor finessed.

The talks also covered an argument about the business name. Troy and others at Old Bridge felt their operation deserved the "Mustang Ranch" title since Sally worked the current site when its illegal status required trailers that could be easily moved over different county lines to avoid sheriffs. The Old Bridge, Wild Horse, and Moonlite Bunny all fought a court battle for the right to license the Mustang name, with Gilman winning the last judgment.

"For now," said Troy ominously.

The Old Bridge Ranch sign prominently listed its location as Mustang, Nevada, hoping to play on its historic connection. By the time *Love Ranch* opened, the Old Bridge closed because of owner David Burgess' child pornography conviction. But the interior's basic design lives on in the look of the cinematic *Love Ranch.*

Much of what the scouting team saw became part of *Love Ranch*, not just physical locations in Reno and at the Wild Horse, but during the story's first twenty minutes, as business logistics are shown.

"I want you to be able to watch this, see the operations, and say 'Yeah, that's how it was,'" Taylor told one of the brothel owners.

He acknowledged discrepancies in various parts of the film.

"The Reno Arch in the movie isn't the one that was there in 1976," he said. "I know that. But it looks like it's from the seventies. It feels right."

Despite his quest for authenticity, *Love Ranch* felt wrong to many critics who covered its June 2010 release.

Some called the movie too predictable. Others dinged it for making the brothel look seedy and dingy, though in reality, the ranch fit photos and descriptions from that era. The reaction surprised Hackford, who said he felt "proud of the film" and remained that way.

"This picture plays for an audience, especially women, but we've been savaged by the critics," he said.

Hackford hopes the critical bandwagon will shift over time.

"It's not the first time they didn't get it," he noted. "*An Officer and a Gentleman* received dismal reviews," he said of his film that went on to be a box office smash and earn two Oscars.

"The true test of a film is longevity. Let's see what the audience says in twenty years."

In the meantime, *Love Ranch* lives on as the name of a place Dennis Hof opened across the highway from Moonlite Bunny Ranch in tiny Lyon County.

Nevada brothels' unique status inspired other projects. Screenwriter Allan Aaron Katz capitalized on Reno's proximity to brothels for his screenplay, *Diamonds*.

"I've never been here before," Katz told me on set downtown. "But I needed a place where three generations of guys could legally go to a brothel."

The brothel visit fits into a family story about a grandfather, son, and grandson who leave British Columbia to find a treasure the older man left behind in Reno during his days as a prizefighter. The men take the Reno trip as a family bonding experience, but fight until they find one place where experience changes attitudes and views—a brothel. Despite its base near various "ranches," moviemakers never planned to film a real brothel for two reasons. Most projects never leap over the first hurdle—without James Cameron's budget for *Avatar 2*, no one can afford charges incurred for the loss of business.

Along with budget concerns, *Diamonds* faced the need for minimal daily commutes since it featured a comeback role for Kirk Douglas, suffering from health issues following a helicopter crash that broke his back and a stroke that tied his tongue. Like the Greek gladiator Spartacus he played on screen, Douglas loved battle and determinedly trained his body to work away physical complications. What broken back? He'd walk again. What speech impediment? He'd talk again. And he'd sure as hell make another movie, even if there weren't a lot of roles for guys over eighty. Receiving a

Film Office greeting at Reno's Bistro Roxie restaurant the night after he completed his first day on set, Douglas warmly encouraged conversation.

"It's great to be back," he said.

He still had trouble speaking in pristine stage tones but a few minutes into the conversation, his rhythms seemed natural and normal.

"It was cold out there today," he said of Reno's late November weather. "But it felt good."

That late fall filming helped Reno win the *Diamonds* project from British Columbia, where heavy rains promised difficulties for Douglas and the rest of the crew. Reno supplied a variety of looks, including a private home on Reno's Kinney Lane that met every clichéd movie image of a brothel. Its Victorian exterior covered an interior featuring walls decorated with nude portraits of its owner. Flocked wallpaper and antique furniture finished the look so well that the production designer let the décor stand.

All the movie's big names showed up on set not far from downtown Reno. Douglas joined his real-life longtime friend, Lauren Bacall as Madame Sin Dee. Dan Aykroyd played Douglas' son, meeting his match with Mariah O'Brien. As the virgin with things to learn, Corbin Allred hooked up with former Playmate and future talk show host Jenny McCarthy.

McCarthy fit her gregarious image and volunteered to help during one lunch break. Douglas just turned eighty-two, and the crew brought a cake. McCarthy stepped in to do a bump-and-grind version of "Happy Birthday," finishing on Douglas's lap. Douglas smiled broadly, and McCarthy concluded the piece by bouncing over and hugging his wife Anne. Despite its fun set and titillating premise, the movie failed to raise box office excitement.

Diamonds joins other projects that prove prurient interests and beautiful bodies never guarantee success. Case in point, 2003's *The Ranch,* bearing no resemblance to a 2016 Netflix series with the same name. Back in 2003, *The Ranch* seemed promising, and Showtime executives hired *Sex and the City* director Susan Seidelman for her flair in working with actresses. Amy Madigan from *Field of Dreams* played the tough, grumpy Nevada madam, though cameras rolled in British Columbia.

Despite the investment, management axed the series before it began and instead cobbled together footage for DVD release in feature film format. This leaves an incomplete story with major plot points hanging. Predictable, clichéd plotting and characters weaken the project, but its deeper problem comes from difficulty in making its characters acceptably sympathetic to mainstream audiences. Some viewers refuse to believe a woman can be both model mother and dynamic prostitute—even though many in the business insist it happens.

According to Moonlite Bunny Ranch owner Dennis Hof, *The Ranch* developed after his negotiations for a Showtime series failed. The network wanted the fictional approach they chose with *The Ranch*, but Hof saw more potential in a reality series and went on to make *Cathouse* with HBO.

"I see the guys at Showtime, and they just shake their heads," said Hof, whose marketing materials included T-shirts with the slogan, "We put the HO in HBO."

The HBO production team rarely needed Film Office help at the Moonlite Bunny Ranch, though production managers occasionally requested a production directory listing locals who worked as crew members.

One exception came when a Los Angeles producer called my office in 2007 and reached my new assistant.

"HBO wants to do a musical," she told me. "They're asking about stages at casinos and schools and places like that."

"Great," I said, and gave her a couple of contacts to call.

The HBO producer called again but this time I heard my assistant greet him by name. I stopped in my tracks and waited until she put the phone down.

"What's the name of this musical?" I asked.

"I don't know. I just have 'HBO Musical.'"

"Call back and get the title," I directed.

She reported back: *Cathouse: The Musical.*

"Tell you what," I said. "Let's stop calling schools."

School districts frown on brothels. For that matter, many casinos hesitate to link themselves directly with brothels, so this project's best bet came at Storey County's historic Piper's Opera House.

Cathouse: The Musical aired in 2008, eventually becoming a four-disc DVD set featuring songs that sound nothing like the pulsing music throbbing through the Moonlite Bunny bar.

Broadway producer Fred Barton chose eleven classics from Cole Porter and similar composers. The program shows Barton guiding the girls and owner Dennis Hof through routines, honing their moves and voices for each number. Highlights include Hof and his then-girlfriend, Brooke Taylor, singing "You're Getting to Be a Habit with Me."

"It was fun," Hof said. "I didn't know I could do it."

Still, neither he nor his girls gave up their day . . . er, night . . . jobs.

The whole *Cathouse* reality show concept started as a special in 2002, returning the next year with *Cathouse: Back in the Saddle.* Eleven episodes aired in 2005, followed by six in 2006. The show ventured deeper into the workings of a brothel than many documentaries, as Air Force Amy and other working girls step into bedrooms with clients for sexual acts—with various anatomical details blurred.

By *Cathouse* standards, any older documentary on brothels looks badly lit and staid. Still, *Mustang: House of Pleasure* offers revealing moments.

Having just moved to Reno in 1976, I watched the newly released documentary in a theater, hoping to learn about a business less than a half hour's drive from my home.

Of course, having been filmed long before digital cameras that work well in low lighting, the cinematography for *Mustang: House of Pleasure* looks awful. Filmmaker Robert Guralnick faced technical limitations but had good access. He reveals sights that might startle those expecting a glamorous, sexy world.

Filmed in 1975, a set of trailers behind a simple chain-link fence comprise the ranch. Inside, cheap plywood veneer walls line "the house that Joe built."

Ceilings hang low. Red carpet smothers the floor, with the same color scheme for furniture.

Joe fits the motif, wearing a red tie and pants, along with a gaudy white sport jacket checked in big black squares.

"I'm trying to bring this business out," he says. "It's not as bad as people think it is."

In another scene, Joe wears an electric blue coat as he sits in a zebra-striped chair backed by a wall of gold and red vertical stripes. He calls out as his wife Sally moves by, insisting the camera focus on her.

"She's the one that runs it," he says. "A woman belongs in a place like this, not a man."

The project also shows several employees in action, catching them with comments about clients.

"They're all the same. They've got the same prick. They fuck the same way."

None of the girls show enthusiasm about lining up for clients to choose.

"Hi, I'm . . . ," the girl says with all the excitement of a comatose victim, her face made up with off-white sparkly lipstick and thick false eyelashes.

Once chosen, the girl takes her client to inspect his sexual tools and assure cleanliness; after all, part of the point of legalizing brothels involves safety.

About this time during the movie, I felt my jaw dropping. Not because of the penis getting washed—that seemed like a good idea.

No, my surprise came from recognizing the guy getting washed as one my coworkers at my new job, reporting news for KOLO radio.

"So I saw that new movie about Mustang Ranch last night," I told him the next day.

His face widened into a big grin.

"Fun, huh?" he asked, no sign of red enveloping his face.

Well . . . different words came to mind. Paraphrasing Dorothy, "I'm not in California anymore." Welcome to Nevada.

14

Showgirls and the Entertainers

She stands tall, strutting with Tina Turner confidence in stiletto heels, rhinestones glittering and feathers swaying, ricocheting off curvy hips and flouncing rounded, protruding breasts. She's a showgirl, an icon of Nevada and its entertainers. You may see her on stage. You might catch her as part of floor entertainment during a trade show or convention. And memorably, you see her on screen in *Showgirls*. *Showgirls* stands out for good, bad, and extreme reasons.

Screenwriter Joe Eszterhas started with a proven plot, doing some heavy lifting from the Oscar-winning *All About Eve* and its competition between an established stage star versus a conniving up-and-comer. The *Showgirls* script expanded on Eve's attributes by calling for an ocean of bare breasts and nearly X-rated sex.

"It is certain to do well," director Paul Verhoeven insisted during scouting.

With a PhD in mathematics, Verhoeven knows numbers, proven by the millions he made in the film industry.

But still . . . talk about a tacky script. Main character Nomi first encounters her soon-to-be best friend in a "meet cute" scene—she pukes on her. Another gross-out involves menstrual blood.

These scenes seemed likely to get chopped since most scripts go through evolutionary steps during production. Yet the *Showgirls* script proves a rare example where the director treats every word with Biblical respect that prohibited any alteration.

As for parts requiring the director's vision to expand vague descriptions, Verhoeven plays off an observation about Nomi's "natural pelvic thrust" by offering an amazing sex scene warranting a warning label,

"Don't try this at home." Frolicking in a swimming pool, lovers resemble sea serpents suffering from an intestinal malady (perhaps a cross between cholera and epilepsy) that induces spasmodic, breaching belly flops. Such "natural pelvic thrust" might make a weapon of mass destruction if some enterprising military expert gets hold of it. As a result of this and similar scenes, *Showgirls* earned stunningly bad reviews plus sweepstake status at the Razzie Awards, which honor each year's worst contributions to movies. That should have ended *Showgirls* and its place in cinema history.

But in a twist of fate, *Showgirls* found its niche as kitsch. Theaters ran *Showgirls* parties, where audiences added their own lines with *Rocky Horror Picture Show* glee. David Schmader performed a comic routine at *Showgirls* screenings, touring the country and adding wisecrack commentary. Bringing his show to Reno, Schmader talked about the movie's running symbolism regarding fingernails, one of Nomi's specialties. Nomi goes into "slave status" when her nemesis wields power over her by demanding a nail job; later, as Nomi sets out to get revenge on a vicious rapist, she fires up by painting really flashy images on her nails—that will show him!

Such scenes gave *Showgirls* enough fans to rate it number thirty-six on *Entertainment Weekly*'s 2003 list of top cult films. Eventually, distributor MGM accepted reality by releasing a campy anniversary DVD set that included a "pin the pasties on the showgirl" game.

No one thought about doing that with the *Sister Act* entertainers, even though Whoopi Goldberg starts the movie as a Reno showgirl. No wait, in real-world dynamics, Whoopi was originally Bette Midler and Reno was Atlantic City . . . or maybe Las Vegas.

Movie deals and screenplays change, so *Sister Act* experienced a variety of switches when the production team came for a quick look at Reno in 1991. By this time, Bette dropped from the project and Whoopi signed on. Producers dumped Atlantic City and wanted Vegas. But they like to mark off options.

"Yeah," scouts say to management. "We checked this and we checked that. Vegas works best."

Reno lacked flashy Las Vegas Stratosphere towers. Reno casinos remained old school, with what locals prefer to call "character" rather than "rundown, in need of updating." People came to Reno to gamble, not admire new developments in architecture.

"This picture will be like the place where we film," director Emile Ardolino said after a morning scouting the handful of casinos comprising Reno's downtown "strip."

"In Las Vegas, we will have bigger stunts and a helicopter rescue at the Stratosphere. There will be many special effects," he said.

"If we use Reno, we will be smaller and have more to do with the musical numbers and characters," he continued.

"Like *Dirty Dancing*?" I asked. His previous hit remains popular today, decades after its original release.

Crinkling his eyes, Emile smiled and issued a drawn out "Yessss. . ."

By displaying character, Reno caught the fish-out-of-water story about a showgirl who hides out with a group of gospel singing nuns.

The premise forced a casino lounge singer to flee quickly for a nearby big city.

"Well," scouts said facetiously as the production team stood underground in the Harolds Club counting room and looked up at a ladder leading to a grate in the sidewalk.

"She could just pop out the grate."

A synchronicity spiraled, with jokes about heroine Delores running down the street to the Amtrak station and catching a train to San Francisco. The grate ended up in the final product, although it required movie magic to transform heavy metal into a foam rubber replica light enough for Whoopi to lift.

Reno's Saint Thomas Aquinas Church on Arlington and Second Streets also made the location in an opening scene. Asked to name the apostles, a young Delores begins well enough by coming up with John and Paul. She pauses and thinks hard.

"George and Ringo," she finishes triumphantly.

Her teacher looks aghast.

"Do you know what happens to girls like you when you grow up?" demands a horrified nun.

Cut to: Delores as a showgirl, singing Motown hits on stage at a small casino called Fitzgerald's. Movie magic combines Fitzgerald's interiors with the Nevada Club exterior. The Nevada Club's art deco exterior appealed to the filmmakers, who made it part of the movie by using the property's marquee to advertise Delores's group, The Ronelles.

As plot has it, Delores leaves town for weeks, then returns. When cameras rolled for the homecoming, someone looked at the marquee and wondered why The Ronelles continued playing without their lead singer. Some movie geek would point out the mistake, highlighting it on a "bloopers" page. No problem—a stagehand rolled up to the board and quickly reworked the letters so the only thing for movie geeks to ponder is why any group would call itself The Leerons.

Other last-minute challenges hit production. Weeks of effort went into an aerial shot of nuns arriving at Reno's downtown heliport. Okay, so no downtown heliport existed in Reno, but an empty parking lot looked good enough to pass as a landing pad. The real problem came from defunct casinos whose darkness prevented the blaze of neon the director wanted. The lights needed to shine for dialogue between a nun and the Mother Superior, played by Maggie Smith.

"It's so beautiful!" cries Wendy Makkena as the youngest nun.

"Reno and Gomorrah," sniffs Dame Maggie in response, perfectly embodying her *Downton Abbey* shock at anything less refined than a British estate.

Turning on lights to appall Dame Maggie proved more complicated than location manager George Herthel imagined. It meant digging up phone numbers to get a closed casino's out-of-country owners to contact both the power company and a specific electrician who knew the system. Less than an hour before the helicopter scene, Herthel joined the Film Office to meet an electrician in a dark alley. Next step, pull boards from the door and head inside.

Flashlights showed the way upstairs to the top floor and a room that felt like a fifties movie spaceship with controls everywhere. The electrician switched levers and pushed buttons, taking time to finish his mission.

"That should do it," he said, pulling a handle upwards.

Heading down carpeted steps toward the main room, no one expected what happened next.

"Freeze!" cried a voice, adding, "Raise your hands!"

Three Reno police officers stood at the base of the stairs, guns drawn and pointed at chest level. Arms edged upwards as one officer looked at George, the location guy.

"Oh, it's you," smiled the officer, holstering the weapon.

The Disney liaison covered all his bases and local cops knew him as a thorough movie professional rather than a robber, the result of an alert neighbor reporting to police after spying people entering the closed casino.

Interior shooting provided other challenges. Even though signs warned about filming on the premises, not every Fitzgerald's customer noticed cameras rolling. Regular gamblers continued playing on the floor, where dinging slot machines pinged and encouraging shouts rose from blackjack tables.

Still, it looked a little odd. The script calls for a batch of nuns to infiltrate the property and rescue Delores. Each nun had a stand-in, so an inordinate number of gamblers wore habits.

One little nun liked the giant dollar machine, her small size forcing her into a mighty leap to grab its handle, her body weight pulling it down. Comedian Kathy Najimy's belly laugh echoed as she hit the slots. Mary Wickes sat at a bar and grinned as she watched her cohorts. With hair and features hidden in the cap of her habit, Whoopi Goldberg played a serious game of craps in between takes.

"Cut!" cried the assistant director as Whoopi switched gears and twisted around to her nearby game table. Her turn as shooter had arrived. Dressed in the conservative black and white attire of a nun, she grabbed the dice.

"C'mon fuckin' seven!" she bellowed, rolling the red squares.

Eyes widened as uninformed passersby marveled at the language coming from a saintly nun.

Max Page, one of the hotel owners, recalled walking through the casino with a friend. Looking around at all the women in black and white, his buddy observed action. Nun at a bar. Nun hanging off a slot. Nun yelling the "f-word."

"You know," the visitor told Max, "the Catholic Church sure has changed since I was a kid!"

Despite the fun, no one expected much more than a pleasant comedy to result. But director Ardolino hit the bullseye with his quest of blending music with characters, and audiences responded to the warmth and catchy gospel music he offered in *Sister Act*. The biggest non-sequel hit of 1992, *Sister Act* briefly turned Goldberg into the highest paid actress of the time when she signed for a 1993 sequel. As the second-rate follow-up opens, Delores plays Las Vegas, where production notes say "she has risen from a second-rate lounge singer to . . . well . . . a second-rate headliner."

But as the joke implies, Las Vegas and other parts of Nevada often lure first-rate headliners. If they warrant a biopic or concert film, the state often shows up as a real location or a faked setting.

Frank Sinatra and the rest of the Rat Pack? Sure, just ask Ray Liotta, Joe Mantegna, and Don Cheadle.

Liberace? Absolutely; Michael Douglas won an Emmy playing him in 2013, re-creating Mr. Showman's act at his Las Vegas Hilton (now Westgate) base.

Kevin Spacey as Bobby Darin; Jim Carrey as Andy Kaufman; Joaquin Phoenix as Johnny Cash; Katy Perry as herself. And The King? Without question, Elvis and Vegas go together, whether it's the real deal, or Kurt Russell or others playing him.

Fictional performers hit Nevada stages, too, including the manipulative magicians in 2012's *Now You See Me* and Steve Carell as *The Incredible Burt Wonderstone* in 2013.

Such projects often work with the Commission on Economic Development's Nevada Film Office. All of which leads us back to *Showgirls* and its ability to develop Nevada's economy.

Cameras rolled during a production number on the onetime Sahara showroom stage at the Horizon (now Hard Rock Hotel). Star Elizabeth Berkley stood in an aisle, glittering in sparkles with fluttery strands, a silvery G-string, and nothing on top. On stage, showgirls danced, bare breasts flouncing.

All around, a roomful of people watched. Some movies might fill those showroom seats with cardboard cutouts, but *Showgirls* boasted the budget to pay actual people to play audience members. There they sat, Nevadans earning money by watching topless women. Now that's economic development.

The *Showgirls* Tahoe Connection

After interviewing location manager Bill Bowling about his extensive career for an article in the Association of Film Commissioners' official magazine, *Locations*, I put in a business plug.

"Call if you ever need a Northern Nevada location."

Bill thought for a moment before responding.

"Well, I'm doing this movie called *Showgirls* but it all takes place in Vegas and they have what we need."

The required marketing comment continued.

"Yeah, Vegas is great. But sometimes it gets busy and Reno has been known to step in."

We signed off and that seemed the end of it until the phone rang a few weeks later.

"Guess what?" Bowling asked.

The world of movies provided far too many options for any answer other than "What?"

"We need a showroom for *Showgirls*. We can't find a stage that's available in Las Vegas."

Local location manager Tim Wilson joined forces for a military-style flanking of all alternatives, eventually targeting Lake Tahoe's Horizon Hotel. Despite lacking the cache of better-known labels like Caesars and Harrah's, the Horizon featured a remarkably large, top quality stage. Elvis played it under its former Sahara logo. Ann-Margret proved her strength and determination there after falling from a twenty-two-foot platform. With a long-running Western extravaganza just about to end, a window of opportunity opened for the movie.

But this movie offered a big challenge: Would Horizon management accept a project destined toward an R-rating or stronger? Dutch director Paul Verhoeven shocked America with a scene that let everyone know Sharon Stone's wardrobe lacked underwear in *Basic Instinct*. He never held back.

"Our high rollers won't mind that," said Horizon marketing manager Ruby Turner.

And so the Vegas-based *Showgirls* arrived off-season, during November 1994, with one week to shoot three different musical numbers. Director Verhoeven wanted his movie to look authentic and hired Michael Jackson's lighting coordinator to make sure tones and colors felt like they would in a concert rather than a movie. Equally complex scenic elements filled the stage. It turned out the set for each number required several days to build, plus more to break down. The math ran longer than one week, and *Showgirls* catapulted into a major Northern Nevada project with multiple requirements.

New questions arose as producers looked for other locations to fill time for each stage transition.

Did any local area resemble Utah, where main character Nomi hitchhikes in the story's early scenes?

Sure. Dramatically tall mountains like Jobs Peak made a perfect Utah backdrop in one sequence near Minden. Another scene used the Sierra ridges on the north end of Carson City across from the Glen Eagles restaurant, with star Elizabeth Berkley hitching a ride.

Sporting more clothes than at any other moment in the movie, she repeatedly ran to the side of U.S. Highway 395, where her designated vehicle stopped on cue.

One hopeful real-life driver, not noticing cameras, pulled over and gaped at this stunningly beautiful woman with her thumb out at the side of the road.

"Want a ride?" he offered.

Berkley giggled and jumped with excitement—she just earned positive demonstration of her acting skills.

Besides hitchhiking territory, Northern Nevada provided warehouse space for sets like trailer interiors. And when major characters end up in hospital rooms? That was also Northern Nevada, but not without a struggle.

"The movie will be rated R?" asked the public information officer at a conveniently located hospital.

Ruminating on *Basic Instinct*, her mental wheels turned, imagining conservative board members glowering at her.

"Yes, but we really, really need this room," I wheedled, counting on our longtime working relationship.

"It's for the good of the state," I punted since film projects enhance economic development. "It means jobs for locals in the community."

She paused.

"Well, I guess we could do it. But you have to promise me one thing."

I take promises seriously.

"What?" I asked cautiously.

"Promise me we won't be in the credits."

I sighed in relief. Production companies dole out highly prized recognition sparingly and most people negotiate for attention.

"No problem," I said, certain no unsolicited credits would turn up.

The hospital remains an unidentified mystery participant in *Showgirls*. Ironically though—and without any request by me—my name runs in the closing credits.

It's a bragging point according to John Waters, the so-called "Pope of Trash" whose unique cinematic contributions include *Pink Flamingos* and *Hairspray*. As far back as 1995, he agreed the movie "will be great trash forever."

Long after *Showgirls* left Nevada, I interviewed Waters about locations in movies, asking him about his favorite trashy films by other people.

Showgirls came up.

"I don't think they were in on the joke," he observed. "And that's what made it so great."

15

Bonanza and the Cowboys

The Original Ranchers

For millions, a map blazes as Nevada's western icon. Every Sunday night for more than a decade, the title "Bonanza" burned like a brand from a "Map of the Ponderosa in Nevada." The Ponderosa stands out in the middle, with Virginia City marked at the top. Reno sits north and Carson City, south. Below, Lake Tahoe dominates as a large swath of blue. The yellow "Bonanza" title retreats back into the map, flames bursting through, with the image changing to a shot of four cowboys—the Cartwright family.

Close-ups linger on each individually. In the first few seasons, Pernell Roberts arrives as Adam Cartwright, the firstborn; a solid, good-looking guy. Dan Blocker smiles next as Hoss, the congenial, easygoing son. Michael Landon arrives as Little Joe, the teenage heartthrob with big hair. Lorne Greene leads the group as Ben "Pa" Cartwright, a man whose stately look belies his difficulty in keeping women alive; it took a different one to produce each son. Covering fourteen seasons, from 1959–1973, meant the opening images changed as cast members moved on or died. Some backdrops used Tahoe Meadows, off Mount Rose Highway in Nevada, while Southern California provided most. But whether original Cartwright "boys" or new additions like Mitch Vogel and Tim Matheson, the Cartwright men made friends, fell in love, defended the innocent, and protected their ranch with its sprawling Lake Tahoe vistas. Lake Tahoe joined the show because it lures tourists.

"My family and I used to vacation at Lake Tahoe and Virginia City," *Bonanza* creator David Dortort explained on set for a television movie based on the series. "I love the history here, and I knew how beautiful and colorful it is," he continued.

Both traits fit the *Bonanza* plan because Dortort and his partner Tom Sarnoff designed the program to help sell a brand-new concept, color television. Though most of the series filmed on Paramount soundstages in Southern California, every season featured location work at Lake Tahoe with deep, rich greens in its trees and a range of blues varying from lapis to electric turquoise shades in the water.

Armed with tightly analyzed scripts of an entire season, the *Bonanza* team arrived toward the end of each summer and handled the whole year's Tahoe shots to insert in every episode. The *Bonanza* team flitted through various locations the first few seasons, but when it reached number one in the ratings, Tahoe landowner Bill Anderson realized the program brought new tourists expecting to find the Ponderosa Ranch. Anderson built a Ponderosa Ranch to NBC specifications on his property at the north shore's Incline Village. After 1967, the new ranch proved a comfortable spot for producers to shoot authentic locations, though it mostly functioned as a tourist destination.

"People come here and talk about the Cartwrights like they were people who really existed," said Anderson, walking his ranch during production of *Bonanza: The Next Generation*.

Until its sale in 2004, the ranch provided the country's first, strongest, and longest-running example of turning television location filming into a tourism bonanza.

Colorful locations enhanced *Bonanza*'s other strengths. Its cast brought together familiar faces plus unknowns with star qualities. The show featured outstanding guests, a list that reads like a who's who of reliable fifties and sixties performers: Yvonne de Carlo, Ida Lupino, Alan Hale, Jack Carson, Stella Stevens, Wayne Newton, Suzanne Pleshette, and Charles Bronson among them. Leonard Nimoy, before his break as *Star Trek*'s Mr. Spock, played a small role as "something of a misfit, a miscreant" in a 1960 *Bonanza* episode called "The Ape."

"It was good work," Nimoy recalled, adding, "I enjoyed doing it; I enjoyed the guys. The cast was an interesting bunch of people."

Some guest stars later won Oscars, among them James Coburn, Lee Marvin, and Jodie Foster.

The show gained credibility by factoring in names of famous historic people from the region. However, *Bonanza* firmly follows the Hollywood tradition of changing facts that inconvenience plotting. This allows Little Joe to fall in love with the title character of an episode titled "The Julia Bulette Story." Virginia City's most prominent prostitute, Bulette found a place in legend because of her brutal murder. The 1959 world of television never mentioned the word "prostitute," so Pa dances around specific reasons he wants Little Joe to find a different girlfriend.

"It's like a scar," says Pa.

Little Joe—a grown man in a town and in times demanding adult qualities—misses the point.

The Cartwrights also interact with leading Nevada figures like "Mr. Henry T.P. Comstock," starring Jack Carson as the man often credited with discovering Virginia City's silver fortune. The episode includes the real-life character Chief Winnemucca, namesake of a town off Interstate 80 in Humboldt County, Nevada. Trouble brews when Little Joe goes all moon-eyed over the chief's daughter Sarah, a big concern to the tribe since Cartwrights only fall in love for one episode, usually with fatal results for the woman. Luckily, Sarah survived Little Joe, and her impressive accomplishments make her one of the few women represented at the US Capitol in Washington, DC, with her own statue.

Anyone expecting a history lesson from *Bonanza* quickly spots inconsistencies by trying to follow that famous map from the Ponderosa Ranch to Virginia City. MapQuest outlines a squiggly pattern resembling yarn abandoned by a playful cat. Starting on State Route 28 in Incline Village, MapQuest sends you to State Route 431, where pines—including ponderosas—bunch along the roadside and stretch into large forests, broken by flat meadows near the 8,911-foot summit. Hairpin curves discourage high speeds on the way down until you get toward U.S. Highway 395 after about twenty-four miles. State Route 431 merges into State Route 341, the Geiger Grade leading up to Virginia City in thirteen winding miles. White crosses and other markers dot accident sites, common on this steep stretch with multiple sharp turns. Alpine terrain transforms quickly to high desert, with reddish soil dotted by squat pinion pines. The route takes an hour to drive, covering thirty-nine miles with elevation changes going up and down 2,000-plus feet.

Lacking MapQuest, the Cartwrights use television magic. In an episode called "The Magnificent Adah," they wait until dark, hitch their horses, and sneak off to Piper's Opera House in Virginia City, a real place where Hal Holbrook played Mark Twain. The boys catch the Piper show and return to the Ponderosa Ranch in Incline that night. If not magic, then the boys rode fuel-injected super equines equipped with headlights since most people allow a full day for horses to cover forty miles.

Bonanza failed its reality check but thrived with affectionate family values in a decade defined by civil unrest and the generation gap. *Bonanza* stands apart as one of the few Nevada projects that succeeded by promoting honesty, integrity, and courtesy. Kids grew up slowly back then, in both the 1960s and the 1800s. Though the fully grown Adam, Hoss, and Little Joe look like men, Pa never stops calling them boys—and they act like it. But the genuine warmth and sincerity of its creators and stars overwhelm plot simplifications. Keeping all that going for fourteen years represented rare success on television, but Dortort needed a break when Dan Blocker died.

"The heart went out of it for me after that," he said. Nearly two decades later, he felt ready to go at it again.

The Next Generation

Dortort and Tom Sarnoff resurrected the *Bonanza* concept with three television movies featuring Pa Cartwright's grandsons, filmed entirely on location in the Tahoe area. The region faced competition from Canada, which put in a strong bid offering tax-saving production incentives. By scheduling production when Tahoe's Ponderosa tourist site closed in fall and winter, producers found readily available, reasonably priced resources available at the story's actual setting.

"My feeling is that *Bonanza* belongs in Nevada," Dortort said in 1988. "It's an American story."

"*Bonanza* shows what the Western genre represents," he elaborated. "Not only in terms of recapturing the beauty of nature by shooting outdoors, but in telling a kind of story which is essentially a morality tale where good, honest values are important."

Original plans for *Bonanza: The Next Generation* brought series regular Lorne Greene back ruling the ranch. Greene died before production began, though, replaced by Western great John Ireland of Howard Hawks' *Red River* as Ben Cartwright's brother Aaron. Ireland enjoyed the role.

"I like Aaron because he's not typically the Western character. He has a background of the sea, a background of painting in Tahiti with Paul Gauguin, and now beginning a new background of managing the Ponderosa, trying to run it and keep it going in the midst of all kinds of problems that arise," he said on set.

The show's series title came from the real-life "next generation" as Michael Landon, Jr. joined the cast to play Little Joe's son, and Lorne's daughter Gillian Greene stepped in for romantic interest.

With roots firmly placed in old-school ideals from the early success of *Bonanza*, the "new generation" hit a cynical era in the eighties. It failed to repeat the success of the *Star Trek: Next Generation* reboot. However, NBC green-lighted a follow-up special, a two-hour *Bonanza* movie in 1993.

The show faced one hitch in project development when John Ireland died. Producers turned to another Western legend, Ben Johnson, one of the many famous names who made a guest appearance in the original series. Producers tapped him to run the Ponderosa in *Bonanza: The Return*.

Johnson, a former rodeo champ who earned the 1971 Oscar for Best

Supporting Actor for *The Last Picture Show*, perfectly embodied the traditional ethics promoted by *Bonanza*.

Johnson sat on location, looking apropos in his movie clothes, the kind of Western shirt, Stetson, boots, and rugged pants he might wear at home. Well over six feet tall and still standing straight, he remained nimble enough to ride his own horse, one he personally drove up for the ten-hour trip from Los Angeles to Lake Tahoe.

Cowboy roots also showed in his overall attitude. Arriving at his Tahoe hotel late one night, Johnson found problems with his room. Rather than raise a movie star hissy fit, he returned to the parking lot and slept in a trailer with his horse.

"It worked out fine," he said later. "It was cold that night, and I was kind of worried about him; he's not used to snow."

The chance to work with Johnson brought guest star Leonard Nimoy to *Bonanza: Under Attack* in 1995.

"Ben Johnson was just a wonderful man," Nimoy said a few years later during his photo exhibit at Sierra Arts in Reno.

Nimoy's turn in *Bonanza: Under Attack* let him play a good guy in the role of a sanitized Frank James, brother to outlaw Jesse.

"This, I think, is a very interesting role for me. It's a departure," said Nimoy on set in a meadow outside Carson City. Sitting back in his chair, he wore a black cowboy hat over perfectly normal, round ears. Nonetheless, he looked much like his most famous screen character, bearing Mr. Spock's thin, high-cheeked elegance.

Bonanza and its movies extended their lives with venues on specialty networks and DVD. By the turn of the century, the old program experienced popular resurgence through Pax TV (later Ion) airings. In 2001, the network began a prequel series called *The Ponderosa*, featuring "the boys" when they really were boys. Producers again wanted Lake Tahoe locations, but their high season, mid-summer shooting made the process too expensive.

They caught low season in Australia instead, where an exchange rate of fifty-four cents on the dollar made their budget go farther. Filmed near Melbourne in Kattemingga, the set looked over rustic buildings and dirt streets backed by tall eucalyptus trees. Known locally as "gum trees," their leaves fluttered with pink parrots. Owner Nola Whitehouse joked about the dearth of ponderosas and pointed to six small pines.

"You should see the way they weave the riders in and out of those trees to make them look like a forest," she laughed.

Shoot low, and that mass of gum trees in the background disappears along with their colorful feathered occupants. Next point, steer clear of kangaroos as they hop by at dusk. It took minimal manipulation to resurrect the Cartwrights. But the first stars remain the favorites and survive in various DVD packages that show them in their original, full-color glory surrounded by the beauty of Lake Tahoe.

The Railroaders

The Cartwrights of *Bonanza* represent settlement, but historically, people moved right through Nevada on their way to the final Western frontier in California. That great Western director John Ford looks at the process with 1924's *The Iron Horse,* a silent film about the famous race between two railroads to link the nation's east and west points. Ford brought period trains to tracks running through undeveloped land only thirty miles outside Reno in Wadsworth. Ford's team built two towns from scratch, and the director experimented by moving his camera to take advantage of their stark isolation surrounded by vast landscapes.

Watching historic movies challenges those used to the chop-cut editing speed in Marvel action movies. *The Iron Horse* holds up better than most silent films, clearly presenting its story using outstanding visuals. With *The Iron Horse,* director Ford already showed signs of the genius that eventually earned him a record four Oscars. He pays attention to detail, intricately re-creating the moment when railroaders hammered a golden spike to join their competing lines. Coincidentally, a major nineties ad for mining company Freeport-McMoRan also ignored Utah's history by bringing the famous golden spike event to Nevada.

As part of the real-life trail of rails, Nevada's historic remnants lure projects needing trains. The Nevada Northern Railway, located near the state's eastern border in Ely, provided track plus an engine and cars for *Once Upon a Texas Train* in 1988. Starring Willie Nelson, it took on the name *Texas Guns* for DVD release.

Nevada's historic Virginia & Truckee Railroad brings Johnny Depp out West with Crispin Glover for 1995's *Dead Man.* The train's exteriors look spiffy as it heads through the V & T tunnel, hiding movie chicanery. With an extremely tight budget, the production company refurbished only the side shown on screen.

Other tricks emerge. Depp rides to "the end of the line" at a fictitious town symbolically called "Machine." He steps off at the Gold Hill, Nevada depot, but editing lets him walk down a street filmed in Arizona. Arriving at the end, Depp magically returns to Nevada and heads into Gold Hill's Crowne Point Mill.

This surreal interior with operational equipment clinched the deal for bringing *Dead Man* to Nevada. Discovering multiple sites where inoperable machines lay frozen in time, producers liked the turns, grinds, and crunches at Nevada's mill. In real life, the mill reduced rock ores to remove precious metals from the region's silver and gold mines, a history that fascinated producer Demetra J. MacBride.

"It's a spectacular place," she announced in production notes, adding the Comstock's history of miners, travelers, gunfighters, bawdy women, and ghosts seemed suited to her project.

The city's reputation for haunted locations encouraged Depp to spend a night at Mackay Mansion in the hope of interacting with phantoms.

"No," he responded sadly the next day when asked if he encountered any ghosts. Thin and pale, his jet-black hair hung lankly for the role. "I stayed up all night but never saw any ghosts."

Foregoing sleep put dark circles under Depp's eyes, but that looked ideal for his role as a fatally injured man forced to get out of town fast. On screen, Depp's every fiber exudes pain and exhaustion in what director Jim Jarmusch described as "a young man's journey, both physically and spiritually, into very unfamiliar terrain."

Riding up Geiger Grade to scout Virginia City, director Jarmusch said he always wanted to make a Western. A bushy-haired Ohio native who pokes fun at Cincinnati in his *Dead Man* script, Jarmusch likes such Western themes as retribution, redemption, and tragedy.

"Westerns have inseparable connection to 'America' in the broadest sense," he said, happy to spin into detailed cinematic analysis of genres and ideas.

A truly independent filmmaker working with an actor who exalts in testing limits, Jarmusch knew he might horrify *Dances with Wolves* fans by presenting a "Dreams with Peyote" sensibility. Despite weak box office results, *Dead Man* steadily builds enthusiasts who appreciate its mythic sense about a hallucinatory trip from the Old West to a world beyond.

The Singers

A more traditional Westerner than Johnny Depp, Roy Rogers found happy trails in Nevada. He started with a "modern" project, circa 1946, for *Heldorado,* a gentle renaming of the famous Helldorado Rodeo event in Las Vegas. Rogers played the Las Vegas sheriff, wearing a cowboy hat and riding his beloved horse Trigger in a curious segment involving the Hoover Dam before any major development. Hearing of a murder, Roy heads thirty-five miles out to the crime scene—on Trigger instead of a speedier car. This should upset taxpayers concerned about time management, but Roy makes it all work out in the end. The story resembles many Rogers' features, which often run only an hour. A mystery sets action rolling, with amusing help provided by sidekick Gabby Hayes, plus musical interludes from Rogers, Dale Evans, and the Sons of the Pioneers.

Heldorado's success encouraged Rogers to come back to Nevada in 1947 to ring *The Bells of St. Angelo*, available on video as part of the Happy Trails Theater. A special feature details difficulties in perfecting the film's new Trucolor system. Having the system turn a black dress green caused few problems, but viewers balked when a horse of a different color showed up. With problems eventually solved, the system brings out gorgeous hues at Red Rock Canyon and the Valley of Fire State Park.

"It really was beautiful up there," recalls Dale Evans, who plays the successful author of a Pulp Western series, much as Kathleen Turner did later when she showed up at Red Rock Canyon for the introductory scene in *Romancing the Stone*.

Evans married Rogers, an Ohio farm boy who worked in a shoe factory before becoming the King of the Cowboys. Like Nevada resident Wild Bill Elliott and other Western stars of the time, Rogers put rugged locations in his titles; he was just as likely to ride *Under California Stars* as *Under Nevada Skies* or spend *Night Time in Nevada*. People called him the Arizona Kid one year and the Carson City Kid the next. Rogers' musical roots in founding the Sons of the Pioneers eventually gave rise to the "Song of Nevada" in 1944.

The Gunfighters

Nevada hosted traditional Western icon Hopalong Cassidy in 1988's *Gunfighter*. The project's more celebrated name came from the movie's producer, Francis Ford Coppola. Coppola, owned rights to the Hopalong books, a popular series written in the early twentieth century by Clarence Mulford, and let his nephew Christopher write and direct under the working title *The Great Bar 20*. Chris found the right spread in Elko's Gund Ranch, plus set up building fronts on a dry lakebed around the Trinity Junction off Interstate 80. He kept costs low with family connections. Cousin Roman operated a camera borrowed from George Lucas, who used it on *American Graffiti*.

The younger Coppola gave himself a cameo as a Mexican bandito and aimed at making Westerns popular again.

"People want heroes," he said on set, his face covered in a scraggly beard as he prepared to shoot another scene on the dusty flats of Trinity Dry Lake.

Coppola saw a revitalized Western hero in rodeo champion Chris Lybbert, whose resemblance to Harrison Ford featured a friendly smile and light-colored hair but failed to include acting. Instead of hiring an outsider,

Coppola should have continued his nepotistic streak and hired his brother to act. But in those days, no one considered Nicolas (Coppola) Cage an action hero.

Nevada's Western link finally saw the screen's most iconic cowboy arrive in 1976 with John Wayne as a notorious gunfighter called *The Shootist*. The story's Carson City setting reflects a small town with a sense of history that remains in neighborhoods near the governor's mansion, where huge trees shade narrow streets. A "Nevada Celebrates Filmmaking" plaque commemorates the film at 500 Mountain Street, where a cardboard cutout of John Wayne stands in a window. The movie itself lives on, more appreciated now than when its nostalgic traditions hit theaters during the groundbreaking, genre-bending seventies.

Though perhaps "old hat" in the seventies, this Western icon generated excitement during his Nevada stay and no one ignored him. Wayne regularly filled copy in local papers, one employing giant pica letters for a headline declaring an inaccuracy:

"Last film? Bull!"

Like the shootist he played, Wayne had cancer. It killed him three years later without a chance to make another film.

Fading Sunsets

The West defied death for years, as director Sam Peckinpah explored in *The Ballad of Cable Hogue*. Highlighting isolation at the Valley of Fire State Park, an hour from Las Vegas, the title character hits the transition from horse to automobile. Left for dead by robbers, Hogue drags himself through hot desert sands until a natural spring saves him. He turns the land into an early rest stop for automobiles, biding his time and hoping for revenge on the men who robbed him. The story contains surprisingly sweet moments considering it comes from the man whose greatest contribution to the Western genre remains the still-shocking bloodbath in *The Wild Bunch*. Changing his tone for *The Ballad of Cable Hogue*, Peckinpah took a self-consciously humorous approach to the West, with hyped-up camera speed and split screens. Repeat viewings emphasize the lyrical sense of a ballad, which—given the title—matches Peckinpah's intentions.

The film also provides a flamboyant role for Jason Robards, plus strong work from Stella Stevens as a prostitute named Hildy. She almost turned the role down.

"I read the script, and Hildy disappears halfway through," Stevens recalled decades later at the Reno Film Festival, still looking trim and wearing a white cowboy hat. "I told Peckinpah, 'She has to come back.'"

The confrontational Peckinpah happily argued any point, but his storytelling instincts recognized how the movie works better with Hildy returning for its final scenes. As for the actual filming process, Stevens found it tough.

"It was really a man thing out there on the desert."

She paused, trying to come up with the best phrasing to explain why it seemed so macho.

"They were all out there peeing in the dust."

Finding a paying audience also proved difficult, despite Peckinpah's status as a critical darling after *The Wild Bunch*. Stevens said Peckinpah's temper and orneriness caused studio executives practically to bury the film. The world ignored *Cable Hogue* in its own time, but the passing of years brought it more attention.

"It really is a good film," Stevens said after watching the movie at a 2009 Reno Film Festival screening, joining her audience in wiping away tears.

Hogue's sense of the fading West returned in 2005 for *Don't Come Knocking* with Sam Shepard as a cowboy star frustrated by his life. Fleeing a Utah film set, he visits his hometown Elko, the perfect place to raise a real-life cowboy. Located on Nevada's eastern side off Interstate 80, Elko features many ranches and captures international fame for its annual winter Cowboy Poetry Festival, celebrating music and lyrics written about life on the range. The setting impressed Eva Marie Saint, the blonde in Alfred Hitchcock's seminal *North by Northwest* who earned her spurs with a television series called *How the West Was Won*. Known for cool elegance on screen, she seemed at home in Elko, where she played Shepard's mother. She walked casually through the local Hilton Garden Inn, when Nevada Film Office staff interrupted to thank her for working in the state.

Instead of just nodding vaguely and moving on quickly, the Oscar winner stopped and smiled warmly, happy to talk about her experience working in this rural community. She loved the food and staff at the hotel. She enthused over filming locations and Elko's rising sun.

"The sunrises here are just so magnificent," she said.

Ironically, her movie dealt with sunsets.

The sun sets in 1979's *The Electric Cowboy*, which also featured a Western actor fleeing his job. The big budget film from director Sidney Pollack stars Robert Redford as fading rodeo champ Sonny Steele, running from a world forcing him to wear a costume rimmed in glittering lights. Sonny feels like the ghost of himself, working in the New West amid the neon excess of Las Vegas. Sitting atop a prize horse in the glow of his own outfit, Sonny turns degradation into triumph as he steals the stallion and rides down the sparkling Las Vegas Strip to the purity of the unadulterated, wide-open desert. Eventually, he finds that despite industrial growth, the Old West survives in hidden corners. Take the time to look, and you find wide-open stretches in which to ride off into the setting sun. Or better yet, enjoy the magnificent rising sun.

Ben Johnson, Gentleman Cowboy

Always a gentleman, Ben Johnson warmly greeted me by name each time he came on set and once told me he enjoyed working on the original *Bonanza* show more than making the movie that earned him his Oscar. I gave him a puzzled look. Actors usually adore projects with Oscar-worthy roles.

Not Ben Johnson. He resisted doing *The Last Picture Show* because of its bad language, a definite contrast to *Bonanza*.

After his explanation for preferring *Bonanza* to *Last Picture Show*, I shot Johnson a second puzzled look. This man helped change the face of Westerns in *The Wild Bunch* with ultraviolent action where blood spurts out of him like a dishwashing nozzle. I said those three words: *The Wild Bunch*, then added my question.

"What about all that blood?" I asked.

"Well," he answered laconically, just the way a real cowboy should. "The West was a violent place and sometimes you had to use your gun."

He paused for effect.

"But you didn't have to swear about it."

16

Maverick and the Top Guns

The engine revs louder, the surrounding sights blur, a beat pumps harder, and the handsome young hero grins confidently as he races into the Danger Zone, a place that might easily be the skies of Nevada. Nevada offered that Danger Zone when *Top Gun* soared to box office heights in 1986, solidifying Tom Cruise as an action hero who found no mission impossible. He joined a vision that sells the Navy's Top Gun school as a place where teachers look hot, classes run short, and field trips zoom into adrenalin-laden flights where Cruise's *Maverick* character satisfies his iconic "need for speed."

The vision worked partly because of an effective blend of rising talent, who still had places to go and costumes to wear. An established headliner, Cruise rocketed upwards in the movie star constellation. Val Kilmer aimed toward *Batman* ears. Anthony Edwards awaited *E.R.* scrubs. Hot off *Witness*, Kelly McGillis sported high fashion glamour. Meanwhile, Meg Ryan spent her pre-stardom supporting scenes stealing attention from everyone else. Tim Robbins made an even briefer appearance without presaging his eventual Oscar win.

Good actors always help, and Tony Scott directed them skillfully after years honing his visual storytelling abilities by producing commercials with his brother Ridley. Most of all, *Top Gun* rocketed to box office heights through spectacular footage of fighter jets soaring, falling, zooming, and zipping in ways never before filmed. Producers lacked resources to run out and buy a fleet of planes at $30 million a pop, so they needed to make nice with the military by acquiescing to script and location stipulations. In accepting their lack of complete control, the *Top Gun* team created a production rarity, a lovefest between filmmakers and the military.

"The Navy was great," *Top Gun* line producer Bill Badalato said a few years later when he returned to Reno for the comedy *Mafia!* The military matched his enthusiasm.

"*Top Gun* was nearly the perfect project for us," noted Phil Strub on a panel for the Association of Film Commissioners International in Washington, DC.

Strub liked the project because the *Top Gun* team answered "yes" to the military's basic questions at the time:

Q. *"Would it benefit the military?"*

A. "Yes! How else could you afford a 110-minute ad starring Tom Cruise?"

Q. *"Could it help with recruiting?"*

A. "Yes! Glamour, excitement, and everything a hot-blooded eighteen-year-old wants shows up here." (The following year's records proved the point with a 16,000-person increase in Navy enlistments by one account, or a 500 percent increase, according to Wikipedia.)

Q. *"Is it in sync with present policy?"*

A. "Well. . . wait a minute. . . what is policy?" filmmakers probably asked.

The military came back with concerns about location, romance, and death. Producers responded cooperatively, with imaginary answers like "Sure, we'll change the opening setting. And, of course we can privatize the love interest. And, no problem changing the death scene. . . . and, what else. . . sure. . . . The answer is *yes*!"

That last question about ever-changing policy often stops projects. A couple of years after working on *Top Gun*, Badalato's assistant Patti Carr came back to Nevada as associate producer for *Steal the Sky* and once again hoped for military cooperation.

The military said "No."

Why? The script put Iraq in a bad light.

"Iraq is our friend," came the military's explanation, since no US troops fought there in 1988. Based on a real-life incident in Iraq, *Steal the Sky* needed to specify the country for plot points. Producers opted to use a private, nonmilitary facility near Reno and call it Iraq.

But the *Top Gun* producers had options. Though the Top Gun school exists, fictional and—more importantly—flexible characters fill the story. Some settings proved mutable. Writers set an opening altercation between Maverick and Soviet planes over Cuba, but the military deemed that too controversial. No big deal for the producers—they just switched out a title to make it read "Indian Ocean."

Next came an issue about a military instructor linking romantically with student Maverick. Not allowed. She transformed into a contractor who gets to wear much more attractive clothing than military uniforms.

Another instance featured a plane crash killing Maverick's friend. Military representatives felt the scene might remind viewers about an excess of recent crashes, so the character dies after ejecting from a plane.

But, when it came to the Naval weapons school known as Top Gun, producers wanted the real thing at San Diego's Miramar Air Force Base. They got it, but also found themselves passing off Nevada as training sites near Miramar. While naval activity in a state with no ocean borders seems strange, using Nevada's Fallon area made sense.

Playing off nearby Reno's famous arch, Fallon Naval Air Station calls itself "The Biggest Little Air Station in the Navy." Its 13,000 square miles of airspace make it the largest station in the Navy, the only facility big enough to train an entire wing group.

Everything needed for the *Top Gun* movie's generic training sequences came more easily in Fallon than San Diego. Fallon worked visually since most audiences see no difference between Northern Nevada desert and the ever-diminishing scrubland surrounding busy San Diego (alert viewers might spot Nevada-style white sand dunes whizzing by the brown hills and flat valleys that define the region's "basin and range" terrain). Overall, the desert looks appropriately expansive, a seemingly vast eternity of undeveloped land where planes buzz without bothering anything but a jackrabbit or coyote.

Built in 1942, the facility covers 84,000 acres of land, with bombing and warfare ranges within a two-minute jet's flight from takeoff. The station features the Navy's longest airstrip at 14,000 feet, the fifth longest in the nation and twenty-sixth longest in the world. Located about an hour's drive from Reno off Highway 50, Fallon offers quick access to city conveniences, yet remains far enough from major population centers where noise and other issues cause problems for residents.

As a result of its combination of accessibility and isolation, Fallon Naval Air Station met *Top Gun* movie needs in 1986. By 1996, it superseded Miramar and became the real-life home for the Naval Fighter Weapons School. This makes Fallon a certified contender when it comes to the long-fabled *Top Gun* sequel.

"We'd love to have *Top Gun* back," base public affairs officers kept telling the Nevada Film Office.

"We're working on it," Tom Cruise reported to *MTV Movie News* in December 2011. He and director Tony Scott scouted the airbase in 2012. A few days later, Scott died, yet again grounding *Top Gun 2*. In early 2016, producer Jerry Bruckheimer Tweeted a photo of himself with Tom Cruise, while both *Variety* and *Deadline Hollywood* headlined stories about a potential *Top Gun 2.*

In the meantime, the Top Gun school remains one of those locations defining Nevada's iconography, a place where action junkies satisfy their need for speed in vast territory that calls to mavericks.

Within the school itself, however, decades affected attitudes regarding *Top Gun.*

"We fine people $5 for saying that title," laughed Lt. Ross "Jackpot" Jackson, when asked about the movie during a tour.

He answered the question because it allowed him to address major fallacies the public developed by watching *Top Gun.*

Looking somewhat like a brother to Maverick's buddy Goose, Lt. Jackson stood lean and straight in an olive drab flight suit covering a black T-shirt. An instructor at Top Gun, he delayed answering immediately, pondering just which inaccuracy to highlight.

"The biggest misconception is that this is an environment for jerks and jocks," he finally answered.

Six years old when the movie was released, Lt. Jackson never worshiped *Top Gun*'s sunset-infused scenes of tough-looking pilots going it on their own and relaxing as they play volleyball shirtless with muscle-toned chests greased and shining.

"This isn't a place for hotshots," he continued. Instead, students face a rigid and time-consuming course program that precludes recess.

"Most of us have families. We don't have a lot of time to spare."

Lt. Jackson participated in a publicity program for visitors at the restricted facility. Security officers prevent drop-ins, but special events and organized tours occasionally mean the gates open for *Top Gun* fans longing to revive movie magic. An airpark with more than a dozen fighter planes features the sleek and shark-like MiG-21 Fishbed, the F-8 Crusader, and the type of F-14 Tomcat used in the *Top Gun* movie.

The tour includes a trip up a tower, allowing an eagle's view of the airfield's record-breaking long strip backed by the Stillwater Mountains in shades of shadowy browns, blues, and grays. Since Fallon has more than 60,000 takeoffs and landings a year, visitors usually see jet action, though it takes a quick eye in many instances since the planes become tiny specks of black in just seconds.

From the tower, the single-story round Top Gun school looks like a modern, but ordinary, educational facility. Nine-week programs run every quarter and visitors only go inside if classes aren't in session. The airy, ivory-colored walls curve around, brightened by windows near the top of a high ceiling. Photos and placards honor various classes, but none resemble the trophy that Tom Cruise and Val Kilmer fight for in the movie. Another of the movie's misconceptions, the trophy came from a screenwriter's ploy to create dramatic tension.

The school's "restricted area" status means no photography is allowed. Visitors commemorate their trip by a pop into a tiny gift shop offering Top Gun school hats, shirts, patches, and mugs. People whisper "in the movie. . ." often enough to make the facetious prohibition against mentioning the film a promising revenue source.

Nevada's real-life role in the Top Gun program meant some early location scouts in Fallon during one phase of the sequel's preproduction. But a site's location never guarantees filming there, as two projects about an evolving type of pilot show. Both 2014's *Good Kill* and 2016's *Eye in the Sky* include a Nevada setting for the people who steer "remotely piloted aircraft," or drones. The link makes sense since Creech Air Force Base lays forty-five minutes north of Las Vegas in Indian Springs and specializes in overseas contingency operations with drones.

Lacking US Department of Defense script approval, *Good Kill* leaves out a specific reference to Creech and re-creates its base on generic desert land. But the movie also shows the Las Vegas skyline and homes near enough for drone pilots to return to after their twelve-hour shifts. Unlike the original *Top Gun* kerosene cowboys who need flashy equipment and dramatic airspace, drone pilots work in windowless bunkers and watch action on screen, transmitted thousands of miles from the aircraft they operate. They miss the need-for-speed thrills but see close-ups of the aftermath of their efforts—mangled bodies (Brandon Bryant, a real-life Creech pilot who provided input on an early draft of the script, told *Newsweek* the military linked him to 1,626 kills). Rather than softening the horrific impact through desensitization, distance provides its own psychological blowback, which *Good Kill* explores by asking questions and taking a thoughtful look at the problem.

Eye in the Sky also asks questions, though with more emphasis on the referring-up process about who deserves responsibility for a drone's civilian victims. Aaron Paul and Phoebe Fox play Creech pilots who delay bombing when they spot a little girl near a targeted site in Kenya. Though low on the food chain, the two newcomers ask a colonel played by Helen Mirren to reconsider her order—a move that seems more in line with dramatic license than military training. While action spans several locations across the globe, writer-director Gavin Hood filmed the entire project in South Africa. Nearby desert, an interior bunker, and a few dull-colored boxy buildings with a sign that reads "Creech" proved more cost effective (but perhaps less fun) than a trip to Las Vegas.

Those Vegas-area military facilities proved unnecessary for other projects, including the 1986 jet fighter movie, *Iron Eagle*. Originally set for a summer release, distributors pushed the movie into theaters early to avoid confusion with *Top Gun*. Earning about $25 million compared to more than $175 million for *Top Gun*, *Iron Eagle* producers failed to get a military "thumbs up" at Nellis Air Force Base for their project, even though star Jason Gedrick looked like a recruitment model. He and his high school buddies hack into the Air Force computer system to fly jets off base on an unauthorized rescue mission overseas, a definite "No" for the military's third question, "Is it in sync with present policy?" Past, present, and future—no policy permits stealing multimillion-dollar jets. Despite big grimaces from military leadership, *Iron Eagle* earned an official Nevada connection by shooting breathtaking flying scenes of a Cessna through the Valley of Fire's rock spires.

The belief that flyboys might hang out in Nevada continued when *Top Gun*'s Bill Badalato cashed in on his air movie credentials with a 1991 spoof called *Hot Shots!*. The connection plays into a gag about a nearly blind pilot who accidentally lands near the Dunes in Las Vegas. Given the nature of his spoof, Badalato knew the military would never approve the project and didn't bother asking.

But the military's inability to take a joke surprised British director Jonathan Lynn regarding a location hunt for his 1996 movie version of *Sergeant Bilko*.

"It makes no sense," Lynn said when discussing the military's disapproval.

"It's just harmless fun," he insisted.

His ire came while scouting a completely different project months after he finished *Bilko*. Time passed, but he still bristled.

Part of Lynn's harmless fun let the sergeant escape his military base to go on "desert maneuvers"—at Las Vegas casinos.

"We don't approve of the gambling and other activities the sergeant engages in," the military's Phil Strub later explained.

In contrast, Vegas venues loved hosting Steve Martin as the irascible sergeant made famous by Phil Silvers in a fifties television series.

Director Lynn warmly praised the Mirage and Las Vegas but used end credits to lash out one last time.

"The filmmakers gratefully acknowledge the total lack of cooperation from the United States Army," reads one line.

Lynn, like *Steal the Sky* producers, used a private facility. *Steal the*

Sky found its home at Nevada's Stead Airport north of Reno. The private Stead facility's starkness from its former days under military jurisdiction increased its official look with a National Guard operation next door. An added bonus came from the Classics in Aviation business at Stead, one of the few in the nation with a real MiG for characters to fly.

Set entirely overseas in Italy, Israel, and Iraq, *Steal the Sky* effectively combines scenes shot in the Middle East with those from Northern Nevada.

"Reno looks very much like a lot of parts of Israel and Iraq," said producer Yoram Ben Ami, a former Israeli soldier. "And it's funny, except for the elevation, Reno itself is very much like the Middle East."

He let the Pyramid Lake region match a Kurdish camp setting, with nearby water pretending to be the Red Sea.

"Actually," Ben Ami said after filming finished, "It would have been easier to shoot the whole project in Nevada."

He liked the state's cooperation, plus found it safer than working in his Israeli homeland. Meanwhile, star Mariel Hemingway enjoyed all her on-site work, including the Middle Eastern hotspots.

"Obviously, people would wonder if Israel is a frightening place to be," she said on set at Stead. "I didn't find it frightening at the time. I think it's a very volatile place to be right now, and it's getting worse every day, but I didn't feel any danger in being there because we were very well protected."

As for Reno, she noted that casinos felt like the Danger Zone.

"My husband lost a hundred dollars last night. In like four minutes, he lost this money."

Scary, but action heroes know Nevada's real Danger Zone brews way beyond the gaming tables. It thrives up in the skies and out in the wide-open spaces of a state whose reputation for going off the beaten path makes it a perfect home for mavericks of all kinds.

17

James Bond and the Spies

When famous movie spies list their job requirements, they specify the need to work in glamorous locations featuring international allure, buxom beauties, powerful criminals, and an endless supply of martinis, shaken, not stirred. Vegas, baby, Vegas, proves the perfect home for a superspy sporting the middle name "Danger." Powers, Austin Powers, gets shaken and stirred by teaming up with Vegas. But wait a minute, what about Bond, James Bond?

Places, preferably exotic ones with hints of risqué danger, play an important role in the Bond franchise: Havana, Venice, Jamaica, Colon, Sardinia, the French Riviera, and finally, in 1971, Las Vegas.

Yet combining the Best Bond Ever, Sean Connery, and Las Vegas failed to mix in perfect martini style.

Diamonds Are Forever ranks as Sean Connery's weakest Bond incarnation. It barely misses status as Bond's worst screen presence. After five decades of Bond, *Quantum of Solace* got the slam-dunk low end of twenty-four official films in a 2012 article by Peter Travers of *Rolling Stone* (*Diamonds* rated number eighteen, also not much to brag about). Meanwhile, insightful critics at *Indiewire* played off the successful title *Skyfall* in an article about bad Bond movies called "Skyfail." *Diamonds* rusted down in the bottom five.

The film critic at Reno's National Public Radio affiliate feels the same way.

"I often prefer cheering the underdog, but it only takes a few *Diamonds* clips for me to feel like Wile E. Coyote grinding heels into the ground and churning up dust before running smack into a cliff's wall."

That's me talking, exercising my three-decades-plus experience analyzing films for a weekly broadcast.

This bruised, banged-up Bond frustration goes back to the original 1971 release of *Diamonds Are Forever*, when millions of fans longed to see

Sean Connery back in the role that made him a star. He previously broke from Bondage, allowing George Lazenby to slip in for what some regard as a top franchise entry, *On Her Majesty's Secret Service.*

"It would have been better with Connery," most thought at the time, believing the actor's return guaranteed success. Massive publicity announced that Connery broke records by negotiating a $1.25 million salary, a stunning figure in the days when psychics never predicted $30 million for a star (though with inflation, Connery probably earned the equivalent in 1971).

Connery took the money on principal, putting much of it toward establishing a Scottish film fund helping locals (like him) work in their homeland. Connery wanted respect. Back then, money got more respect than Bond, an attitude that changed as ever-increasing entries evolved into one of the most successful and durable film franchises of all time.

Connery also wanted challenges. Bond no longer grabbed Connery's passion, as his flabby presence and performance indicate.

"He's fat," many said then—though viewed with hindsight, he looks pretty slim. Still, by Bond standards, Connery lets everything slip, from his taut abs to a dark toupee and enthusiasm about the project.

Yet with superstar magnetism, "Sexiest Man Alive" panache, and Oscar-quality acting skills, even a bored Sean Connery offers watchable moments. And, quick to attach itself to anything with the fame and glamour of James Bond, Las Vegas happily claims credit as film location. A 2012 *Nevada Magazine* article rated *Diamonds Are Forever* one of the top ten movies made in the state, which may be a pro-city blindness resembling a mother porcupine describing her baby as soft and cuddly. The bragging slows when you consider major problems in *Diamonds Are Forever.*

- A vapid villain—Ernst Blofeld, the series' most frequent bad guy, usually menaces with his bald head, scarred features, and nasty habits like killing Bond's favorite wife. All that seems forgotten in *Diamonds,* where Charles Gray plays him with jutting jaw and mouth clamped on an elegant cigarette holder, much in the manner of real-life power monger Franklin Delano Roosevelt.
- A Bond bimbo—Bond girls work best when they combine beauty with smarts, like Diana Rigg in *On Her Majesty's Secret Service.* With *Diamonds,* Jill St. John looks great in a bikini but opens her mouth and sounds more like Betty Boop than the slick jewel thief she portrays.
- Cartoonish chicks—Bambi and Thumper use Olympic-quality gymnast moves to attack Bond with visual style. It looks so good they

stop, seemingly to admire one another. In that time, even Bugs Bunny could nail them.

- A ridiculous ride—Bond traditionally escapes in an exciting and flashy vehicle, like a bobsled or helicopter, tank, speedboat, or even a space shuttle in *Moonraker.* But with *Diamonds,* Bond crashes a space exploration center in the desert and rides away in an awkward moon buggy, whose bouncing red ball and sluggish pace look like a toy. The childish element continues when Bond leaps from the buggy and jumps on a tiny dirt bike that forces the tall man's knees up at an angle resembling a kid who outgrew his tricycle. Spotting Bond on the scene, a scientist asks, "What is this, amateur night?" It certainly looks it.
- A crazy chase—Bond movies celebrate exciting, fast, mind-blowing chases highlighted by speed, destruction, and inventiveness. Think an ice race on an Austrian lake in *Die Another Day.* Or a tank demolishing everything in sight around St. Petersburg in *Goldeneye.* Or a Lotus Esprit turning into a submarine for an underwater race in *The Spy Who Loved Me. Diamonds* puts a Ford in a parking lot. It starts with the moon buggy and dirt bike. Jumping off his three-wheeler when he spots the Bond bimbo waiting for him in the middle of the desert (don't ask), Bond leaps into a red Ford (okay, a cool-looking Mustang Cobra) and drives to downtown Las Vegas, where the chase finishes with a moment rating as one of the biggest bloopers in action film history. Forced into an alley too narrow for any street vehicle, Bond tells his bimbo to lean over, enabling him to tip the car on its right wheels and drive on through the tiny space. That's not the outlandish part. The car emerges on two left wheels. Everyone on set failed to notice the mistake when it happened. Rather than spend more money doing it again, producers settled for a cheap insert shot of the car appearing to drop into a normal position. However, this fails to explain how (or why) the car shifts to the other side in such a tiny space. Decades later, another agent with the initials J.B.—Jason Bourne—totally showed up Bond with a chase that completely shut down the Strip for two nights.

And finally:

- Las Vegas—Ouch. Back in 1971, Las Vegas lacked Bond proportions. Director Guy Hamilton worked hard to make the few blocks of Fremont Street look massive enough for a daring chase, but he

> ended up with half the action consolidated in a parking lot, where cops drive like customers in amusement park bumper cars that purposely crash into one another. Granted, 1971 Vegas lacked the huge-scale neon Strip that superspy Jason Bourne closed for his fifth film and a massive chase in January 2016. Bond's Strip, shown in aerial shots, features vacant lots and desert. The International stands out as the biggest structure, known today as the Westgate and dwarfed by nearby buildings. Nothing near the size and elegance of the Aria existed, so *Diamond*'s gaming scenes shot at the Riviera, a place better known for Pia Zadora movies.

By the time *Diamonds Are Forever* ends, Bond scuttles up the joke ladder. After all, the movie showcases a bored middle-aged hero fighting a beloved US president plus two Disney characters. Our hero makes his way on a tricycle; he races through a parking lot; he goes to extravagant locations like Circus Circus. At least he doesn't emerge from the casino carrying a fluffy, pink stuffed toy.

Watching *Diamonds Are Forever* makes any true Bond aficionado cringe with embarrassment. It puts average viewers to sleep. But one man found a way to make *Diamonds* pay off.

"I've always wanted to play a swinging character who wears sideburns and skin-tight, crushed velvet bell-bottoms," said Mike Myers, explaining his motives behind making *Austin Powers: International Man of Mystery*.

Keeping with that sixties theme, he also wanted to spoof one of its icons, James Bond. By the time Myers developed his screenplay in 1997, twenty Bond movies offered him scenes to spoof. Yet one film served as a major blueprint: *Diamonds Are Forever*.

Already able to pass as self-parody, *Diamonds* provided the basis for chases that looked like jokes. It role-modeled laughable bad guys and girls. Its bad guy had a pussy and a gray suit. And compared to other worldwide hotspots, *Diamonds* featured an affordable Las Vegas location. It suited a low-budget lampoon where a sixties secret agent named Austin Powers and his nemesis Dr. Evil emerge from a time warp to find themselves in the nineties.

Since the *Diamonds* plot never mattered much, Myers wrote broad strokes, sending his bad guy to a Nevada desert missile base similar to Blofeld's Silver State base.

"Here's the plan," says Dr. Evil in his Nevada lair, petting his white pussy as he addresses henchmen, including Jill St. John's husband, Robert Wagner.

"We get the warhead and we hold the world ransom for . . . *one million dollars.*"

It resembles Connery's salary for *Diamonds Are Forever.*

Times obviously changed in thirty years, and Myers makes the most of culture shock as Powers and Dr. Evil repeatedly underestimate the new world they live in.

Austin finds remnants of the past when he romances his new love interest by riding down the Strip in a red British double-decker bus, complete with a serenading Burt Bacharach. Bacharach's Bond connection goes back to writing Herb Alpert's trumpet opening theme for the 1967 version of *Casino Royale.* Mostly though, Powers redefines the fish-out-of-water metaphor to one in paisley bell-bottom pants at a white tie affair. The humor inspired two follow-up films.

Neither Powers nor Bond represent the first or last of their kind in Nevada movies. Nor did Bond corner the market on diamond dealing in the state. Credit for first mixing spies and diamonds goes to James Garner in 1968's *The Pink Jungle* when he repeatedly denies any connection with the CIA. Garner lands in South America on a fashion shoot for a new, non-melting lipstick called Pink Jungle, but gets sidetracked by a treasure hunt for raw diamonds in the nearby desert. Rather than travel out of the country, producers decided the tufa rocks and swirling sands of Northern Nevada's Pyramid Lake look like exotic South American locales.

Agents continued spy adventures in Nevada with *Return of the Man from U.N.C.L.E.* in 1983. Inspired by a sixties television series, which in turn used James Bond as its springboard, the television movie brings back Robert Vaughn as the title character.

"Solo," he introduces himself, tongue firmly in cheek as he gambles at Caesars Palace in Las Vegas. "Napoleon Solo."

Bad bets ruin his retirement plans, and he re-enters U.N.C.L.E.'s superspy payroll with partner Illya Kuryakin, a trim David McCallum, who later played "Ducky" in *NCIS.*

Predating Mike Myers and Austin Powers, the *U.N.C.L.E.* team jokes around with sixties espionage shows. Patrick Macnee, the spy Mr. Steed in the *Avengers* television series, plays *U.N.C.L.E.*'s new leader. Later, a specially equipped Aston Martin DV5 with the license plate "JB" whizzes in to help Solo out of a mess. George Lazenby, the Bond Connery replaced after *On Her Majesty's Secret Service,* drives the car.

Other Bonds find business in Las Vegas, as Daffy Duck and Bugs Bunny discover during *Looney Tunes: Back in Action.* Heroes seek to thwart a dastardly plan to turn all humans into monkeys in this comedy mixing animation with live action. The animals get key information from Timothy

Dalton, the serious Shakespearian actor who always made playing James Bond look like it involved a severe case of constipation. Yet in Las Vegas, he smiles and has fun handling spy stuff with a talking rabbit and sputtering duck. Too bad he never applied the same ease to his Bondage.

Dalton proves one point with *Looney Tunes*: Bond and Las Vegas can work together comfortably. That other J.B. spy, Jason Bourne, proved it in 2016, finding huge cooperation from city officials and casino managements.

"This production had access and ability to close down a large portion of a casino floor at Aria and even shut down the strip for a couple of nights, which you can imagine is no easy task!" recalled Ed Harran, assistant director of the Nevada Film Office.

Bourne also took advantage of the empty Riviera casino.

"They used a SWAT car to crash into the Riviera, which they dressed as a fully functional casino with all the machines, signage, and, I believe, 1,200 extras," continued Harran, adding the project ranks as one of Nevada's biggest in terms of total budget.

So, if Bourne did it, why not Bond? James Bond and Las Vegas should write off *Diamonds Are Forever* as a bad "starter marriage" that deserves better. Bond arrived when Vegas acted like a gawky teenager with a taste for Bud Light. The ugly duckling transformed into the world's largest strip of giant casinos and diamond-sparkling lights, emerging as a slick, sleek swan who prefers a martini, shaken, not stirred. Bond and Las Vegas are made for each other.

18

Rain Man and the Road Trippers

Need to find yourself? Make a quick buck? Get some nookie? All that and more happens on road trips down Nevada highways.

Among road trippers, *Rain Man* rides high, learning lessons and making money during a Las Vegas stop. Besides being one of Nevada's most honored movies with Oscars for best film, director, screenplay, and acting, *Rain Man* follows classic Road Picture requirements.

Three basic road rules define the genre:

1. Oddly paired partners
2. Scenic routes
3. Distinctive vehicles

After all, who wants to spend two hours watching Mr. and Mrs. Blah nod off on a gray straightway in their dirty white Kia?

Far better to focus on handsome young Tom Cruise joining Dustin Hoffman in top acting form. They look dynamite as their pale yellow '49 Buick whisks by. They stand out in the glittery midst of Nevada State Route 604, better known as Las Vegas Boulevard, definitely not a fast, efficient road for getting to their California destination.

The plan for a quick trip from Ohio to California falls apart for Tom Cruise as Charlie Babbitt.

Charlie's vague memories of someone in his past called Rain Man take solid form when he discovers his older brother Raymond at a mental institution. Worse yet for arrogant and chronically broke Charlie, he learns his father left a $3 million trust to Raymond, an autistic savant.

Hoping to get that money, Charlie kidnaps Rain Man in Ohio and heads west, little foreseeing how many "are we there yet?" moments occur when your traveling companion babbles incessantly.

Raymond quotes plane crash statistics and refuses to fly west, putting the two in their father's old Buick. Raymond annoys Charlie by obsessing about underwear from Kmart. And Raymond counts toothpicks.

"How many toothpicks are in that box?" Charlie asks during an "aha!" moment at a small desert diner (set in Arizona but filmed in Pahrump, Nevada).

Irritation changes to insight as Charlie's features light up and he asks a key question. If Rain Man easily counts hundreds of toothpicks, what about cards in a Las Vegas casino?

A series of quick shots establishes the setup as Charlie and Rain Man race through striking desert scenery and pass the famous diamond-shaped "Welcome to Fabulous Las Vegas" sign.

They find a pawnshop where Charlie bankrolls his gold watch. Classical Roman statues of Caesars Palace look on while mismatched partners rush into the resort's luxurious shopping area where designer suits line racks of hangers.

The two ride down escalators as director Barry Levinson aims his camera on their well-shod feet and rises upwards, revealing the dynamic duo in similar pale gray suits and bright white shirts.

"Rain Man," says Charlie as they hit the casino floor. "Let's play some cards."

Charlie panics when Rain Man takes a queen on his eighteen. Casinos, he knows, call the game twenty-one, not twenty-eight.

"That was my queen," grumbles Charlie, looking at his six and four.

Rain Man shrugs.

"There are lots of queens."

Rain Man nails it, baffling casino security and thrilling onlookers by knowing every card in a six-deck shuffle.

The two win $85,000 and cement themselves as the envy of blackjack players across the world.

A classic road picture, *Rain Man* travels through seven states. Most viewers recall a couple of them, but everyone remembers Nevada.

It makes sense. As official names like The Loneliest Highway in America and The Extra-Terrestrial Highway indicate, Nevada steps in as road picture heaven, with asphalt ribbons covering thousands of miles in dramatic landscapes making infinity feel real. Nevada's roads promise change, taking drivers to new places mentally and physically.

That allure means that many travelers, besides Charlie and his brother Rain Man, follow road rules.

The one about mismatched partners? Try Robert De Niro and Charles Grodin in 1988's *Midnight Run*, capitalizing on a *Rain Man* link. Martin Brest, like Steven Spielberg and Sidney Pollack, signed on to direct *Rain Man* before Barry Levinson took over. Rather than waste everything he learned during *Rain Man* scouts, Brest shifted his locations to *Midnight Run*, where two bickering men travel from New York to Los Angeles. The duo stops in Southern Nevada's Lake Mead and at the now-defunct Aladdin Casino in Las Vegas. Locations add sparkle to the film, but its highlight remains rapport between Grodin and De Niro, the first time audiences discovered the raging bull laughs.

Road Rule number two and distinctive vehicles? *Vanishing Point* pushes that button in 1971 when Barry Newman races away from pursuers in a classic Dodge Challenger R/T with a 430/375 horsepower engine. The movie plays up isolated Nevada in Austin and Goldfield, with Cleavon Little as a disc jockey at radio station KOW. The film's cult ranking solidified decades later in 2007 when director Quentin Tarantino used the same model car in *Death Proof*.

Another cult favorite, 1992's *Roadside Prophets*, features noted lawbreakers David Carradine, Arlo Guthrie, and Timothy Leary in a project carefully following all road rules.

The story features two strangers as mismatched partners, riding classic motorcycles on obscure Nevada highways and hunting for a mysterious "Eldorado." Amiable, though self-consciously existential, *Roadside Prophets* celebrates the highway's freedom and its strong spirited, "I'll do it my way" sagebrush rebels.

Focusing on the *E* and *l* in their "Eldorado" goal, the mismatched prophet hunters check out Ely and Elko, throwing in McGill for good measure. They also find Jackpot, featuring Cactus Pete's Casino and a John Cusack cameo. Director Abbe Wool gives audiences an extensive look at rural Nevada, all on vintage motorcycles using narrow state routes. She spotlights Nevada's hidden beauty in sequences at the Valley of Fire, a dramatic canyon composed of striking red sandstone hills, and cliffs pictured on the film's original poster art.

Other druggies obeying road rules include Cheech and Chong in 1982's *Things Are Tough All Over*. Promoted with the tagline, "The original high rollers hit the Strip," the mismatched partners ingest massive amounts of peyote while driving a limo on desert highways leading to Las Vegas. Stranded on a desolate road, they intend to flag down another car but get sidetracked singing their trademark out-of-sync lyrics. They eventually find the seventies epitome of a Vegas ride when comedian Rip Taylor picks them up and practices his casino stage show on them. He hauls out props such as a giant aspirin he claims belongs to porn star Linda Lovelace. Tears stream down Chong's face.

"Stop! Don't encourage him!" shouts a horrified Cheech, thinking his partner is crying tears of laughter.

But the shaking squalls come from agony at hearing such bad jokes, a staple of Taylor's popular Nevada showroom engagements.

Cheech and Chong belong to the era Hunter S. Thompson wrote about in his *Rolling Stone* magazine "Fear and Loathing" series. Both the 1972 presidential election and Elko, Nevada inspired panic and repugnance in Thompson's writings, but Las Vegas warranted the writer's most beloved terror and hatred in a story featuring classic road picture elements. Two decades after its best-selling book incarnation, *Fear and Loathing in Las Vegas* put the dazed and confused Johnny Depp and Benicio Del Toro on a scenic highway to Nevada in a cherry-red convertible. The film's theatrical release came too late to exploit pro-drug bizarreness popular in the seventies, but a cult following grew in the afterlife of streaming and rentals, warranting a two-disc DVD release in 2003. Special features include director Terry Gilliam's audio commentary explaining why the film meets road picture qualifications.

"You've almost got to let yourself go and forget about narrative, forget about normal storytelling," he advises.

"Take the ride."

One winner follows this advice in 2005's Darwin Awards.

"The award is given annually to the person who has caused the most catastrophe and passed away in perhaps the stupidest way," explained writer/director Finn Taylor on set in Reno.

"So it's people who could essentially be helping the gene pool by removing themselves from it."

Millions already knew about the awards; outrageous Darwin Award tales thrive virally on the web, even after experts disproved many, labeling them urban legends.

Taylor frames his premise around two stuffy insurance investigators on a road trip exploring sites of strange claims, including a famous one about a Chevy Impala loaded with a jet-assisted takeoff (JATO) rocket system.

Taylor hoped to replicate the incident on a Nevada highway featuring desert scenery within a reasonable distance of his San Francisco base. However, he scheduled the stunt for January in a region where expert weather forecasters display their own Darwin Awards collection of failed prognosticating. A snowstorm ruined the warm, desert ambiance on Pyramid Highway, where Taylor planned to film the scene. Taylor punted and used snow-sprinkled highway for shots of stars Joseph Fiennes and

Winona Ryder driving frigid northeastern roads. The rocket scene followed sun in Southern California.

Besides including Pyramid Highway, Taylor filmed at Twin Cities Surplus in Reno, a perfect road stop for his Darwin recipient to buy a rocket. Taylor loved the location.

"From a filmmaker's point of view, it is totally untapped beauty," he told a group visiting the set.

"You couldn't have asked for better production design than this," he said, waving his arm around the shop jammed with boots, camo wardrobes, and motorized equipment.

"It just had the feel of a kind of magical, mystical place."

For *Mythbusters* (Discovery Channel) stars Adam Savage and Jamie Hyneman, a store full of gadgets seemed a natural setting to play salesmen.

The two participated because they reenacted the JATO myth in their program's first episode, "Jet-Assisted Chevy/Pop Rocks and Soda."

"It's my personal favorite because it was just so darn much fun to do," said Hyneman, sporting his usual droopy mustache and wearing camouflage military fatigues instead of his trademark beret.

"I need a grinectomy," said a smiling Savage while staging the event in 2003.

Strong believers in survival of the fittest, the Mythbusters protected themselves by using remote control on a car that reached 3,000 horsepower for twelve seconds, rising over a dry lakebed.

In contrast, the Darwin recipient reportedly got in his car and drove it down a road.

"Most of the driver's remains were not recovered; however, small fragments of bone, teeth, and hair were extracted from the crater, and fingernail and bone shards were removed from a piece of debris believed to be a portion of the steering wheel," reports the official website, darwinawards.com.

However, the Mythbusters lived up to their name and proved the incident impossible.

Even so, David Arquette played the driver as if he really took off in that car, reaching into his acting skills to understand motivation.

"He just feels like his life's not meaningless, but he hasn't done anything profound with it," said Arquette, bearing a slacker look with his lanky dark hair, a scruffy beard, and a sloppy military jacket.

"He gets this idea," explained Arquette.

"He wants to make a mark. He wants to sort of have his life stand for something, so he does this wild act of attaching a rocket to the top of his car and tries to beat the land speed record," Arquette continued. "I get that."

The driver's search for meaning ends on the road.

A search bore different meaning for Jimmy Stewart in *The Magic of Lassie* after the famous dog disappears from Sonoma County, California. Tracking Lassie east, Stewart takes a break from his hunt by stopping at a coffee shop at Boomtown in Verdi, a few miles from the Nevada border.

Serving his meal in her role as a waitress, musical star Alice Faye came out of retirement and sang "When You're Loved" during the Boomtown scene. Richard Sherman and Robert Sherman wrote the song and arrived on set in Nevada to see their new work performed. Few composers travel with films, but the Sherman Brothers earned clout composing the *Mary Poppins* soundtrack, winning an Oscar for Best Song for "Chim Chim Cher-ee." They proved as perky and chipper as their music.

"The overtone is that no one can really own a person, no one can really own an animal or any living thing," Richard said, cheerfully talking about his newest work.

Dogs and music promised a happy project according to producer Bonita Granville Wrather.

"The public needs something like an entertaining Lassie film," she said, likening her project to the then-popular Benji dog series.

"People just adore it. It's entertaining, and it's good and clean. That's basically what we believe in."

The movie bombed, but the Boomtown road stop generated one success. "When You're Loved" earned yet another best song Oscar nomination for the Sherman brothers, a duo just as nice as shown in the Emma Thompson/Tom Hanks film about making *Mary Poppins, Saving Mr. Banks.*

Road stops often provide movie highlights. *The Doctor* found one in Nevada.

"Trees." "Mountains." "A great vista."

Producers asked the Film Office to find all those for the doctor and his friend to see at Lake Tahoe, so location manager Janice Polley took a state-sponsored ride around the seventy-two-mile body of water.

Tahoe gleamed and proclaimed itself the most striking alpine lake in the continental United States.

Janice acknowledged Tahoe's magnificence, but questioned whether it met *The Doctor*'s stark, dramatic needs.

With no time to travel anywhere else, she settled for some file folders filled with photos of nearby Pyramid Lake.

"I must confess, I took one look at the pictures," recalls cinematographer John Seale, "and I just said, 'That's it, that's gotta be it, that's exactly what we're after.'"

Janice returned to Reno the next morning and spent the day exploring the inland desert lake, whose turquoise blue spreads in startling contrast to the surrounding desert flats and odd volcanic rock formations called tufa. No doubt: Pyramid looked perfect. The doctor was in—Nevada.

The new location meant a couple of script changes, resulting in a phone call from another location manager, Lori Balton.

"So, we need the doctor to explain where he's going," she said. "How do you get to Pyramid?"

Easy question.

"You head out of Reno on I-80 toward Winnemucca," came the instant Film Office response.

"Winnemucca?!" she cried. "What's a Winnemucca? How do you spell it?"

The funny-sounding-name conversation made an impression since the movie features a similar routine from "Doctor" William Hurt in a phone booth.

He gets directions, but rather than drive all the way to Winnemucca, the doctor and his friend stop in an idyllic spot for a sunset dance. Though the location seems right off the interstate, getting there requires leaving I-80 in Wadsworth and catching State Route 447 to Pyramid before taking a dirt road to the lake. But accuracy rarely matters in movies. More importantly, Pyramid looks good on screen.

The location entranced everyone on set and their fascination followed up in the project's production packet where director Randa Haines notes how, before arriving at Pyramid, the doctor stays in safe, controlled, vertical environments.

"The desert is the visual opposite of his life. I wanted the place to be spacious and open, horizontal, beautiful and frightening, at the same time."

Cinematographer John Seale expressed similar thoughts when he returned to the area to pick up second unit shots on State Route 447.

"Pyramid looks gorgeous in the picture. And it's exactly what the film needed, this beautiful sunset on the edge of the lake in the desert. In the various previews, it's been always the best scene."

Seale, an Oscar winner for *The English Patient*, loved shooting in orange "magic hour" lighting.

"Of course, that's a gorgeous time at any time in the desert. But Pyramid Lake is special. That water, and that little island in the middle . . . using that as a backdrop, you couldn't lose, really."

Similarly, you couldn't go wrong with Gerlach as an ideal stop on a road trip *Far from Home*, (1989), though the tiny town missed the first round of scouting because producers wanted a location no more than an hour from Reno and an airport. As a result, the film's location manager,

Alicia Alexander, joined the Nevada Film Office for a scout of small towns near Reno. She covered Dayton, Hazen, Virginia City, Silver City, all kinds of dusty little places off the beaten track but close to Reno.

After seeing Wadsworth, the scouting team headed north on the Pyramid Highway to appreciate the road's emptiness, stopping at a spot just past the lake where highway reaches straight out, grabbing the horizon and disappearing into the sky.

Staring into the distance as a bright cerulean sky contrasted against the desert's sandy yellows and tans, she went no further because the nearest town—Gerlach—lay another hour away.

This predated Burning Man's annual celebration that turned Gerlach into a world-famous last bastion of civilization for 50,000 revelers setting up camp in Black Rock Desert. Few outsiders ever heard of Gerlach or knew what it looked like back then.

More importantly, Gerlach broke the project's time boundaries at well over two hours from the Reno Airport. Alicia considered her Nevada scout complete and left for Utah.

It seemed Nevada lost the project. But Alicia called a few days later, noting several things happened.

"We scouted all day in Utah and stopped for a drink afterwards, but they wouldn't serve us any beer," she observed about the Mormon-run state.

"And we didn't really see the right kind of town," she added. And then came the kicker.

"When I describe the location, people tell me about Gerlach," she said.

Often, film commissioners win projects by urging moviemakers to overcome their hesitations.

Other times, telling them they can't do something makes them want to show they can. This proved one of those times.

"What about the Reno Airport being so far away?" came a Film Office question.

"We can hire a small plane and use the airstrip in Gerlach," Alicia responded.

"There's only one motel. That's motel with an *m*, not *h*. And it only has forty rooms."

"That's okay," she said. "A lot of our people have their own RV's. We'll use those."

"There's no warehouse to build sets or handle props."

No problem, just use the woodworking shop at Gerlach High School.

So cast and crew descended on Gerlach, setting up little bands of temporary RV parks.

"It was so much fun," actress Jennifer Tilly recalled years later.

The dark-haired beauty and killer poker player gets her spot-on comic timing from her sense of playfulness.

"We couldn't go anywhere else or do anything, so we just hung out with each other at our little trailer parks. The most exciting thing was when I got killed in a car explosion. We all showed up to watch the fire and cheer."

Not much different from Burning Man—except everyone wore clothes.

The movie's star, Drew Barrymore, adapted to Gerlach's isolation surprisingly well for a teenager weaned on the Beverly Hills lifestyle.

"There was no way out, you know, and at first you feel resentful 'cause you're in such a small town when you're used to a big world. Then you start to know the people, and you start to like it. I'm a very independent person, I'm always doing something, and I kind of found it hard there, but I really liked it," she recounted in her trailer after the crew moved from Gerlach to Carson City.

The return to civilization meant she explored places like the now-defunct Ormsby House casino. There, Drew practiced mathematical skills by playing twenty-one. Granted, Drew's curves belonged on an adult's body, which later made her part of the *Charlie's Angels* trio. But back then her unlined, youthful face belonged to someone who should be carded.

Not only that, the dealer recognized her from *E.T.*, made seven years previously when Drew was seven. A dealer with skills at counting to twenty-one should add better.

Retelling the incident provided a rare moment for Drew, who usually bore the serious concentration of a seasoned professional on set. For a moment, she abandoned her adult mode and did what any little girl would under the circumstances.

She giggled, beaming pride over flaunting authority.

Drew's real-life underage gambling showed one way to break rules in road pictures; B-movie auteur Roger Corman found another when he brought *Grand Theft Auto* to Nevada in 1977.

"Well, maybe we didn't get *every* permit we needed," he admitted decades later when we reflected on complications involved with a stunt-laden project.

Production statistics proclaim twenty-four explosions, twenty-three destroyed cars, and eleven stolen vehicles, but Corman brags more about giving future Oscar winner Ron Howard his first directing gig in the story of a young couple who steal a Rolls Royce and aim for a Las Vegas wedding chapel.

In another instance of rule breaking, *Joy Ride* filmmakers jettison the one favoring obscure highways.

They called the Film Office in Carson City at the end of a workday, a surprise since they kept to themselves about the project. They went out on their own joyride, hunting down ideal locations for their story about college students terrorized by a psycho truck driver. After spending a day joyriding across Nevada, the moviemakers asked the Nevada Film Office for a spur-of-the-moment dinner meeting.

The team included producer Patrick Markey, a film commission success story because he left his government job in Ohio for production work with Robert Redford.

Director John Dahl joined the group, happy to be back in the region where he made his first feature film, *Kill Me Again*.

Joy Ride screenwriter Clay Tarver, who partnered with a pre–*Star Trek/ Star Wars* J. J. Abrams on the script, also spent the day driving for locations.

At dinner, the group members pulled out video images each of them liked along the Interstate 80 corridor.

Traditionally, barren old two-lane highways lure scary stories, but the *Joy Ride* team wanted to mix up expectations.

"Real students don't want to spend time on the road getting to college," explained the writer. "They'd use an interstate."

Higher traffic counts on interstates sometimes make them more difficult to maneuver than smaller roads, a point of concern for a key stunt. The gimmick required running a distinctive 1972 Chrysler Newport into a ditch. Location manager Tim Wilson liked the way Nevada's Highway Patrol made everything work smoothly.

Besides an interstate, the project needed road to pass by a diner in Nebraska, where the *Joy Ride* stars made a memorable entrance. Set dressers refurbished an abandoned Winnemucca gas station so well that actual drivers stopped in, hoping to sit down and drink coffee. Instead, the real-life travelers found a movie set featuring Nebraska postcards.

The set appealed to locals called as extras for a scene where a psycho truck driver directs Steve Zahn and Paul Walker to shed their clothes and stroll into the café naked.

Many know Zahn as a comic cutie from *Sahara*. Though a few years off from *The Fast and the Furious* franchise, Walker stood out as tall, blond, and blue-eyed, with toned abs showcased with his bathing-trunk wardrobe during *Into the Blue*.

Both men wore mini G-strings for their scene. Women pounded their fists upwards in glee when a filming glitch required everyone to come back another day for reshoots.

In all, director John Dahl thought Nevada captured what he wanted for his road picture.

"I realized that I really was in the middle of nowhere," he said shortly after production.

"I felt vulnerable, because it seemed like anything could happen, and it could have been hours before anyone came along. Every truck and auto seemed to have a menacing presence. To me, being on a highway in Nevada is more terrifying than being in New York City at 3 a.m."

Locals use more-favorable adjectives, though, when describing the state highways that lead them away from urban areas. Buildings and houses disappear from Nevada's gambling centers, quickly becoming vast, open spaces dancing in shifting shadows caused by white puffs of clouds sailing against bright blue sky. The long highway stretches for seemingly endless miles, gradually easing into a wispy vanishing point. Infinity lies out there. Anything seems possible.

Lassie Loses It

Before my film commission days, I visited the *Magic of Lassie* set as a reporter writing one of those "Hollywood comes to Nevada!" stories for a local weekly.

The press conference included a piano concert by Richard and Robert Sherman, characters in the *Saving Mr. Banks* movie about the making of *Mary Poppins*.

The duo played their Oscar-winning "Chim Chim Cher-ee" from *Poppins* as well as upcoming music from *The Magic of Lassie*.

Waiting in a food line with the Shermans afterwards, I described driving my mother crazy by relentlessly singing their "Let's Get Together" (yeah, yeah, yeah) song from the original *Parent Trap* movie.

"You must be twenty-three," said Richard.

"Richard!" admonished his wife. "You don't talk about a woman's age."

He turned and looked at her with eyebrows raised innocently.

"But every seven-year-old loved that song," he said, then pointed at me and shrugged. "So I know how old she is."

I found the Shermans much more engaging than Lassie, though I adore animals. This Lassie, sixth generation, acted like a bitch. A transvestite since he was a boy playing a girl, Lassie kept his own pet poodles.

"Lassie likes it, to run around with these little poodles, and we've always had little dogs with him all of his life. Every Lassie I've had has had a little dog," explained trainer Rudd Weatherwax.

But things got slightly tense on set, perhaps an omen of Lassie's box office future. At one point, the star only half-heartedly lifted his paw for a classic cute dog pose as I snapped a photo. Arriving like a fast-frame vampire ready to bite my neck, trainer Weatherwax zipped to my side and tried to jerk the film out of my camera, saving the world from the image of a lackadaisical Lassie. Since I righteously protected my film, I like telling that story.

I replayed it for *Lassie* television mom June Lockhart when I bumped into her years later at a Reno restaurant.

Introducing myself as the local film commissioner, I recounted what happened.

"No shit?!" responded Lassie's sweet television mother. "You kept the film? Good for you!"

My shots provided visual evidence of Lassie's fallibility. As it turned out, the movie itself reveals Lassie's shortcomings.

Motels Along the Roads

Road trips mean road stops, often at the motels along Nevada highways.

"Reno has the most amazing array of motels and signs," noted director Taylor Hackford while filming *Love Ranch* with Helen Mirren in 2008. "The city is like a motel museum from the sixties and seventies—it's a stylistic gift, and I'm trying to use every one of them in my movie."

From art deco lines to cool-looking cars, motel signs, and motor lodges, design adds character to such projects as *Hard Eight* and *The Cooler*. But for a title that defines the concept, nothing says it more than *The Motel Life*.

Though the story's brothers go on the road only briefly from Reno to Elko (played by Virginia City), the real focus examines an underclass lifestyle in residential motels.

"I just lived it rough," says *The Motel Life* author Willy Vlautin, a former Reno resident who moved to Portland, Oregon to pursue a music and writing career.

He left Reno after difficult times but maintains a strong fondness for his former home.

"I lived in Reno 'til I was twenty-seven. I was a failure in Reno, a failed musician, a struggling writer. It was a pretty isolating place as far as the arts, but I loved Reno, and Reno is still my favorite place."

Vlautin's move proved fruitful. He plays gigs regularly with his band and published several novels, selling movie rights for all of them.

He knows those sales mean giving up control, but he pushed some ideas when the Polsky Brothers, Alan and Gabe, obtained rights to *The Motel Life*.

"I always felt *The Motel Life* couldn't be shot anywhere else," Vlautin said, adding that his belief guaranteed nothing regarding places to film.

"I sell the rights to my books, but they don't put it in writing about the locations. I kind of begged them to do it in Reno. I showed them around Reno," he recalled.

"To me, Reno was one of the main characters. I felt the Polsky Brothers in the end realized that."

They also understood the story, one likened to the style of *Barfly* author Charles Bukowsky, whose writing explores an underclass in society.

"They really wanted to make it, for a story that's pretty intense and dark, it's a labor of love. I don't think they thought they were going to make a fortune."

Granted, the Polskys found recognizable names to participate, including Dakota Fanning, Emile Hirsch, and Kris Kristofferson, but the story of two brothers struggling from hand to mouth with no place to go bears little resemblance to typical box office hits.

The concept came from Vlautin's own experience, partly inspired because his mother often found the money to put him up at Reno's Holiday Hotel before it was the Siena.

"Balconies faced the river. Every morning I would stand outside and see men emerging at the banks. Drifters, they weren't quite homeless. That part of Reno felt like the way I felt in my heart. I felt kind of damaged. *The Motel Life* is a study in defeat. When you think like a beaten man, nothing comes from it."

Vlautin's ability to convey loss and loneliness with empathy and compassion translated into a sensitive film that generated positive reviews and—as expected—minimal box office play (though it gained fans on Netflix).

Filming itself involved the usual location challenges, especially for a story that requires specific weather.

"I came down the first Friday of filming," explained Vlautin. "It was sixty-five degrees in January at first, like spring. It was supposed to be winter. Sunday night it started snowing, exactly where the book takes place. I thought that meant Reno was not pissed at this movie."

The Motel Life remains a film he can feel proud about, plus it gave him a bucket-list experience, the chance to meet one of his lifetime heroes.

"They knew I was a big Kris Kristofferson fan, so they let me come down for the first three days of the movie. They were nice enough to say, 'We really want to have you two guys meet.'"

The opportunity melded with another plus, showcasing a special location.

"I grew up going to the Halfway Club. It was the first restaurant I ever ate at by myself. Almost thirty years later, Kris Kristofferson is sitting in the same seat I used to sit in. Kris Kristofferson is one of the greatest guys of all time. I got to meet him. And during filming, it felt like I helped Reno and the Halfway Club, even if it was just for a day. To feel I had some kind of impact was good. It's fun—exciting and fun."

Some of Vlautin's other location favorites showed up in the film, including the Elbow Room Bar, the casino floor of the Club Cal Neva, and the Sandman Motel, with its iconic sign featuring an old car.

"The Sutro and other residential motels are leaving. At least they're documented in the film now."

And how effective are those locations?

"They should make all movies in Nevada. It's really beautiful. I like Reno. It just looks beautiful on film."

EPILOGUE

Putting Nevada's Movie Icons on a Cell Phone Selfie

I want to see icons take a selfie defining Nevada movies. What a shot it would make: Elvis. Marilyn. A space alien. The Duke. Rocky. A Godfather. Mustang Ranchers. And Bradley Cooper could click it, just like he did for Ellen DeGeneres at the Oscars one year. White teeth gleaming, rhinestones glittering, green skin shimmering, Elvis, Marilyn, and other icons blazed new trails and fought battles their own way through eleven decades of Nevada movies.

But so far, only a couple of these icons have participated in really good—let alone great—Nevada films, and none of them fully define the home I know and love.

"What movie captures Nevada best?" a young guy named Paul asked me in the days before he took the name P. T. Anderson and earned Oscar nominations for writing and directing movies like *There Will Be Blood.*

Without a beat, I shot back, the work of Oscar winner Jonathan Demme. "*Melvin and Howard.*"

Resembling a teenager, ready to grant a fossil fountain-of-youth points for coming out of the Jurassic era, Paul brightened immediately.

"Right!" said the then twenty-three-year-old whiz kid.

He also bypassed such iconic titles as *The Godfather* movies, *The Misfits*, and *Viva Las Vegas* as his favorite Nevada film, leaning instead toward the kind of character-driven story he likes to make.

For my part, I appreciate *Melvin and Howard* because it travels all over the state, from Las Vegas to Reno with Gabbs along the way. Few movies, not even those with Rocky, go that distance.

But more than locations, *Melvin and Howard* picks up on Nevada's mentality with a character whose life completely changes overnight. Perhaps with money, or possibly from a marriage beginning or ending, Nevada offers the chance to ignore mundane routine. Sudden wealth. Sudden poverty. Sudden freedom. They all happen daily in Nevada venues.

Melvin and Howard reveals such extremes, but despite its Oscar-winning screenplay, it never captured a huge, mainstream audience.

That success goes to *Ocean's Eleven* or *The Hangover*, neither stepping out much beyond Las Vegas and neither focusing on people who live here.

Paul said he hoped to make a definitive Nevada movie, and his *Hard Eight* ranks as one of the best.

But the movie with everything, the crowd and critic pleaser using statewide locations and capturing Nevada's blend of craziness, normalcy, and distinctiveness?

Still waiting. In the meantime, I like imagining that selfie of Elvis, Marilyn, and a space alien.

Viva Las Vegas!

Finding the real places you watch on screen in Las Vegas simply means opening your eyes along the Strip and Fremont Street. Walking along these streets provides more visuals than any other block in the country—and that's just from the outside. Whole worlds replicate inside each facility, and most aim to keep you fully entertained in just one spot. Las Vegas succeeds partly by keeping ahead of the game and changing frequently, so many screen sites disappear (indicated by parentheses). Titles include:

The Strip

Drive-chase shots	*Austin Powers: International Man of Mystery*
	Jason Bourne
	L.A. Without a Map
(Starting on the southwest side of Las Vegas Boulevard and traveling north)	
(Hacienda)	*Blasted in Nevada*
	Top of the World
Mandalay Bay	*CSI*
	Las Vegas
	Ocean's Eleven (2001)
	Play It to the Bone (boxing match)
	Rocky Balboa
	Undisputed
Luxor	*Mars Attacks!*
	Showgirls
	Synthetic Pleasures
Excalibur	*Leaving Las Vegas* (one of many Strip exteriors used)
New York, NY	*CSI*
	(*Lethal Weapon 4* crew stayed here)
Monte Carlo	*Dance with Me*
	Dodgeball

	Southpaw
	X-Files ("Three of a Kind")
Aria	*Bosch* (season 1)
	Last Vegas
Bellagio	*CSI*
	Ocean's Eleven, Twelve, Thirteen
	Hangover
	What Planet Are You From?
(Dunes)	*Blasted in Las Vegas*
	Fallout: New Las Vegas
	Harley Davidson and the Marlboro Man
	Hot Shots!
	Oxford Blues
	Vega$
Caesars Palace	*City Slickers II*
	Electric Horseman
	Fools Rush In
	Friends
	The Hangover, 1 & 3
	Get Shorty
	The Guilt Trip
	Hearts Are Wild
	Hell's Angels '69
	History of the World, Part 1
	Iron Man
	Joan Rivers and Friends Salute Heidi Abramowitz
	McMillan: All Bets Off
	My Giant
	Ocean's Eleven
	Oh God, You Devil
	Percy Jackson and the Olympians
	Players
	Pleasure Palace
	Portrait of a Showgirl
	The Pretender
	Pumping Iron 2: The Women
	Rocky III
	Rain Man
	Showgirls (Forum Shops)
	Southpaw

	The Strip
	Think Like a Man Too
	Where It's At
	Wild Card
	You Ruined My Life
Mirage	*Bogus*
	Bosch
	Sergeant Bilko
	Pure Country
	Vegas Vacation
Treasure Island	*Miss Congeniality 2: Armed and Fabulous*
	Knocked Up (*Mystère* show)
	The Island Adventure Begins
Frontier	*Heldorado* (as Last Frontier)
(Stardust)	(home to real-life "Casino")
	Fear and Loathing in Las Vegas
	Feeling Minnesota
	Saved by the Bell: Wedding in Las Vegas
	Showgirls
	Swingers
Circus Circus	*Baby Geniuses*
	Bosch (Seasons 1 and 2)
	Diamonds Are Forever
	The Grasshopper
	Las Vegas Lady
Stratosphere	*Fever Pitch*
	Las Vegas Caper

(Cross the street, start on the northeast side of Las Vegas Boulevard, and travel south)

Sahara	*CSI*
	Heat (as Club Bingo)
	Garry Shandling: Alone in Vegas
	Ocean's 11 (1960)
	Painting the Clouds with Sunshine (as Club Bingo)
	Stripper
(Riviera)	*21*
	3000 Miles to Graceland
	Amazing Colossal Man (peering through window)
	Austin Powers: International Man of Mystery
	Beyond Desire

	Bob & Carol & Ted & Alice
	Casino
	Subliminal Seduction (aka *The Corporation* (as the Royal)
	Double Exposure
	Fear and Loathing in Las Vegas
	Girls' Night
	Go!
	The Godfather
	The Hangover
	Nevada Heat
	Ocean's 11 (1960)
	Sexual Roulette
	Showgirls
	Vegas Vacation
(Desert Inn)	*Con Air*
	The Godfather Part II
	Ocean's Eleven
	Lost in America
	MacShayne: Final Roll of the Dice
	MacShayne: Winner Takes All
	Perry Mason: The Case of the Defiant Daughter
	Rush Hour 2
	Twogether
	Vega$
Venetian	*CSI*
	Get Carter
	Rat Race
Wynn	*Paul Blart 2: Mall Cop*
(Sands)	*Blasted in Las Vegas*
	Con Air
	Demonoid: Messenger of Death
	Kiss Me, Stupid
	Meet Me in Las Vegas
	Oceans' Eleven (1960)
	Picasso Trigger
	Stark: Mirror Image
	(home to The Rat Pack, Sinatra)
Imperial Palace	*Hell Squad*
	Lost in Las Vegas
	Love Streams
	Stripper

Flamingo Hilton	(Bugsy's original Las Vegas creation)
	C.C. and Company
	The Girl Rush
	Godzilla (2014)
	My Friend Irma Goes West
	Ocean's Eleven (1960 & 2001)
	Viva Las Vegas (pool scene)
Barbary Coast	*Jocks*
	Oceans Eleven (2001)
Bally's (MGM)	*Honeymoon in Vegas*
	Fever Pitch
	The Incredible Burt Wonderstone
	The Life and Death of Sam Kinison
	Lookin' to Get Out
	Lucky Chances
	Rocky IV
Paris	*Six Feet Under*
	Step Up: All In
	Think Like a Man Too
(Aladdin)	(real life: Elvis married Pricilla here)
	Alias
	CSI
	Dancing for Dollars: The Bolshoi in Vegas
	The Girl Rush
	Going in Style
	Midnight Run
Planet Hollywood	*Get Him to the Greek*
	Queen of Versailles
	Race to Witch Mountain
	Somewhere
	Think Like a Man Too
	What Happens in Vegas
	Wild Card
MGM Grand	*Diva Las Vegas*
	The Extreme Adventures of Super Dave
	The Great White Hype
	Now You See Me
	Ocean's Eleven
	Vegas Vacation

Tropicana	*Bogus*
	Diamonds Are Forever
	Funny Bones
	The Godfather
	Seven Days
	This Is My Life
	The Vegas Strip Wars
	Viva Shaf Vegas

Non-Strip Properties

(Maxim)	*Delusion*
	L.E.T.H.A.L. Ladies: Day of the Warrior
	Hard Vice
	The Messenger
	Mugsy's Girls (Delta Pi)
Golden Gate Hotel	*Pay It Forward*
Golden Nugget	*Wild Card*
Palms	*Bosch* (Season 2)
	MTV's *Real World*
Rio	*Guns*
	The Stand
Hard Rock	*Honey, I Blew Up the Kid*
	Tomcats
Convention Center Westgate (originally International and Hilton)	
	Above the Law
	Behind the Candelabra
	Diamonds Are Forever
	Elvis: That's the Way It Is
	The Entertainers
	Funny Bones
	Indecent Proposal
	Kill Me Again
	Mickey Spillane's Mike Hammer: Murder Takes All
	Lucky Chances
	Over the Top
	VIP
UNLV	*8 Seconds*
	Knocked Up
	Viva Las Vegas

McCarran Airport	*21*
	Amazing Race
	Bosch
	Casino
	Diamonds Are Forever
	Fools Rush In
	The Mexican
	Midnight Run
	Ocean's Thirteen
	Prizzi's Honor
	Rat Race
	Vegas Vacation
San Remo	*Best of the Best II*
Red Rock Resort	*21*
Neon Boneyard	*The Amazing Race* ("Do You Believe in Magic")
	Anthony Bourdain's *No Reservations*
	Bachelor Party Vegas
	Fools Rush In
	Hangin' Tough
	Last Vegas
	Mars Attacks
	Now You See Me
	Vegas Vacation
Fremont Street	*Best Night Ever*
	Heldorado
	The Incredible Burt Wonderstone
	Leprechaun 3
	My Giant
	Night of the Running Man
	Vegas Vacation
	Viva Las Vegas (race)
	King Ralph
	Reckless Kelly
	The Stand
	Bosch (Season 2), "Victim of the Night" (Downtown Container Park shopping area)
Binion's	*Another Stakeout*
	Aria
	Truth or Consequences, New Mexico
	Father Hood

	Fear and Loathing in Las Vegas
	The Incredible Burt Wonderstone
	Last Vegas
	Lucky Town
	Lucky You
	Pay It Forward
	Pokertown
Four Queens	*Confessions of a Hitman*
Mint	*Diamonds Are Forever*
Union Plaza	*Another Stakeout*
	Bible & Gun Club
	Casino
	Confessions of a Hitman
	Cool World
	The Mexican
	The Stand
	Starman
	Stark

MOVIE LOCATION GUIDE

Waking Up in Reno—
A Downtown Walking Tour

It takes less than a mile to walk in the footsteps of Marilyn Monroe, Clint Eastwood, Robin Williams, and Jack Nicholson throughout downtown Reno. "Walking up in Reno," so to speak.

Silver Legacy–Sierra Street Entrance between Fifth and Sixth

Waking up in Reno let the late Natasha Richardson transform herself at the Legacy spa before riding up escalator banks in the casino's downstairs valet lobby. The Legacy also provided more than the usual amounts of food from its buffet in 1997's *Kingpin*.

North to:

Circus Circus along Sixth Street

A wedding chapel when *Promised Land* filmed in 1986, characters played by Meg Ryan and Kiefer Sutherland got married here. Reno weddings also occur in:

Breaking the Rules (1992)

Desert Hearts (1986)

Melvin and Howard (1980)

My Blue Heaven (1990)

Circus Circus provided its steakhouse for a romantic pairing between Maria Bello and William H. Macy in 2002's *The Cooler*. Other interiors shot at the former Flamingo Hilton, now transformed into privately owned condominiums.

East along Sixth Street to:

University of Nevada, Reno (UNR) from North Virginia and Ninth Streets

Stay on Sixth Street and look north for a good view of the school where producers appreciated the location's Ivy League appearance during the forties and fifties. The 1946 movie *Margie* turned Morrill Hall into a high school with students played by Jeanne Crain and Alan Young. Young, who went on to become Mr. Ed's best friend on television, hid his Scottish Canadian accent in the movie, his first ever. He later returned to Nevada for what he described on his website as "another all-American boy" role, joining Natalie Wood in *Chicken Every Sunday* with Minden and the V & T Railroad creating the sense of Tucson, Arizona around 1910. Young then went back to UNR, with Shirley Temple for 1948's *Mr. Belvedere Goes to College*. Temple recalled the project fondly: "I was slowly growing up!"

UNR's movie connection also includes:

Apartment for Peggy (1948), with William Holden and Jeanne Crain

Andy Hardy's Blonde Trouble (1944), with Mickey Rooney

5 Against the House (1955), with Kim Novak

Hilda Crane (1956), used students as extras, including future Nevada governor Richard Bryan

Mother Was a Freshman (1949), with Loretta Young and Van Johnson

Since producers chose UNR for its Ivy League resemblance, the school primarily stood in for non-Nevada locations.

Walk to Center Street, turn south (right).

The National Bowling Stadium–300 North Center

Turning onto Center Street reveals the National Bowling Stadium, which offers producers a unique visual—the biggest set of lanes in the country. The stadium draws thousands of bowlers every year for major national bowling competitions. The interior's eighty Brunswick lanes lie under forty-four-foot-high ceilings. Downstairs, the lobby includes the Kingpin Club, recalling the facility's major movie. *Kingpin*, a crazy comedy from the Farrelly Brothers, plays off Martin Scorsese's ultraserious *The Color of Money*. Really. Woody Harrelson takes on the Paul Newman role as a former hustler who gets beat up after a winning game. His hand irreparably damaged after the beating, Harrelson seeks a protégé but must eventually face his nemesis. Movie magic allows Harrelson to make the strikes needed to overcome that evil opponent, played by Bill Murray. Harrelson's real-life bowling ball merely edged down the alley slowly, hitting a few pins. In contrast, Murray always got a strike.

Continue south.

Railroad Station–East Commercial Row and Center Street

A refurbished station includes museum displays covering the city's historic railroad connection. Bits of the original depot façade used in *Desert Hearts* remain from the opening of the 1985 movie starring Helen Shaver.

Continue south on Center, turn east toward Lake Street.

National Automobile Museum and Old Reno Arch–10 Lake Street

The museum boasts movie ties inside with displays of cars owned by stars like Mary Pickford, Elliott Gould, John Wayne, and James Dean. Exhibits feature the Thomas Flyer, the car that inspired 1965's *The Great Race*, plus one hauled all the way to Rosarito Beach in Mexico as part of the background for the launching of 1999's *Titanic*.

Combining the museum's auto focus with Reno's famous "Hot August Nights"–period car festival, the location proved an ideal home for the original Reno Arch. The serendipitous relocation came about through 1994's *Cobb*, about the famous baseball player who lived at Tahoe. After locating the sixties-era arch in a city dump, the *Cobb* team spent $30,000 to repair and relocate it on East Fourth Street. During that week of filming, locals started coming to the set, not to watch the moviemaking process, but to take pictures underneath the arch, leading civic groups to find a permanent site for the restored artifact.

Cross Lake and Center by Siena to South Virginia Street.

Mapes Site

The Mapes once stood on an empty lot across the street and kitty-corner from the Riverside. Imploded on Super Bowl Sunday 2000, the Mapes remains only a memory, commemorated by plaques. The biggest, most glamorous hotel during the forties and fifties, it provided the elegant Sky Room for a *Desert Hearts* party. It also hosted a private poker game in 1976's *California Split* with Elliott Gould and George Segal. *The Misfits* contributes to its fame. Its cast and crew stayed there, plus Clark Gable specifically mentions the hotel casino in the movie.

Cross Virginia Street to:

The Riverside–17 South Virginia and Washoe County Courthouse

Reno's most historic corner long featured a hotel/casino like the Riverside, though the building currently provides lofts as part of a Sierra Arts Foundation and Artspace project, aimed at bringing residents back to downtown. In its early days, the Riverside provided rooms for people to wait out their divorces, among them Clare Boothe Luce, who juggled her experiences into 1939's *The Women*. The hotel shows up in 1954's *Johnny Dark* with Tony Curtis and Piper Laurie. Other film appearances include a lovemaking scene in *Desert Hearts* and a casino scam in 1989's *Blind Fury*.

Next door to the south stands the old Washoe County Courthouse and a plaque about the city's divorce trade, which earned Reno international renown from the twenties through the sixties and beyond. The courthouse appears in 1960's *The Misfits* when Kevin McCarthy tries to stop Marilyn Monroe from divorcing him. The divorce comedy *Pffft!* sends Judy Holliday by the courthouse to split with Jack Lemmon. The title—however you pronounce it—comes from a phrase columnist Walter Winchell coined about famous couples breaking up. Louise Fletcher issues marriage decisions from her podium as a judge inside the courthouse during *Edie & Pen*.

Return north on Virginia to Truckee River

The Truckee River runs by the Riverside and joins Nevada's divorce lore as the place, symbolically, to end a marriage. Called "The mythological divorce capital of the Western World" in a 1996 *Smithsonian* magazine article, Reno created traditions during the decades when the fastest way to end a marriage meant establishing a six-week residency in Nevada. One involved throwing wedding rings off the downtown bridge into the Truckee River. Urban legend? State Archivist Guy Rocha saw a mix of fiction turning to fact. He traced the first ring-throwing episode back to the 1929 novel *Reno* by Cornelius Vanderbilt, Jr., who came to the city for a divorce in 1927. The book inspired short-time residents to do the same. My husband Fred found evidence to back up the stories. A mining engineer, Fred took his gold dredge under the Second Street Bridge and pulled up about 120 rings, plus some teeth with gold fillings. Somehow, the tradition of throwing one's teeth over the bridge never caught on. The historic bridge, seen in *The Misfits*, gave way to a refurbished version in 2016.

Continue north to Virginia and Second Street

This corner offers a view of other film locations like the Nugget (233 North Virginia), where Michele Pfeiffer's sister Dede works in 1996's *Up Close and Personal*. Two years later, *Mafia!* producers dressed the signal at Virginia and Second Street like a slot machine, requiring visitors crossing the street to pull the slot handle and come up with the right icons. Nearby, set designers hauled trash into an alley for 1999's *Diamonds*. The real deal looked too pristine for a scene where a mugger attacks former boxing champion Kirk Douglas.

Cal Neva/Virginian–140 North Virginia Street

The last of the city's traditional small casinos, Cal Neva's Western-looking casino floor attracted producers of *Waking Up in Reno* (2000) for a gambling scene with Patrick Swayze, Billy Bob Thornton, Charlize Theron, and Natasha Richardson. The building's outside marquee showed up in a remake of *In Cold Blood* (1996), announcing a performance by Louis Prima. The marquee promoted the fictitious lounge performer Pony Cobb in *Edie & Pen*. No one cares about Pony Cobb, but many still listen to the man who played him, Randy Travis. In another project, reflections of the Cal Neva marquee bounce off a car window when Patrick Swayze visits Reno in *Letters from a Killer* (1998).

Harrah's Reno–219 Center Street

Sister Act viewers clearly see Harrah's, via aerial footage of Reno, while *The Misfits* includes a coffee shop scene. A plaque remains on an outside wall to honor both movies. *Matilda* (1978) shows Harrah's as the venue for a bout between the world heavyweight champ and a kangaroo. *E.R.* hunk Goran Višnjić gambles in Harrah's high rollers slot area during 2001's *The Deep End*.

Harrah's Plaza (formerly Harolds Club)

Harrah's co-opted the old Harolds Club and turned it into a plaza showing few remnants of a famous past. Once known for its *Harolds or Bust* billboard marketing campaign, the old casino opened in 1935 and last appeared in 1996's *Fathers' Day* with Robin Williams and Billy Crystal. Back in 1955, Harolds robbers attacked in *5 Against the House* with Kim Novak. Harolds also provided interiors for frequent *Dexter* director John Dahl in his first movie, *Kill Me Again*, from 1989. Right next door, the Nevada Club provided the exterior casino look for *Sister Act*. Until it closed in 1998, it still had an upstairs room filled with mechanical nickel slot machines, helping it play a 1950s casino in the 1995 feature *Imaginary Crimes* with Harvey Keitel.

Whitney Peak Garage

Parking garage top floors offer good views, sending director Sean Penn to the one at Virginia and First Street, shooting a scene of Jack Nicholson walking in a crosswalk by the Reno Arch for *The Pledge*. Nicholson slung his baseball cap low over his forehead, and not a soul recognized him during the several hours spent getting the shot.

Since garage heights provide such good views, I scouted several when a production company asked me to find a spot where a character could consider jumping to his death, backed by lots of neon.

"We want him to have a dramatic backdrop while he thinks about killing himself," the production staffer requested.

Following up on the call, I drove up to various top floors, clicking shots from rooftop edges.

"What are you doing?" asked one security operator.

Without thinking, I answered with the nonchalant ease of someone in my location-scouting business.

"Oh, I'm just looking for a good place to commit suicide."

His dropping jaw made me elaborate and explain about movie location work.

The movie mantra: "Not really, just make believe!"

Reno Arch–Virginia Street Downtown

Almost any recent movie set in Reno announces its location with a shot of the pink neon glow from the downtown arch that serves as a gateway to the city. Designed for the Transcontinental Highway Exposition in 1926, the first Reno Arch celebrated paving the Lincoln and Victory highways across the nation. Replacements occurred over the decades, with the newest, primarily pink, variation erected in 1987. The base includes a plaque commemorating 1992's *Sister Act.*

Sister Act incorporates the Reno Arch as a bevy of nuns scurry under it on their way to the Nevada Club, a casino that no longer stands. The arch brought 2010's *Love Ranch* to Reno, despite initial plans to film the entire project in New Mexico. Though the current arch arrived in the eighties, director Taylor Hackford noted that its seventies sensibility felt authentic and fit his project. He ended up incorporating more of downtown Reno, including the now-defunct Fitzgerald's Club. Fitzgerald's opened in 1978, but its interiors remained total seventies to viewers in the new millennium. Other works with this current arch include:

Body and Soul (1997)
Breaking the Rules (1989)
Diamonds (1999)
Edie & Pen (1996)
El Cortez (2006)
Fathers' Day (1997)
Into the Wild (2007)
The Motel Life (2012)
The Pledge (2001)
Smith (2006)
Tricks (1997)

Up Close & Personal (1996)

Waking Up in Reno (2002)

The previous arch, with four diamond shapes for each letter of Reno, moved to the city of Willits in California but remains visible in movies shot between 1963 and 1986, including:

California Split (1974)

Matilda (1978)

Melvin and Howard (1980)

Stacy's Knights, (1984)

Stacy's Knights, also known as "*Double Down,*" stars Kevin Costner in his first leading role, and features shots of him walking downtown with the old Harolds Club sign clearly in the background.

Melvin and Howard, featuring an Oscar-winning performance by Mary Steenburgen, led *Magnolia* director Paul Thomas Anderson to pay homage to it at the defunct Downtowner Motor Lodge on Second Street. Nearby, the El Cortez gave title to a 2006 project starring Lou Diamond Phillips.

Whitney Peak Hotel (formerly Fitzgerald's)–255 North Virginia

Fitzgerald's, next to the Reno Arch, provided interiors for the casino Harvey Keitel owns in *Sister Act.* As opening credits roll, Whoopi Goldberg sings in the Moonlight Lounge, a little stage that never again starred someone of her stature. In fact, this casino never again saw so many nuns at once, let alone the kind who look like Kathy Najimy and Maggie Smith.

"I can't believe I'm here," Smith said, stroking her habit as we met on set.

The winner of multiple Oscars who hails from Great Britain looked around with a grimace perfectly suited to the *Downton Abbey* matriarch she played years later.

Other performers, like Whoopi Goldberg, got right in the mix and spent their time between takes putting money in slot machines or on tables.

Besides welcoming singing (and gambling) nuns, Fitzgerald's hosted a catfight for *Waking Up in Reno.* The scene, filmed in early 2000 near casino elevators, has Natasha Richardson's character losing it when she finds out her friend, played by Charlize Theron, has been sleeping with her husband. Patrick Swayze picks up Charlize and thrusts her in the elevator as Natasha storms out. The fight occurs while they are waiting for the elevator to arrive—a seemingly inordinate amount of time, but accurate. Real-life signs, in fact, apologized for long waits. A few years later, *Love Ranch* gave a last view of the casino floor before Fitzgerald's became a sports center, with a rock-climbing wall outside.

Eldorado Hotel–345 North Virginia Street

The Eldorado Hotel Casino put up a fake glass window for Clint Eastwood to crash through in 1989's *Pink Cadillac*. The chase and its camera trickery makes Virginia Street seem as long as the Las Vegas Strip. The Eldorado casino floor and convention center became part of the action for the 1998 cable remake of *Body and Soul*. The movie stars welterweight champion Ray "Boom Boom" Mancini as—surprise—a boxer. He fought in a ring set up for the film in the convention center, but the casino floor looks about the same.

This finishes the tour near the easy-access parking at the Silver Legacy.

MOVIE LOCATION GUIDE

Joy Ride through Rural Nevada

Road trips sweeten Nevada's movie scene, so I invented a long one that covers rural filming locations. This goes well beyond the *Joy Ride* movie with its college kids who cross Nevada making multiple stops on Interstate 80. My film fantasy joyride requires multiple gas stops to cover hundreds of miles—and projects. One big circle works for most of it, but numerous side trips ruin any nice, neat geometric shape for a simple-looking map. In any case, travel options abound.

Vegas from Arizona

From Arizona, get on U.S. 93 west to Nevada. Exit at State Route 172 for Hoover Dam at the state border. The dam boasts more than one hundred projects. Among them:

The Aliens Are Coming (1980), featuring extensive interior shots

The Amazing Colossal Man (1957), using process shots

Diamonds Are Forever (1971), with Sean Connery as James Bond

Domino (2005), with Keira Knightley as a bounty hunter

Father Hood (1993), with Patrick Swayze kidnapping his kids

Fools Rush In (1997), with Matthew Perry and Salma Hayek falling in love

Heldorado (1946), with Roy Rogers and Trigger showing their love

Lost in America (1985), with Albert Brooks and Julie Hagerty challenging their love

Saboteur (1942), with director Alfred Hitchcock viewing the dam as a prime target

Superman (1978), with Christopher Reeve failing to protect the target

The Transformers (2007), with Hasbro toys

Vegas Vacation (1997), with Chevy Chase on a dam tour

Universal Soldier (1992), which lets Jean Claude Van Damme scale the structure's face and demonstrates amazing cooperation from the Feds, who control dam access.

Things tightened after the September 11 terrorist attacks; Alfred Hitchcock and Lex Luthor got it right—Hoover Dam makes a damn good target. Even so, you can still take a dam self-guided tour. People reduce to specks on top of the massive curve of what looks like remnants of an alien craft. The dam blocks views of surrounding desert; a flow of water below gives no hint of its real quantity—enough to supply the city of Los Angeles, 270 miles away. Hoover Dam remains one of the world's official engineering marvels, a creation that works spectacularly and looks stunning.

Vegas from California

Entering Nevada from California puts you on Interstate 15 and terrain highlighted in many films, including:

Destination Vegas (1995)

Fear and Loathing in Las Vegas (1998)

Grand Theft Auto (1977)

The Last Stand (2013), as former California Governor Arnold Schwarzenegger gives up politics and takes on his first starring role after leaving office

On the outskirts of Las Vegas, take the Blue Diamond Road to Red Rock Canyon, where such colorful names indicate why the locations both end up on screen so often. With Rainbow Mountain looming against the West, this region adds depth and texture to such films as:

The Ballad of Cable Hogue (1970), with Jason Robards

The Bells of San Angelo (1949), with Roy Rogers

Megaforce (1982), with Molly Ringwald

Over the Top (1986), with Sylvester Stallone

Play It to the Bone (1999), with Antonio Banderas

Romancing the Stone (1984), with Michael Douglas

Sheriff of Las Vegas (1944)

The road takes you to Spring Mountain Ranch where free roaming burros waylay tourists for spare Doritos. A Bureau of Land Management center, with exhibits on local wildlife, plants, and geology, provides more information about the area.

Both Red Rock Canyon and Hoover Dam provide more than enough to explore and photograph in a single day, justifying an overnight stay in Las Vegas, where hundreds of movies also filmed (see the "Viva Las Vegas" list).

Valley of Fire

Set another day aside for a different geologic wonder and natural movie set, Valley of Fire State Park, about an hour's drive north of Las Vegas on I-15. A visitors' center provides basic information about the area, whose striking looks fit films in several genres, including Westerns and science fiction. Among them:

Beer (1985)
Billion Dollar Threat (1979)
Bite the Bullet (1975)
Duets (2000)
Father Hood (1993)
The Good Son (1993)
The Hitcher (1986)
Iron Eagle (1986)
Just Visiting (2001)
Little John (2002)
Nightwing (1979)
One Million B.C. (1940)
The Professionals (1966)
The Stalking Moon (1968)
The Stand (1994)
Star Trek: Generations (1994)
They Ran for Their Lives (1968)

Some movies, such as *Little John*, feature scenes lasting only minutes and comprising Nevada's entire claim to hosting the film. In contrast, *Star Trek* spent weeks on site and still lures fans looking for their favorite series' locations.

U.S. 93–North of Vegas

From the Valley of Fire, the film fantasy joyride moves north on U.S. 93. Wide basins and mountain ranges, reaching heights of nearly 10,000 feet, fill the route. Desert shifts at the Pahranagat National Wildlife Refuge, with its two bodies of water providing bright green trees in summertime.

You need to turn off the main highway if you want take an iconic Area 51 alien adventure. Near Alamo, turn on State Route 375, the official E.T. Highway. If you keep your eyes open, you should spot a white mailbox known as The Black Mailbox on the south side of the highway, about twenty miles in. That dirt road leads to one of Area 51's well-guarded borders. To avoid dirt, travel another twenty miles into Rachel (as seen in various documentaries) and buy a guide at the Area 51 Research Center or the Little A'Le'Inn, which served as a model for a set in the 2011 movie *Paul*. Printed guides include directions to Tikaboo Peak, a high point that provides something of a view of the buildings within the top-secret military facility.

Back on U.S. 93 north, you follow much of the route seen in 1992's *Roadside Prophets*. The highway provides access to five state parks, revealing such desert surprises as waterfalls and lush greenery. Cathedral Gorge stands out with clay drizzles that look like a good home for some of Area 51's reputed residents. Caliente and Pioche offer lodging.

The U.S. 93 junction at Major's Place allows another side-trip opportunity to a onetime film location, Great Basin National Park on U.S. 6/50. A National Park Service brochure describes the region as "a superb example of a desert mountain island." Created in 1986, the Great Basin National Park draws comparatively few visitors in the system and offers undeveloped wilderness ranging upwards to Wheeler Peak at 13,038 feet. One trail leads to a large stand of twisting bristlecone pines that have weathered extremes for nearly 5,000 years. A chainsaw got to one called Prometheus in 1964, before researchers analyzed it and discovered the oldest living thing on earth just died.

The park's major tour goes through part of the Lehman Caves (technically a cavern) and adds another project to the screen list, 1965's *The Wizard of Mars*, also called *Alien Massacre* and *Horrors of the Red Planet*. The cavern reminds me of another science fiction movie, 1979's *Alien*, which used sets that resemble the dark, warbled dribbles along walls and passageways. Stalagmites, draperies, and shields cover the cavern, making it too delicate for big crews. Outside, the park's lodge and diner offer an expansive view of the Great Basin that still looks like the countryside filmed in 1923's *The Covered Wagon*.

Ely

Backtracking on U.S. 6/50 takes you into Ely, where several motels offer the chance to stay overnight and imitate Natalie Portman in 2007's *My Blueberry Nights* by gambling at the old Hotel Nevada.

You can also emulate Willie Nelson and ride the train used in 1988's *Texas Guns*. The Northern Nevada Railway depot also appears in 2001's *Rat Race* with Whoopi Goldberg and Cuba Gooding, Jr.

Ely previously tasted film fame in 1950's *Operation Haylift* and its surrounding region inspired Stephen King's *Desperation*.

U.S. 50–the Loneliest Highway

From Ely, you can cross most of the state on U.S. 50, the Loneliest Highway in America. This takes you through Austin, where *Vanishing Point* visited in 1971. The "living" ghost town parades its Western roots with remnants of wood and stone buildings.

Highway 50 also features access to the Fallon Naval Air Station, though you need permission to enter the home of 1986's *Top Gun* and *Kerosene Cowboys*. Referring to Top Gun pilots, *Kerosene Cowboys* shot some scenes on the base in 2009, but it took until 2014 before the movie came out on DVD as *Red Sky*.

Fallon maintains a picturesque, fifties-style look on its main street, drawing *The Wizard* in 1989 and a first-season episode of *Route 66* ("Like a Motherless Child") many years earlier.

Heading west past Fallon, you might notice remnants of the Roper Drive-In Theater. The dilapidated site attracted several projects:

The Making of the Misfits (2001)
Pink Cadillac (1989)
Trail of Tears (1995)
The Wizard (1989)

Nearby Hazen was briefly a film center:

Cobb (1994)
Joy Ride (2001)
Kill Me Again (1989)
Pink Cadillac (1989)
Trail of Tears (1995)
The Wizard (1989)

Fallon leads to Reno in another hour's drive.

Rewind: U.S. 93 from Ely to Wendover

Say you woke up in Ely and instead of taking U.S. 50, you headed north on U.S. 93. This leads to McGill, which plays Pioche in *Roadside Prophets*;

some say Drew Barrymore filmed 1992's *Guncrazy* there, though no records confirm it. Frozen in time, McGill still looks like a small company town from the forties. The next big stop on U.S. 93 comes at Wells, home of the Ruby Mountain Brewing Company and a difficult half-marathon run up to Angel Lake on a road used for car commercials.

Wendover: Nevada . . . and Utah, Too

I-80 provides access to a significant side trip with an easterly drive to West Wendover where the large Wendover Will welcomes visitors a la Vegas Vic. This surprising bastion of filmmaking at the Utah border offers large resort casinos with big-city amenities. Montego Bay, the Peppermill, and the Rainbow have hosted crews and been in films:

Heaven or Vegas (1997)
Independence Day: Resurgence (2016)
Money Plays (1998)
Promised Land (1988)
The Runner (1999)

Producers prefer to lodge in these full-service Nevada accommodations, even though they film in Utah. Just over the border lies the old Wendover Air Base, known as home to the Enola Gay, which dropped the bomb on Hiroshima to end World War II. The base hosted several projects:

Con Air (1997)
The Core (2002)
Independence Day (1996)
Independence Day: Resurgence (2016)
The Incredible Hulk (2002)
The Philadelphia Experiment (1984)
Mulholland Falls (1995)
Wind (1992)

These projects share Bonneville Salt Flats filming with others:

Bonneville (2006)
Independence Day (1996)
Independence Day: Resurgence (2016)
Letters from a Killer (1998)
Pirates of the Caribbean: At World's End (2007)

Tree of Life (2011)

The World's Fastest Indian (2005)

The West Wendover Visitors Center in Nevada sometimes exhibits stills from these films. The film fantasy joyrider can easily spend a night in West Wendover, imitating stars like Johnny Depp, Will Smith, Nicolas Cage, and Anthony Hopkins.

Interstate 80 to Elko

From West Wendover, the joyride continues west on Interstate 80 to Elko. Projects drawn to the area include:

After the Game (released on DVD as *The Last Game* in 1997)

Brigham Young: Frontiersman (1940), with Tyrone Power as the Mormon leader

Don't Come Knocking (2005), with Sam Shepard as a cowboy star

Gunfighter (1998), featuring the Hopalong Cassidy character

The region's early movie connection came when Bing Crosby bought property and showed up often enough to earn an honorary mayor of Elko title. The city's museum displays his specially made blue denim tuxedo.

Interstate 80 West to Fernley

Heading west on I-80 means you cover the same route as the doomed man at the wheel in the *X-Files* episode "Drive." I-80 exits include Battle Mountain, which steps in as Nebraska during the 2001 movie *Joy Ride*. Nearby, the Marigold Mine almost turned into a site for 1997's *The Postman* when Kevin Costner scouted it with me. Negotiations fell through, but it's surprising to realize that such a big-name star toured this isolated spot, 408 miles from Las Vegas and 218 from Reno.

An hour east on I-80 from Battle Mountain brings you to Winnemucca, named for a respected tribal chief. Rolling off the tongue easily, Winnemucca's many syllables almost force you to finish the name with a smile. The town name spills out of William Hurt's mouth in 1991's *The Doctor* as he heads to a tribal event.

The region gained national fame in the eighties when local trapper Claude Dallas killed two game wardens in the wilderness outside Paradise Valley about an hour away. With all the makings for a screen show, 1986's *The Manhunt for Claude Dallas* indeed turned into a television movie-of-the-week—but using Colorado locations. Nonetheless, Paradise Valley boasts a movie connection as home to a costar of many Charlie Chaplin films,

Edna Purviance. Penelope Ann Miller played her in the 1992 biography of the comedian with Robert Downey, Jr. The Humboldt Museum in Winnemucca displays photos of Purviance as well as shots of the region's biggest production, 1927's *The Winning of Barbara Worth*. *Joy Ride* provides a more recent film connection at the west Winnemucca exit for its popular scene wherein its two well-muscled male heroes are forced to walk naked into a now-demolished building and order hamburgers.

Continuing west on I-80 leads to Lovelock and Pershing County. Just beyond Lovelock at the junction with U.S. 95 comes another *Joy Ride* site on the north side of the interstate. Once the Trinity Truck Stop, the operation burned down a few years after filming. Across the highway from the old truck stop, *Joy Ride* director John Dahl filmed Michael Madsen terrorizing Joanne Whalley at a rest stop in 1989's *Kill Me Again*. Just past the modernized restroom, the Humboldt Sink stretches to the horizon, with flatland used to build a Western town front for *Gunfighter*. The scene features director Christopher Coppola as a bad guy in a sombrero, appropriately dressed in a landscape displaying Spaghetti-Western desolation.

Continuing east on I-80 connects you with Highway 50 at Fernley, where *Joy Ride* stopped at the Truck Inn. Fernley connects you to S.R. 447, the Pyramid Highway.

Side Trip: State Route 447 to Gerlach

Leaving Fernley on S.R. 447 for about thirty minutes, you pass Nixon and see Pyramid Lake, an incongruously blue body of water that looks like it springs from nowhere among miles of dirt and sand (actually, the Truckee River connects it to Lake Tahoe). Just past the lake, an overview of highway stretches into infinity.

Vandals forced closure of a nearby dirt road, preventing access to the tufa pyramid that names the lake. Tufa's oddly shaped volcanic rock formations create intriguing film images in several projects:

The Doctor (1991)

The Disappearance of Nora (1993), with Veronica Hamel waking up in the middle of nowhere

The Greatest Story Ever Told (1965)

Steal the Sky (1988)

Trail of Tears (1995)

The Wizard (1988)

Taking S.R. 447 eventually leads to Gerlach, seen in 1989's *Far from Home*. Just beyond town lies the Black Rock Desert, where *Far from Home* and 2003's *Sin* filmed. The desert gets more intense recognition as base for the Burning Man art celebration, a topic of many documentaries.

From Gerlach, backtrack to I-80. Hook over to S.R. 446 out of Nixon for more terrain familiar from movies that shot on private property:

Desert Hearts (1985), at Capurro Ranch

The Misfits (1961), at Quail Canyon Ranch

Sin (2003), at Capurro Ranch

Interstate 80 to Sparks

Once on I-80, head west toward Sparks. Billboards and signs point out locations that make Nevada unique as the only state with legal brothels; however, laws prohibit advertising. As a result, billboards recommend the bar at the Wild Horse Saloon or a museum at the "World Famous Mustang Ranch," both off the Tracy exit. There's an entry booth for stating your business.

"I want to tour the museum," for example, works. That might run a $5 tip; other activities cost a lot more.

Across the parking lot from the Mustang, the Wild Horse Adult Resort provided a pool setting for Taylor Hackford's *Love Ranch*.

Continuing west, the Mustang exit leads to remnants of Joe Conforte's original Mustang Ranch. *Charley Varrick* (1973) filmed scenes there when the ranch still thrived. Abandoned buildings from the Old Bridge Ranch stand nearby.

More I-80 travel leads to the Nugget Casino Resort, site of:

Hard Eight (1997), Paul Thomas Anderson's first feature

Magnolia (1999), Anderson's fourth feature

Pink Cadillac (1989), with Clint Eastwood

Starman television series (1986), with Robert Hays

Reno as Seen from Interstate 80

The freeway provides a Reno skyline vista, plus jutting towers of outlying casino-resorts like the Grand Sierra Resort, the Peppermill, and Atlantis. Under its former names MGM Grand and Reno Hilton, the Grand Sierra Resort welcomed numerous projects:

. . . All the Marbles (1981), with Peter Falk

A Brand New Life (1989), with Barbara Eden and Don Murray

Disappearance of Nora (1993), with Dennis Farina

Edie & Pen (1996), with Stockard Channing

Jinxed (1982), with Bette Midler
Mafia! (1998), with Jay Mohr
Trail of Tears (1995), with Pam Dawber
The Wizard (1988), with Fred Savage

The Peppermill, off the Plumb Lane exit on Virginia, also worked with many projects:

Breaking Vegas (2005), where the History Channel showcases the events that inspired *21* in Las Vegas
Going for Broke (2003), with Delta Burke as a compulsive gambler whose addictions changed the rules
Hard Eight (1996), with Gwyneth Paltrow as a working girl
Jesse Hawkes (1989), with Robert Conrad as a bounty hunter
The Last Don (1997), with Jason Gedrick running a casino
Mafia! (1998), spoofing mob movies
Stacy's Knights (1984), giving Kevin Costner an early screen break
The Wizard (1989), allowing kids to direct a gambler's moves

On the south side of the horizon near the convention center, the Atlantis tower rises, its casino floor featured in *El Cortez* and *Sin*.

Interstate 80 to Tahoe

Travel literature often hyphenates the area as Reno-Tahoe, for good reason. No one should miss the chance to take a side trip out of Reno around the Tahoe basin, even though it maps out like someone went crazy making squiggles on an Etch A Sketch.

Part of Washoe and Paiute territory before John Fremont formally discovered it in 1844, the lake quickly lured visitors like Mark Twain. People loved it early, building too many houses and businesses to qualify it as a national park. Nevada and California state parks plus the U.S. Forest Service protect remaining wilderness.

Tahoe's California Locations

Traveling west on I-80 from Reno provides an extra bonus if you cross state borders past Truckee, California to Donner Lake, named for travelers famously stranded in the wilderness during the winter of 1846–1847.

Besides providing a campsite for the family in 1989's *A Brand New Life*, the lake hosted a 2009 feature film about its namesake, *The Donner Party* and a 1992 *American Experience* episode from Ric Burns. In 2015, the

Weather Channel made *Dead of Winter*, with commentary from Reno author Frank Mullen. The production company used Nevada desert and faked Illinois farmland in the greenbelt area of Douglas County.

If you take the old highway out of the north end of Donner Lake, you find a narrow road going up in a twisty set of curves. Surrounded by dramatic, hovering granitic mountain faces, Old Donner Pass boasts an impressive resume when it comes to movie titles:

Cobb (1994), with Tommy Lee Jones as the iconic baseball player

Bushwacked (1995), with Daniel Stern

Dead on the Money (1991), with Corbin Bernsen

Jack Frost (1998), with Michael Keaton

Misery (1990), from Stephen King's book

Love Ranch (2010), with Helen Mirren

The Adventures of Rocky & Bullwinkle (2000), with animated hitchhikers

True Lies (1994), from a pre-*Titanic* James Cameron

Donner Pass provides a turnaround point with two travel options around Lake Tahoe.

California State Route 267 to Crystal Bay

S.R. 267 leads to King's Beach where you can head to the California/Nevada border at Crystal Bay on S.R. 28. The Cal Neva lies in both states. Once owned by Frank Sinatra, the property drew famous names like Marilyn Monroe. The lodge turns up in 1988's *Things Change*, and *Cobb* from 1994. The 1998 HBO project about *The Rat Pack* includes action set but not filmed there.

Next door, Crystal Bay's Nugget let teenagers celebrate 1986's *Welcome to 18* starring Mariska Hargitay before her *Law & Order: SVU* run. Nearby, Crystal Bay Club opened its floor to a 2005 Court TV show about a magician trying to fool the casino.

California State Route 89 to Tahoe City and the West Shore

Rewinding back to Truckee, S.R. 89 leads to Tahoe City and areas used by 1998's *Jack Frost* and 2001's *The Deep End*. Just past Tahoe City, near Homewood, you see the gated entry to Fleur du Lac, once known as the Kaiser Estate. Original buildings included the house used in 1974's Oscar winner for Best Picture, *The Godfather Part II*. The boathouse remains, with multimillion-dollar, high-end luxury condos replacing the movie's other key sites. Moving along south on 89, you come to Sugar Pine Point State

Park, where Ehrman Mansion plays the stately home of wealthy characters in *Cobb, Dead on the Money*, and *Things Change*.

Beyond Sugar Pine Point, Emerald Bay stands out as a favorite drive-by shot for any project with a Lake Tahoe setting. A walkway from the parking area leads to Vikingsholm and small forests like those in 1951's *A Place in the Sun* with Elizabeth Taylor and *Rose Marie*, which provided a 1935 musical hit, "Indian Love Call." The movie also features Reno-area Native Americans dancing the Busby Berkley choreographed number "Totem Tom Tom" at Fallen Leaf Lake.

S.R. 89 proves fatal for Meg Ryan in 1998's *City of Angels*. The two-lane highway leads to Fallen Leaf Lake Road, a narrow drive that goes into an upscale vacation area where Ryan hooks up with Nicolas Cage using the same house Whitney Houston retreats to in 1992's *The Bodyguard*.

On the lakeside of the highway, Camp Richardson and its complex of buildings, plus Valhalla Lodge, served as base for *High Mountain Rangers*, a 1987 television series with Robert Conrad.

The South Shore: Back in Nevada

S.R. 89 continues from California to Nevada. The shopping center right at the border appeared in *City of Angels*, though that's hard to tell since renovations have changed it so much. Nevada's Stateline provides a long list of projects:

Assassination (1987), with Charles Bronson

High Mountain Rangers television series (1988), at the Horizon (Hard Rock) and Lakeside Inn

A Howling in the Woods (1971), with vistas of the lake from the restricted Glenbrook Lodge off Highway 50

Forty Pounds of Trouble (1963), with Tony Curtis at Harrah's

Man in the Moon (1999), with Jim Carrey at Harrah's

One Shoe Makes It Murder (1982), with Robert Mitchum

Payoff (1991), with Keith Carradine and John Saxon at Harvey's

The Seduction of Gina (1984), with Valerie Bertinelli

Showgirls (1995), with Elizabeth Berkley at the Horizon, now the Hard Rock Hotel

Smokin' Aces (2006), with Ryan Reynolds and Chris Pine at Montbleu

Surrender (1987), with Sally Field and Michael Caine at Harvey's

Things Change (1988), with Don Ameche and Joe Mantegna at Harrah's

Welcome to 18 (1986), with Mariska Hargitay at the Lakeside

Leaving Stateline on Highway 50 and winding along the lake leads to sites suited for screen action. James Caan finds misery after checking into an old Forest Service facility at Round Hill. Future Jack Ryan Chris Pine kills former Jack Ryan Ben Affleck at the Cave Rock boat launch in *Smokin' Aces*.

State Route 28–the East Shore

Over at Spooner Lake State Park, by the junction of Highway 50 and S.R. 28, Ben Johnson, John Ireland, and other cowboys ride in the *Bonanza: The Next Generation* (1988–1995) television movies. The park also provides access via North Canyon Road to Flume Trail, one of the nation's most popular bike rides.

Beyond Spooner to Sand Harbor Lake State Park brings a key location for *The Deep End*, where Tilda Swinton ignores the movie title and dumps a body in some of the shallowest water found in the region (actually, the title works as a metaphor for her troubles, as well as the name of a fictitious Reno bar she visits). Area backdrops highlighted Suzanne Somers' television series, *She's the Sheriff* (1987–1989).

Past Sand Harbor, the entrance to the Ponderosa Ranch once played home to *Bonanza*. Closed in 2004, the park provided tours of the ranch house, used for the television series toward the end of its run. All three follow-up television movies shot at the ranch as well.

Outside the Ponderosa Ranch, S.R. 28 leads to a junction called S.R. 431, the Mount Rose Highway. A right turn here starts the path that resembles Etch A Sketch squiggles.

The Mount Rose Highway

About five miles up the first set of hills, a vista point deserves pulling over for photography or gaping at beauty. This view shows up in several road movies, including 1989's *Breaking the Rules* with Jason Bateman and *The Wizard* with Christian Slater.

Back in your vehicle, driving along Mount Rose feels treacherous to the uninitiated. A more famous route, the Road to Hana in Maui, gives a similar sense.

"Wasn't that the most awful, difficult drive you ever made—can you believe it?" a stranger asked me as our paths crossed past the end of the Hawaii drive.

Pitiful and sweat-drenched, he looked like he just suffered a roller coaster trauma ward and maybe knew only straight roads in Florida.

"We-e-ell," I paused, trying to spare his feelings. "I've driven worse."

That would be the Mount Rose Highway, where elevation changes and the occasional blizzard exacerbate hairpin curves. Turns become a racecourse in 1954's *Johnny Dark*, with Tony Curtis, and make a perfect site for *E.R.* hunk Goran Višnjić to crash his car in *The Deep End*.

Despite hazards, I love the road. Its leveling-off point comes at Tahoe Meadows, seen in some seasons' opening *Bonanza* titles. The popular winter playground also flourishes in summer as a fabulous spot for wildflower hunting with intricate elephant heads, Sierra rein orchids, and the pink/yellow combination of shooting stars.

The Mount Rose Highway finishes just south of Reno on U.S. 395. Crossing 395, the road becomes Geiger Grade, or S.R. 341.

Geiger Grade and Virginia City

Geiger Grade takes you through more curves and altitude changes into Virginia City, famous long before *Bonanza* existed. The series never filmed there, but real Virginia City makes its way into television programs *History's Detectives*, *Believe It or Not* with Jack Palance, and the daytime soap, *Santa Barbara*. The V & T Railroad, which operates during the summer, steamed through 1998's *Mark Twain's America*, 1995's *Dead Man*, and *Unbeatable Harold* from 2006.

Highway 50 Again

Virginia City leads to Gold Hill and Silver City before getting to Highway 50A (*A* for alternate). Turn left on 50 and you find Dayton, whose Main Street remains recognizable from several projects:

Honkytonk Man (1982)

A Howling in the Woods (1971), as Stainesville

The Misfits (1961), with Marilyn Monroe's famous paddleboard game at the Odeon Hall.

Misfits Flat, further up Highway 50, opens via Pinto Lane near Stagecoach. Named for the Monroe movie, it maintains the barren sense it provided for the spectacular finale involving wild horses. The flat also served as an ideal backdrop for *The Making of the Misfits*. It turns up in 2001's *Sin* when bad guy Gary Oldman drives his car into quicksand. Dry Nevada provides little quicksand in reality, so filmmakers dug a pit and filled it with squishy decomposed granite.

Backtracking from Misfits Flat, Highway 50 goes past signs promoting bars and lounges at brothels in Mound House. Love Ranch got its name from the Taylor Hackford movie with that title. Moonlite Bunny Ranch became home to HBO's *Cathouse*. A drive toward the brothel features specialized traffic signs, like a yellow one with the silhouette of two bunnies demonstrating their procreating skills. Park and ring the buzzer if you want to check out the gift shop, lounge, or whatever.

Carson City

Highway 50 eventually leads to Carson City, Nevada's capital. The governor's office at the state capitol on the main drag played set for the never-finished *Pretty Hattie's Baby* (1991), with Alfre Woodward in a role she described as her best work to date for a 1993 article in the *Washington Post.* She played an alcoholic mother who adopts a mixed-race baby, only to discover the girl is white. Moviemakers decided to use the governor's office for a scene of the girl seeking her father in a Southern California executive suite.

Then-governor Bob Miller agreed to let his space be a film set since his schedule took him out of town the day cameras rolled. Bad weather prevented his flight. Instead of forcing a reschedule, Governor Miller simply moved all his papers to a table set up in the capitol hallway and proceeded to work. Visitors find it easy to tour the capitol, which includes exhibits on Nevada's natural and human history.

The capitol also played a helpful role in Robert Conrad's 1993 television movie, *Sworn to Vengeance,* and 1949's *Chicken Every Sunday* with Celeste Holm.

West of the main drag (take Telegraph to Mountain), a marker designates another film site in Carson City, 1976's *The Shootist. Pledge of Allegiance* also used the house at 500 Mountain Street in 2003.

The city drew projects to Fifth Street and the imposing stone walls of its former maximum-security prison (now closed). Projects include:

Black August (2007), with Gary Dourdan as George Jackson at San Quentin

Death Watch (1950), with Leonard Nimoy pretending to be in a French prison

Flesh and Blood (1979), with Tom Berenger

An Innocent Man (1989), with Tom Selleck

State Penitentiary (1950), with Warner Baxter

Other Carson City movie credits include:

Cobb (1994), with 340 Minnesota serving as a Georgia home for Tommy Lee Jones as a famous baseball player

Far From Home (1989), with Drew Barrymore finding a killer on top of McClellan Peak

Honkytonk Man (1982), with Clint Eastwood pretending to play at the Brewery Arts Center

The Corbett-Fitzsimmons Prizefight (1897), providing Nevada with its first film topic and becoming a cinematic landmark

A Howling in the Woods (1971), with Barbara Eden and Larry Hagman reteaming after *I Dream of Jeannie*

The Motel Life (2012), with Dakota Fanning

Pink Cadillac (1989), with Clint Eastwood dressed as a clown at Fuji Park's defunct rodeo grounds

The Remarkable Andrew (1942), with William Holden at the Rinkle House on Curry Street and an opening shot of the Laxalt tourism building, formerly the state library

Roar of the Iron Horse (1950), featuring the Carson and New Brunswick Canyon lines of the V & T Railroad

Route 66 (1961), season one's episode "Like a Motherless Child" at Stewart and Fifth Streets

Showgirls (1995), with Elizabeth Berkley hitchhiking near the Lone Eagle Grille

Train to Tombstone (1950), using Carson City's old portion of the V & T Railroad

U.S. 95 Back to Vegas via Tonopah

From here the film fantasy joyride gets a little tricky and squiggly since you need to get back on U.S. 95—assuming your plan includes the entire circular tour back to Las Vegas. The next major film stop waits until Tonopah with movies that never earned big audiences:

Tonopah Stampede for Gold (1913)

Family Reunion (1989)

Cherry 2000 (1988)

The Stranger (1995), with kickboxing champ Kathy Long whipping ass

Just twenty-six miles beyond comes Goldfield, featuring *Cherry 2000* and *The Stranger* plus:

Butterfly (1981), with Pia Zadora overwhelming the Razzies

Desert Blue (1998), with Kate Hudson in an early role

Vanishing Point (1970), at the Goldfield Hotel

Beatty

Continue south another 108 miles until Beatty for:

Homer and Eddy (1988), with Whoopi Goldberg

Midnight Run (1988), with Robert De Niro

Confessions of a Hit Man (1991)

Never Leave Nevada (1990)

Ramona! (1993)

Side Trip to Rhyolite

Continue south on U.S. 95 to Beatty, then take S.R. 374 for the eleven-minute ride to Rhyolite, where ruins of a once-thriving community frequently lure filmmakers.

The Air Mail (1925)

The Arrogant (1987)

Cherry 2000 (1988), with Melanie Griffith (again)

The Island (2005), with Scarlett Johansson and Ewan McGregor

Ramona! (again)

The Reward (1965)

Rough Riders Round-Up (1939)

Six-String Samurai (1998)

Ultraviolet (1992)

U.S. 95 from Beatty to Vegas

Returning to Beatty from Rhyolite puts you 185 miles from the film fantasy joyride starting point in Las Vegas. The route back to the city lets you pass by Amargosa and into the Devil's Hole portion of Death Valley National Park off S.R. 373, where dunes were used in *Cherry 2000* and *The Arrogant*. Farther south on U.S. 95 leads to Indian Springs, where C. Thomas Howell spent time in jail for the first *Hitcher* movie, released in 1988.

The exit marked "Mercury" enters the Nevada Test Site, the setting in name only for many projects. Prohibited from pulling off the road and dropping in for a visit, you need advance arrangements to ride a tour bus from Las Vegas, which also houses an enlightening Atomic Energy Museum run in part by the Smithsonian.

U.S. 95 leads to the Mt. Charleston ski area via a junction at S.R. 159 and mountain terrain used to duplicate Utah in *Anywhere But Here*, a 1999 drama with Susan Sarandon and Natalie Portman.

Las Vegas lets the film fantasy joyride end, unless you need to see Laughlin for 1995's *Leaving Las Vegas* or the Jean Dry Lake for 1967's *Hombre,* among many others.

The Joy of Riding

My travels on this itinerary took many separate trips with overnights in different communities and exploring from there. Austin, Beatty, Elko, Ely, Eureka, Fallon, Gardnerville, Goldfield, Hawthorne, Lake Tahoe, Paradise Valley, Rachel, Tonopah, West Wendover, and Winnemucca led me to intriguing locations to photograph and scout after first taking a morning jog. I love getting out on foot as dawn breaks, easing through these communities while smelling the scents of eggs, bacon, and engines coming to life. Wake-up time provides a sense of how a community operates. Some rarely see a woman in running shorts. Some move so leisurely you know no one has a day calendar with appointments. Some communities thrive on fast-food time with mad rushes.

Taking the time to absorb surroundings inspired a Nevada resident I met when we appeared on a television program promoting the arts. University of California Professor Leo Buscaglia bore the world famous "Dr. Hug" nickname by the time he retired and moved to Lake Tahoe in the early nineties. His book *Living, Loving and Learning* ranked as one of the top ten sellers of the entire eighties, gaining an audience through clear and heartfelt expressions about the value of appreciating life. Leo felt we should learn something new every day—easy enough if we just take the time to look at the sights in front of us.

With that in mind, he asked me to help him explore his new home in Nevada since my job made me a location expert. Even though we never met before, the request seemed natural because we felt like old friends who knew a lot about each other—I read his books and he listened to my radio show. Within a few weeks, we took a full day jaunt to the Black Rock Desert and nearby Gerlach, where the owner of Bruno's Country Club personally cooked us dinner while his assistant Doobie toured us around the region. The trip emphasized the joy of exploring our own Nevada backyard. And with the seventh-largest square footage of any state, Nevada provides a *big* backyard. Much as I know the state, I realize more lies out there just waiting to be seen in person and on screen.

Sources and Recommended Reading

Amaral, Anthony, *Movie Horses, Their Treatment and Training*. New York: The Bobbs-Merrill Company, Inc., 1967.

Buscaglia, Leo, *Living, Loving and Learning*. New York: Fawcett Columbine, 1982.

Conforte, Joe and Toll, David, *Breaks, Brains and Balls, the Story of Joe Conforte and Nevada's Fabulous Mustang Ranch*. Nevada, Gold Hill Publishing Company, 2011.

DuVal, Gary, *The Nevada Filmography*. North Carolina: McFarland & Co., 2002.

Farley, Terri, *Wild at Heart*. Houghton Mifflin Harcourt, 2015.

Levy, Shawn, *Rat Pack Confidential*. Broadway Books, 1999.

Heston, Charlton, *The Actors Life*. Dutton, 1978.

Internet Movie Data Base, www.imdb.com. Titles, dates, spellings, and awards come from this website. IMDB data is occasionally unreliable or confusing regarding locations. Projects listed may have only a passing reference to the location without filming there or using it as a setting.

Medvid, Harry & Michael, *The Golden Turkey Awards: Nominees and Winners, the Worst Achievements in Hollywood History*. New York: Perigee Books, 1980.

Medvid, Harry & Michael, *The Hollywood Hall of Shame*. New York: Perigee Books, 1984.

Miller, Arthur & Serge Toubiana, *The Misfits: Story of a Shoot*. Pennsylvania: Phaidon.

Mullen, Frank, *The Donner Party Chronicles*. Halycon/Nevada Humanities Committee, 1997.

Peary, Danny, *Cult Movies 1*. New York: Dell Publishing Company, 1981.

Peary, Danny, *Cult Movies 2*. New York: Dell Publishing Company, 1983.

Peary, Danny, *Guide for the Film Fanatic*. New York: Simon & Schuster, 1986.

Pileggi, Nicholas, *Casino: Love and Honor in Las Vegas*. New York: Simon and Schuster, 1995.

Squier, Jason, ed., *The Movie Business Book*. New York: Prentice Hall, 1983.

Thomson, David, *In Nevada: The Land, the People, God, and Chance*. New York, Knopf, 2000.

Twain, Mark, *Roughing It*. Penguin Library, USA, 1981 (from original 1872 edition).

Video/DVD/streaming options: Many Nevada-related projects are listed at www.amazon.com, www.netflix.com, www.moviesunlimited.com, and www.bigstar.com. Out-of-production titles sometimes show up on E-bay and YouTube.

About the Author

Robin Holabird spent more than twenty years directing the Reno-Tahoe Branch of the Nevada Film Office, a government agency that encourages movie and television producers to use the state's locations and services. During her career, she worked on hundreds of projects, dealing with artists such as Paul Thomas Anderson, Clint Eastwood, and Taylor Hackford, and on ventures such as *Sister Act, CSI*, and *Love Ranch*. After studying film and journalism at Humboldt State University (and later earning a master in public administration from the University of Nevada, Reno), Robin also began reviewing movies for newspapers, radio, and television. She continues broadcasting a weekly radio show on KUNR, 88.7 FM, every Friday morning at 5:30 and 7:30.

A former board member with the Association of Film Commissioners International, Robin edited the organization's magazine *Locations* for ten years, interviewing filmmakers and traveling to popular film sites throughout the world. Having lived in Nevada for more than forty years, Robin travels the state extensively, where she explores and photographs popular locations as well as obscure ones. An outdoor enthusiast, she regularly hikes the region's trails, and she has run the Boston Marathon six times.

Index